CORRUPTION AND CORRUPTION CONTROL

Corruption in politics and public administration is pervasive and difficult to eliminate. It has a strong effect on public attitudes toward government and is at the same time badly understood. A clear, comprehensive understanding of corruption is critical to the goal of ethical government that is trusted by the public.

In this short and accessible text, Staffan Andersson and Frank Anechiarico demonstrate how the dynamics of life in organizations both generate corruption and make it difficult to prevent without undermining the effectiveness of government. They argue that how we define corruption, how we measure it, and how we try to combat it are strongly interrelated and should not be seen as separate issues. The authors demonstrate how this integrated approach, together with a focus on the damage caused by corruption to civic inclusivity and participation, can serve as an entry point for understanding the quality of democracy and the challenge of good governance.

Using examples from mainly the United States and Sweden, Andersson and Anechiarico establish that recent anti-corruption reforms in public administration have often been narrowly focused on bribery (exchange corruption) and law enforcement approaches, while doing too little to other problems and forms of corruption.

Corruption and Corruption Control: Democracy in the Balance will be of great interest to all students of politics, public administration and management, and ethics.

Staffan Andersson is Associate Professor of Political Science at Linnaeus University, Sweden. His research and teaching focus on public administration and comparative politics. Andersson has published widely on issues of risk vulnerability in public organizations, and the measurement of corruption, in journals including *Political Studies* and *Public Integrity*. He was the principal investigator for the National Integrity System Assessment of Sweden (2012).

Frank Anechiarico is the Maynard-Knox Professor of Government and Law at Hamilton College. He is editor and co-author of *Legal but Corrupt: A New Perspective on Public Ethics*, co-author with James Jacobs of *The Pursuit of Absolute Integrity: How Corruption Control Makes Government Ineffective*, and author of articles in *Public Administration Review*, *Urban Affairs Quarterly*, *Administration and Society*, and other journals.

"After three decades of anti-corruption activism that has produced only modest results, it is time to reassess key aspects of reform thinking. Andersson and Anechiarico launch that process by distinguishing between exchange and governance corruption, identifying causes and consequences of those problems, and spelling out political and institutional challenges of reform in a realistic yet positive fashion. In the process they identify core dynamics of corruption that are visible in a variety of settings, and show how lasting reform requires not just punishing misconduct but rather building better relationships between state and society."

— *Michael Johnston, Charles A. Dana Professor of Political Science, Emeritus, Colgate University, USA*

"Distinguishing 'governance corruption' from 'exchange corruption' makes a new, important and stimulating contribution to scholarship about corruption and policy making directed at corruption control. A valuable book that is a must read for corruption scholars highly accessible for students. Bravo."

— *James B. Jacobs, Chief Justice Warren E. Burger Professor of Law, New York University*

"The authors have created something extraordinary: A popular book on corruption! Engaging and accessible content from an international perspective, with original case studies sure to spark discussion, this is a book for students of corruption at every level. The contemporary focus and broad overview make this an on-point and dynamic learning resource."

— *Carole L. Jurkiewicz, Ph.D., University of Colorado, Colorado Springs*

"Andersson and Anechiarico's *Corruption and Corruption Control* represents a major achievement not only in the literature on corruption but in the study of political cultures more generally. Their democratic approach is laudable in itself but it also drives home the need for vigilance against the ideas that corruption is always simple graft and that cultural and ethical dysfunctions can be solved through coercive force alone."

— *Dr Ciarán O'Kelly, Queen's University Belfast*

CORRUPTION AND CORRUPTION CONTROL

Democracy in the Balance

Staffan Andersson and Frank Anechiarico

Routledge
Taylor & Francis Group

NEW YORK AND LONDON

First published 2019
by Routledge
52 Vanderbilt Avenue, New York, NY 10017

and by Routledge
2 Park Square, Milton Park, Abingdon, Oxon, OX14 4RN

Routledge is an imprint of the Taylor & Francis Group, an informa business

© 2019 Taylor & Francis

The right of Staffan Andersson and Frank Anechiarico to be
identified as authors of this work has been asserted by them in
accordance with sections 77 and 78 of the Copyright, Designs and
Patents Act 1988.

All rights reserved. No part of this book may be reprinted or
reproduced or utilised in any form or by any electronic, mechanical,
or other means, now known or hereafter invented, including
photocopying and recording, or in any information storage or
retrieval system, without permission in writing from the publishers.

Trademark notice: Product or corporate names may be trademarks
or registered trademarks, and are used only for identification and
explanation without intent to infringe.

Library of Congress Cataloging-in-Publication Data
Names: Andersson, Staffan, author. | Anechiarico, Frank, author.
Title: Corruption and corruption control : democracy in the
    balance / Staffan Andersson & Frank Anechiarico.
Description: New York, NY : Routledge, 2019. | Includes
    bibliographical references and index.
Identifiers: LCCN 2019000722 (print) | LCCN 2019009045
    (ebook) | ISBN 9781351206990 (Master) | ISBN
    9781351206983 (Adobe) | ISBN 9781351206976 (ePub3) |
    ISBN 9781351206969 (Mobi) | ISBN 9780815383000 (hbk) |
    ISBN 9780815383017 (pbk) | ISBN 9781351206990 (ebk)
Subjects: LCSH: Political corruption. | Political ethics.
Classification: LCC JF1081 (ebook) | LCC JF1081 .A537 2019
    (print) | DDC 364.1/323—dc23
LC record available at https://lccn.loc.gov/2019000722

ISBN: 978-0-8153-8300-0 (hbk)
ISBN: 978-0-8153-8301-7 (pbk)
ISBN: 978-1-351-20699-0 (ebk)

Typeset in Bembo
by Swales & Willis Ltd, Exeter, Devon, UK

For Karin, Disa, and Tova
−SA

For John and Simone
−FA

CONTENTS

ILLUSTRATIONS

Figures

Tables

Boxes

PREFACE

Bell, California, is a largely Latino, working-class town in Los Angeles County with a median annual income of $36,000. In an unpublicized special election in March of 2005, 400 voters approved a new city charter that removed caps on the salaries of municipal officials. Five years later, the shocking, uncontrolled greed of the city council, mayor, and other principal officers got the attention of the State Attorney General Jerry Brown and the L.A. County District Attorney Steve Cooley. As Cooley put it, "they used the tax dollars collected from the hard-working citizens of Bell as their own piggy bank, which they looted at will … [it was] corruption on steroids" (www.cnn.com/2010/CRIME/09/21/california.bell.arrests/index.html). The city manager was paid $800,000 a year, while council members received $100,000 salaries for part-time work (the standard for council members in California is about $5,000 a year) (www.latimes.com/local/la-me-bell-salary-20100715-story.html). Ultimately, eight current and former Bell officials were convicted of misappropriating $5.5 million of public funds. The local population was furious and demanded maximum sentences.

Unless they are in on it, people are made angry by corruption. They should be angry; what happened in Bell and elsewhere is humiliating. Victims of corruption are played for fools by inside dealers, extortionists, and thieves who are operating in governments of any size, everywhere. Public humiliation is a painful injury, but humiliation of the public is a dangerous one. When it is widespread in a political system it leads to fearsome, violent consequences. Those in power at the moment are rejected: exiled, imprisoned, or killed. But all too often, when the dust settles the next gang of thieves is waiting for their turn at the trough. This is a story that has been repeated again and again from the French Revolution to the Arab Spring.

But in other societies, anger and humiliation caused by corruption becomes a regular part of political life; anger stays at a simmer. In these societies, cynicism and dejection erode governance and repress civic engagement. Where this happens, as it has in the industrialized West, it entails more than bribery and graft. Cynical passivity erodes the bonds that attach citizens to each other and to governing institutions. This is often called a problem of government legitimacy, but legitimacy is largely the problem seen from the top down. Seen from a citizen's perspective, the problem is even more fundamental. It is a lack of caring and a lack of care leading to civic enervation and pessimism. In this circumstance, as in the aftermath of revolutionary reactions to corruption, state and community are ripe for opportunists of the left or the right promising simple solutions and a return to probity.

In either circumstance—active, even violent reaction or passive, depressive inaction—opportunists are at large and democracy has little chance. As we look around us, the world is filled with civic anxiety and even desperation. We reject simple, opportunist solutions and finger pointing. This book is based on three, connected premises that guide our inquiry.

- First, the root and effects of corruption must be clearly understood in order for a defense of public integrity to be effective.
- Second, a defense of public integrity is based on identifying the damage done by corruption to democratic governance.
- Third, the damage to democratic governance is understood as denial or limitation of popular participation in political decision making.

The key element for us—and what we consider the bottom line in the study of public integrity—is the quality of democratic governance. Studying corruption gives us a way to understand the problems of democratic governance by identifying both outright theft and also the more subtle exclusionary mechanisms related to official misconduct. This covers a lot of territory. Even error and simple neglect, if left uncorrected, will cause harm to the quality of governance.

But why should popular participation in political decision making be a central concern in a book about corruption? We believe that policies and other official behavior that remove people from a role in shaping the conditions of their own lives are humiliating and dehumanizing in a way that fits the definition of corruption as the purposeful destruction of public value. A further problem in making the case that such exclusion is critical is that it is so widespread that it is hardly noticed by policy makers and researchers. It is the background noise of modern public administration.

ACKNOWLEDGMENTS

The authors are embedded in a community of scholars that has enriched their work over the years. This group includes those we have met at conferences and those with whom we have worked on edited volumes and co-authored publications. Most particularly, we would like to thank the following colleagues for their advice and inspiration: Guy Adams, Danny Balfour, Torbjörn Bergman, Gjalt de Graaf, Luís de Sousa, John Dehn, Melvin Dubnick, Gissur Erlingsson, Mia Falk, Rose Gill Hearn, Paul Heywood, Leo Huberts, James B. Jacobs, Michael Johnston, Ciarán O'Kelly, Carole L. Jurkiewicz, and Lydia Segal.

This book grew out of discussions we have had over the past several years in Upstate New York and in Växjö and Pukavik in Sweden. Our meetings were supported by the Office of the Dean at Hamilton College and by Linnaeus University. We would also like to thank the participants in the research seminar at the Department of Political Science and the research group on sustainable governance, ethics, and corruption at Linnaeus and the Thursday Night Club at Hamilton.

In the latter stages of the project we were fortunate to have the research and administrative assistance of Nico Yardas and advice and assistance on book design from Karin Bäcklund Andersson. We would also like to thank Natalja Mortensen and Charlie Baker at Routledge for their support and professionalism.

The ideas discussed in the pages that follow have been developed in courses on corruption and related topics that we have taught jointly and independently over the years. Perhaps our greatest debt is to our students, for taking our ideas seriously and for providing us with the reactions and criticism that form the core of this book. But we will not hold them, or anyone else thanked here, responsible for any apparent errors in what follows. That responsibility is ours.

1

DEMOCRATIC GOVERNANCE, CORRUPTION, AND CORRUPTION CONTROL

The purpose of this book is to investigate the way in which public administration becomes corrupt and which reforms are best suited to restoring the ideal of public service. This introductory chapter will outline the problem of corruption in national and international settings and open a discussion of the causes and effects of corruption that will continue in later chapters. We will also define corruption and explain how the definition of corruption is related to the way we understand official misconduct, efforts to prevent it, and the way the definition needs to change as public administration itself is changing.

The Best and the Worst

A good way to start this book is with a provocative quote from the Enlightenment philosopher David Hume (1889, Section X): "The corruption of the best things gives rise to the worst." Hume was referring to the way that the "best" of religious faith and charity can be corrupted into the "worst" of idolatry and hatred. But what he says about religion applies to all important values and institutions like justice, education, and defense; once they are corrupted, they become devious, dangerous, and, in some cases, deadly.

The ugliness of official, political corruption is caused by despoiling trust. In the absence of trustworthy government the only guarantees of life, liberty, and property are force and violence. Thomas Hobbes noticed this in the wake of the English Civil War in the 17th century and we can see it for ourselves today in a number of places around the world. The devastation of Syria by warring factions, foreign powers, and its own government has forced Syrians by the hundreds of thousands to seek refuge where stable, honest governments will allow them to rebuild their lives.

The longer Hume's "worst" continues, the harder it is to recover important, public values. In Syria that recovery will be extraordinarily difficult. Syria, before the beginning of the civil war in 2011, was ruled by decree under emergency powers granted to the president in 1963. It has been governed, according to most accounts, by a corrupt, autocratic regime. The corruption in Syria that can be directly connected to the outbreak of the civil war was of two types. First, there was what we might call exchange corruption: every interaction, from ordinary license applications to trouble with the police, would be accompanied by requests for bribes. In most instances, the routine was so well known that no request was necessary. This kind of ordinary, daily corruption rots governance from the bottom up. Over time, "government" becomes a synonym for "corruption" and the expectation of fairness and neutral justice morphs into cynicism.

The second kind of corruption in Syria is related to the first but even more damaging. That is the exclusion and oppression of individuals or groups (Gersh, 2017). Syria was characterized as a model of ethnic and religious tolerance up to the onset of the civil war. The Alawite ruling elite, however, reacted to pro-democracy demonstrations during the 2011 Arab spring by playing on sectarian distrust of the large Sunni majority.

> The first demonstrations attracted hundreds of thousands of people of different faiths. So the regime stoked sectarian tensions to divide the opposition. Sunnis, it warned, really wanted winner-take-all majoritarianism. Jihadists were released from prison in order to taint the uprising. As the government turned violent, so did the protesters. Sunni states, such as Turkey, Saudi Arabia and Qatar, provided them with arms, cash and preachers. Hardliners pushed aside moderates. By the end of 2011, the protests had degenerated into a sectarian civil war.
>
> (The Economist, 2018)

This is governance corruption. Once the Assad regime made it clear that it saw Sunnis as instigators of unrest, rather than as participants in peaceful protests, which they were at first, the bottom fell out. As in Tunisia and Egypt, the prime motive behind the early demonstrations and rallies was exchange corruption. In December 2010, when a fruit and vegetable seller in a rural Tunisian town was unable to pay bribes demanded by the police, his cart was seized and he was slapped and berated in public. Humiliated and deprived of his livelihood, he stood in front of a government building and set himself on fire. The protests that followed toppled the government, but did little to deal with the underlying culture of bribery and extortion. However, in 2018 another anti-corruption movement started in Tunisia.

Governance corruption includes bad and abusive official behavior, as the above examples indicate, but *only when it is intentionally used to exclude individuals or groups from taking part in decisions that critically affect them.* There are lots of errors, mistakes, and abuses that emanate from public agencies that are harmful but do not fit our definition because they are not intentional and which, though harmful, are not exclusionary. This will be explored in more detail in later chapters. But one question should be answered before we go further: can a dictatorship avoid the governance corruption label? The answer is, not for very long. There is a period after a government comes to power through a *coup d'état* or broader revolution—or even an election—when its leaders are faced with a choice. Either they decide to open participation in governance by recognizing opposition parties and holding elections or they decide to consolidate power and justify their authority as the embodiment of the people's will. The French Revolution was followed by a brutal dictatorship and then the creation of the empire under Napoleon. The American Revolution was followed by a weak, central government under the Articles of Confederation and then a stronger one that recognized opposition parties (though they were not organized as such until 1800) and held elections. The Communist revolutions of the 20th century in Russia, China, and Cuba all had broad support at first, but chose one-party rule and never recognized opposition.

Once an authoritarian direction has been selected, the process of exclusion begins. Political enemies, both individuals or groups, are identified, watched, and punished by banishment, internal exile, prison, or death. This radical exclusion is the hallmark of governance corruption in dictatorships and other authoritarian regimes. Singapore's government, often mentioned as an example of "clean" authoritarianism because of its intolerance of exchange corruption, has a long history of summary punishment for those considered a threat to the government's power. Thus, while the international non-governmental organization Transparency International (2018) rates Singapore as the sixth least corrupt country in the world in 2017, in terms of its reputation regarding exchange corruption, Human Rights Watch sees Singapore quite differently:

> Singapore's political environment is stifling. Citizens face severe restrictions on their basic rights to freedom of expression, association, and peaceful assembly through overly broad criminal laws and regulations. In 2017, the country tightened the already strict limits on public assemblies contained in the Public Order Act, which requires police permits for any 'cause-related' assembly outside the closely monitored "Speakers' Corner."
>
> Leaders of the ruling Peoples' Action Party (PAP), which has been in power for more than 50 years, have a history of bankrupting opposition politicians through civil defamation suits and jailing them for public protests. Suits against and restrictions on foreign media that report critically on the country have featured regularly since the 1970s and restrictions on public gatherings have been in place since at least 1973.
>
> *(Human Rights Watch, 2017)*

What looks like a "clean" government from the perspective of exchange corruption looks very different when we include governance corruption. The example of Singapore makes it clear that that our standard for integrity in governance should be democratic inclusion.

These examples indicate the necessity of using a broad definition of corruption that includes both more traditional exchange corruption as well as governance corruption. A definition that relies only on exchange corruption would be clear and relatively distinct from other governance problems, but confining the definition to exchange corruption would also ignore the injustice and lack of accountability of dysfunctional politics caused by exclusionary governance. A narrow definition of corruption and the tendency to equate it with bribery will have consequences not only for how we understand the problem but for how we approach reform as well. We argue that far too often anti-corruption campaigns focus on rooting out exchange corruption while neglecting governance corruption that is far more damaging. A narrow focus tilts the measures adopted to fight corruption toward laws, regulations, and sanctions of individual transgression and away from measures based on shaping and regulating the institutional structures and organizational dynamics that determine ethical behavior.

Contemporary Corruption Issues and Problems

Ethical misconduct by public officials, corporate executives, and leaders of prominent non-profit organizations has become a staple of media coverage. The release in 2016 of the Mossack Fonseca Papers, the so-called Panama Papers (Garside, Watt, & Pegg, 2016; Harding, 2016) deservedly received enormous coverage around the world. The Papers contained detailed information about the financial arrangements in tax havens used by individuals in the political and economic elites to avoid paying taxes at home, which was illegal in some cases, especially when the tax havens were used to conceal conflicts of interest and the proceeds from exchange corruption. Similar revelations resulted from the leak of confidential documents in 2017 labelled the Paradise Papers (Garside, 2017; Hopkins & Bengtsson, 2017). These documents revealed offshore investments to reduce or avoid paying taxes by major international corporations and by elite individuals.

Also in 2017, the #MeToo Campaign exposed widespread sexual assault and harassment and how powerful men (and a few women) used their positions of power not just to commit sexual harassment and assault but also to cover them up. The Campaign also raised the question of how to deal with accusations of harassment and ethical transgressions directed toward public officials and those in the private sector who are possible targets of politically motivated charges (e.g. Teachout, 2017).

Another, execrable example of an abuse of power followed by a cover-up is the sexual abuse of children by clergy in the Catholic Church. This abuse started to get attention in the 1980s and 1990s, first in Ireland, Canada, the United

States, and Australia, and later in other countries. Revelations concerned the abuse itself but also how in a great many cases Church authorities, abetted by state authorities, had covered up cases to protect the Church, instead of seeking justice for the child victims and preventing further abuse. At a meeting in 1975, presided over by an Irish archbishop, children who were victims of abuse signed vows of silence concerning accusations against a pedophile priest (BBC News, 2010). Similarly in Australia an archbishop was found guilty by a court for having covered up sexual abuse of altar boys by a pedophile priest in the 1970s (BBC News, 2018b). The Vatican and local Church authorities were slow to respond and when they did they labelled the allegations as exaggerated. But the truth began to come out around the turn of the century. By 2018 all of the Catholic bishops in Chile offered their resignation after an investigation by the Pope criticized them for neglect in handling of sexual abuse cases (BBC News, 2018a). Here, as in the other examples in this section, violations of the law are shielded from public view, which expands the harm done and ensures the political exclusion of victims.

Corruption Is World-wide

There are examples too numerous to mention of corruption scandals with huge implications for countries in all parts of the world, but we will raise a few to illustrate the consequences of exchange and governance corruption, when they engulf a political system. In Brazil, corruption allegations have been directed toward two recent presidents, Lula da Silva and his successor Dilma Rousseff, concerning their connection to the state majority-owned oil company Petrobas. In 2018 Lula was sentenced to prison for corruption while leading in opinion polls for election to another term as president, while Rousseff was impeached and removed from office during her second term for breaking budget laws and for knowing or choosing not to know about huge payoffs by Petrobas to politicians (Cowie, 2018; Phillips, 2018). Also, Michele Temer, Rousseff's successor, was charged with accepting bribes and obstructing justice, but the lower house of Congress voted not to refer the case to the Supreme Court (Associated Press, 2017). One result of all this was the paralysis of Petrobras. Contracts were cancelled, lawsuits were brought by investors seeking compensation for returns siphoned off by corrupt officials, and over 120,000 Petrobras workers lost their jobs (Watts, 2016).

Corruption played an important part in spurring the overthrow of corrupt regimes in a number of places in addition to those affected by the Arab spring. The "Orange Revolution" in Ukraine toppled the government of Viktor Yanukovych, whose looting of the country's treasury funded an estate worth several hundred million dollars, complete with a full-size replica of a Spanish galleon (Armitage, 2014). In Zimbabwe the Mugabe government, ousted in 2017, frequently spoke out against corruption, while media reports detailed systemic corruption in the government itself (e.g. Zaba, 2016). In China, the Communist regime regularly initiates high-profile anti-corruption campaigns. Nonetheless, citizen distrust of the central government is worsening (Hatton, 2013; Lockett, 2016); bribery and extortion are commonplace and government employees with *guanxi* (connections) have a "straw in the milkshake" of economic growth and grow wealthy (Zúñiga, 2018).

In the United States, corruption scandals are chronic in both government and the private sector. The perception that money corrupts elections has long been widespread in America. In the 2016 presidential election, corruption-related issues were at the forefront in discussions of campaign finance and the extent to which wealthy donors, rather than citizens in general, influence the political agenda and the priorities of political parties and candidates. Both Bernie Sanders and Donald Trump, fighting for the nomination of their respective parties, argued that the acceptance of big money donations corruptly influences politicians. Sanders made campaign finance reform a key issue in his campaign and railed against the U.S. Supreme Court decision (*Citizens United*) which validated unlimited corporate political donations as expressions of free speech. Sanders opted not to have a SuperPAC[1] and made a point of accepting only small donations from millions of individuals, famously averaging USD27 (Bump, 2016). Trump, fighting for the Republican nomination, often referred to his competitors as "owned" by donors, while he was "self-funded" and therefore independent. By the end of the campaign, however, Trump had accepted a substantial amount of both small and large donations (Kaplan, 2017; Narayanswamy, Cameron, and Gold, n.d.). The Trump presidency has from the beginning been beset by allegations of conflict of interest: between family and business interest on one side and government interest on the other. Though he resigned his position as chief executive of several Trump-branded companies, he retains ownership of them, including Trump International Hotel, in Washington, D.C., which is popular with those having business with his administration (see, for example, Leonhardt & Philbrick, 2018).

In Italy, Greece, and Spain, established political parties have been hit by corruption scandals that have led to distrust and even rejection of established politics. This has caused major changes in the political landscape, including the party system, with new or former marginalized parties gaining strength and then coming to power. In Italy in the 1990s, revelations that started in Milan and spread to national politics concerned systemic corruption across established political parties. The judicial investigation "*mani pulite*" (clean hands) exposed an intricate system in place to divide contractor kickbacks among the political parties according to certain quotas. The investigation led to the indictment of more than half the members of the Italian Parliament.

There is an old stereotype of European governance that imagines that corruption begins at the Alps, north of which it is seldom found. Recent major scandals indicate otherwise. Political scandals have erupted in the United Kingdom, France, and Germany. In the UK senior politicians were caught using the parliamentary expense system for all kinds of personal expenses, including cleaning the moat and lighting the stables on the manorial estate of one MP (Prince, 2009). In Germany, the Christian Democratic Party in the 1990s used secret funds to finance elections campaigns, implicating the long-term former chancellor Helmut Kohl, who refused to give evidence in the case.

Even countries often referred to as among the very least corrupt, like Sweden and Norway, have experienced corruption scandals both in the private sector and government. Large, industrial interests in Norway (oil and gas) and in Sweden (armaments) have been involved in big international corruption scandals. In Norway, the agribusiness giant Yara International, based in Oslo, was caught in 2011 for paying over USD8.5 million in bribes to high-ranking Libyan and Indian public officials to secure sales contracts. The practice of buying business preferment from foreign governments is illegal in Norway, throughout the European Union, and in the United States, but still surfaces on a regular basis. Yara was fined USD48 million by the Norwegian government and several of its executives were jailed (Cassin, 2015).

Returning to Germany we find a similar scandal, but on a much larger scale. The German engineering and equipment firm Siemens allocated USD1.4 billion from 2001–2007 for over 4,000 payments to public officials around the world to encourage them to buy Siemens products and services (U.S. Securities and Exchange Commission, 2008).

These examples show first that corruption is an important issue across the globe—in established democracies, including countries we often think of as being very honest. Second, that corruption comes in many forms other than bribery, such as conflicts of interest, favoritism, and the abuse of power. Third, that corruption does not just involve governments and public agencies but also private companies and non-governmental organizations. Building and maintaining the public good is increasingly not a task for government alone but must be done in cooperation with non-public organizations, which warrants the broader term "governance" (Huberts, 2014, p. 6).

Corruption is detrimental to the integrity of governance, to trust in democratic processes, and to effective decision making and administration. *Integrity* in this context can be defined as behavior, processes, and procedures that are in line "with [the] relevant moral values and norms" (Huberts, 2014, p. 4). Of course, we need to know what "the relevant moral values and norms" might be. Historically, the values and norms that guide official behavior range from strict loyalty and adherence to authoritarian rule to democratic inclusivity. We argue in this book that the norm of democratic governance is both the *practical* and the *humane* choice. It is practical because, without the oppositional forces that check the exercise of power in a democracy, the extent and even the existence of corruption will be hidden, denied, or used to jail dissidents; without democracy, corruption is whatever the regime says it is. And it is the humane choice, because democracy is based on rules of equity and equal treatment that will, in principle, prevent those in power from using the lives of others as means to their own enrichment.

As noted at the beginning of this chapter, a broad definition of corruption is an important starting point for the argument of this book. This is in order not to leave out important aspects of corruption and to be able to address critical questions about democracy, accountability, good governance, and corruption reform. Once we understand the role of exchange and governance corruption in the determination of public integrity, we are faced with a number of interesting and important questions. Is it possible to assess corruption with any accuracy? Is exchange corruption the same across countries and across various sectors in society or does it change form as contexts vary? Is governance corruption avoidable, even in stable democracies?

These questions together with the hidden nature of corruption raise a number of thorny methodological issues of identification and measurement. But one additional question is perhaps the most important. What can be done to control and prevent exchange and governance corruption?

The first general point we make in this discussion is that corruption of politics and public administration is pervasive and difficult to eliminate. Corruption, as history shows, is not a time-bound phenomenon: it has been around as long as government and other structures established for collective action. It is not restricted geographically. It affects society at all levels and impacts people in their daily lives. Its relation to power, the relationship between private and public matters, and what is fair governance puts it at the core of our interest in democracy and democratic governance.

The Impact of Corruption

That corruption has a negative impact on society might seem obvious, but it is a claim that has taken a long time to validate. There is a long tradition in philosophy of concern about self-dealing and favoritism in government. In the West, this concern begins with reference to the Aristotelian ideal of virtue, but it also emphasizes the way that corruption affected the state and political history. The Italian diplomat and political philosopher Niccolò Machiavelli (1469–1527), whose influence is still strong in realist theory, pointed to the way that the integrity of public officials was constantly under threat of corruption. However, Machiavelli saw corruption and instability as cyclical and inevitable. His grim view of political evolution is summed up in his account of Florentine history.

> [Provinces] having been reduced by disorder, and sunk to their utmost state of depression, unable to descend lower, they, of necessity, re-ascend; and thus from good they gradually decline to evil, and from evil again return to good. The reason is, that valor produces peace; peace, repose; repose, disorder; disorder, ruin; so from disorder order springs; from order virtue, and from this, glory and good fortune.
>
> *(Machiavelli, 1526/1990, Book V, Chapter 1)*

Jean-Jacques Rousseau (1712–1778), the French Enlightenment thinker, was also a realist, but was more optimistic than Machiavelli about the possibility of avoiding public evil and disorder. Rousseau clearly understood the tendency of political systems to corrupt officials as they strive for power. His solution was the need for strong laws, written specifically to inhibit the abuse of power by ambitious officials.

> The general will is always in the right, but the judgment which guides it is not always enlightened. It must be got to see objects as they are, and sometimes as they ought to appear to it; it must be shown the good road it is in search of, secured from the seductive influences of individual wills, taught to see times and spaces as a series, and made to weigh the attractions of present and sensible advantages against the danger of distant and hidden evils. … This makes a legislator necessary.
>
> *(Rousseau, 1913, Book II, Chapter VI)*

Are we caught in Machiavelli's cycle or can we rely on the power of law, as Rousseau did? If we agree with Machiavelli, our approach to corruption is likely to be punitive: severe penalties, intense scrutiny, and, above all, distrust of anyone in power. Because, if we know that evil and disorder are just around the corner, we will try to protect ourselves, by force if necessary. But, if we agree with Rousseau, we are more likely to concentrate on laws that are less about punishment than about the protection of liberty and the balance and limitation of power. Government employees, under Rousseau's rule of law, are selected for their ability to understand and comply with integrity rules. The way the contrast between these two positions is often characterized in the study of public integrity is as a difference between a law enforcement approach and a values-based approach.

One additional observer of government ethics must be quoted at this point. Lord Acton's famous dictum should be kept in mind by anyone interested in protecting public integrity: "Power tends to corrupt and absolute power corrupts absolutely" (Acton Institute, 2016).[2]

Justifying Corruption

But there are those, particularly some microeconomists, who argue that corruption is not always bad—it reduces transaction costs by cutting bureaucratic red tape and allocates resources to those who indicate that they want them most by their willingness to pay for them (Leff, 1964). The usual term used by corruption defenders is "lubricant" for a system that creaks and grinds and sometimes simply stops. The prospect of money-on-the-side, it may be argued, works to jump-start allocations. Suddenly a permit or license is granted, zoning is approved, or a sewer connection is completed. It is also pointed out that in some developing countries a "gift culture" provides cultural support for bribes. Evaluation of this argument requires careful review of just who benefits from bribery, what the specific circumstances are, and whether there are problems with thinking of corruption as lubrication (Huntington, 1968, pp. 59–71; Nye, 1967).

Anyone reading this book might have been frustrated by slow, neglectful public officials who have dozens of reasons for not doing what you want. This is the root of bribery and extortion: exchange corruption. But exchange corruption is not a simple matter of lubrication. It has serious, immediate costs. Here are a few questions that indicate the downside of corrupt lubrication:

- Will there be any interest in repairing a slow, inefficient system, if it becomes well known that USD500 will do the trick?
- What about those who want and also deserve a government benefit that now requires a bribe, but cannot pay it?
- Will the long-term effect of exchange corruption improve or damage public trust in government fairness?
- How can the work of an agency known for bribe-taking be considered an effective or even rational use of public funds?
- Can those defending exchange corruption and rule avoidance ensure that the service rendered—construction inspection, for instance—will protect public health and safety?
- Won't government employees slow down their work and increase public frustration in order to extract bribes?
- Won't public resources be allocated to areas where it is easier go get corrupt dividends for those involved?

The assumption of microeconomic theory about market exchange is that it is voluntary, and that assumption underlies the positive view of bribery. But exchange corruption is very often involuntary. Take the example of a person in need of emergency hospital treatment who is given the choice of waiting at risk to his or her survival or paying an unofficial fee to get treatment—or a driver being wrongly accused of speeding by a police officer, who is given the choice of either paying a bribe or being charged with an offense. Given the questions above and the problem of coercion, the defense of exchange corruption should be rejected.

Moreover, if we look at the impact corruption has on society, government, and the economy, recent research is overwhelmingly negative about its impact. Corruption has been shown to be related to lower GDP and investment, and to depress growth[3] (Mauro, 1995, is a classic study of this), reduce trade, and increase poverty. It is of course difficult to estimate with precision the economic impact of corruption in monetary terms, but it is clear that the impact is substantial. The World Bank (2016) has estimated that annually about USD1 trillion is paid in bribes and the overall loss to corruption is much higher. Also, the poorest citizens suffer most from corruption. If we consider that poor people are more likely to have fewer resources such as education and connections to influential people and organizations at their disposal, not least in developing countries, they will be more vulnerable to corruption than more resourceful citizens who are often more aware of their rights, and have the resources to take countervailing actions.

International Efforts to Control Corruption

Among international organizations the OECD (Organisation for Economic Co-operation and Development) was an early advocate of common approaches to reduce corruption in international business and trade. The Convention on Combating Bribery of Foreign Public Officials in International Business Transactions, adopted in 1997, provides for trying and punishing international bribe-payers in domestic courts (OECD, 2016). The United Nations followed by stressing the importance of anti-corruption issues more and more. But the most notable change in international policy was by the World Bank. Until the mid-1990s the Bank regarded its own rules against interference in political issues as a prohibition against dealing with corruption. Now, however, the Bank views corruption as a key hindrance to economic development (Kim, 2014; Marquette, 2004; Wolfowitz, 2006).

In addition, Transparency International has become very influential. It was instrumental in putting the issue of corruption on the international agenda. One of its initiatives, the publication of its annual Corruption Perceptions Index (CPI), a measurement of perceived corruption across countries, has very high visibility and has had a noticeable impact on national and international ethics management strategies.

Unfortunately, corruption is often sensationalized, especially when it involves officials and politicians in high office. It is a topic that quickly attracts the label "scandal" and comes to dominates public attitudes about politics and government. But corruption is still badly understood. A clear, comprehensive understanding of corruption—the goal of this book—is critical to the goal of an ethical government that is trusted by the public.

Organizations and Corruption

The dynamics of life in organizations generate corruption and also make it difficult to prevent without undermining the effectiveness of government. Large organizations generate corruption, whether they are public bureaucracies, chartered/quasi-public authorities, or private companies that are paid to provide public services or are of such importance to the society that they serve a public function. Sociologist Robert K. Merton (1940) explained how the ideal type of bureaucracy described by the great German sociologist of the last century Max Weber, aiming for rationality, effectiveness, and impartiality in administration, also leads to negative side effects. These include delay, inflexibility, and brute impersonalism. People working in large organizations are urged to protect the prestige of the working group—to be loyal—not least when dealing with harmful mistakes. The demand for loyalty and each individual's regard for his or her place in the organization and career mobility will lead to cover-ups rather than apologies and corrections. Merton found that over time, formal organizational goals (public safety, clean streets, safe construction) will be displaced by the need to protect organizational status and individual careers. Goal displacement explains the apparent blindness to corrupt activities by managers and organizational leaders. Once formal goals have been displaced, recognizing corruption is considered disruptive and disloyal and will be ignored or punished.

A second sociologist, Diane Vaughan (1999), also studied the unexpected and negative effects of organizational structures and processes that are intended to ensure certainty, compliance, and goal achievement. Vaughan (1999, p. 273) labels such effects "organizational deviance":

> an event, activity, circumstance, occurring in and/or produced by a formal organization, that deviates from both formal design goals and normative standards or expectations, either in the fact of its occurrence or in its consequences, and produces suboptimal outcome.

This broad definition includes mistake, misconduct (corruption), and disaster. She looks at how critical choices are shaped by organizational culture, history, and leadership. In doing so she identifies the pathology of routine non-conformity with norms and values. As organizations mature and are confronted with constraints that threaten their status, they will come to accept dangerous shortcuts, rights violations, or technical errors, if that acceptance enhances their status. Vaughan (1996) calls this acceptance "normalized deviance".

When normalized deviance and goal displacement become entrenched, traditional corruption controls, which focus on individual behavior, will not help (see Warren, 2015, p. 47). What Vaughan and Merton are saying is that without internal controls and intensive monitoring, the culture and operation of large organizations will become corrupt. This is a variant of governance corruption, whereby the purpose for which public organizations in particular are established and toward which governments allocate funds and personnel is displaced and the people's will is violated or excluded.

Dealing with the Downside of Organizations

Stopping the drift of public organizations toward pathology and corruption is assigned to public integrity units of government, as well as prosecutors and auditors. However, the tools used to prevent and detect corruption can so limit organizational flexibility and discretion that not only is corruption prevented, but so is service to the public (Anechiarico & Jacobs, 1994, 1996; Klitgaard, 1988). The anti-corruption reforms of the last generation in public administration have done too little to punish those responsible for undermining public trust in government and too little to extend the reach of the law to emerging problems of interest conflict and abuse of democratic process. We also argue that this outcome is strongly connected to the dominating view of putting the focus (only) on exchange corruption and bribery. This is important to remember when thinking about how to build public integrity into organizations.

In addition, the changing nature of public administration, its organization and operation, has changed how corruption manifests itself and requires changes in how corruption is controlled. These changes begin in the late 19th century and include the idea that political decision making and public administration can and must be separated. The idea was that administration should be based on professional, non-partisan values which would enhance effectiveness and eliminate favoritism and conflicts of interest (Weber, 1946, pp. 196–198; Wilson, 1887/2007). A century later, the New Public Management (NPM), as administrative reforms in the late 20th century came to be called, advocated increased use of market mechanisms and business-like operations in public administration to reduce bureaucratic inefficiency (Hood, 1991; Kettl, 2005; Osborne & Gaebler, 1993). During this period the term "governance" came into use to describe the broad arena of public affairs beyond government agencies, reflecting the role that non-governmental organizations have in public administration and in determining the quality of public life (e.g. Rhodes, 1996).

Economic Values and Public Values

But the NPM, which used the prevalence of organizational pathologies to argue for more agile, market-oriented government, also has a downside. In the United Kingdom, one of the earlier adopters of the NPM agenda, costs seemed to be higher and performance and perceived fairness of public administration somewhat worse in market-oriented agencies (Hood & Dixon, 2015, pp. 180–183). The British found that NPM reforms required external controls that were quite similar to those for which bureaucratic administration had been criticized. But most critically, studies in the UK and elsewhere have found that NPM emphasizes market values like cost-cutting and profit over values of public interest and citizenship (Denhardt & Denhardt, 2000, p. 557).

The modern mix of public and private actors involved in public administration is a challenge for official accountability (cf. Ingram & Schneider, 2008, p. 182). Who is in fact accountable for decisions and the implementation of public policy when most of the work is done by a profit-seeking corporation? Who is held responsible for harmful mistakes and corruption when public officials sign a contract giving government power to a private corporation (Andersson & Anechiarico, 2015; Johnston, 2005)?

As public administration changes, the definition of corruption cannot remain static. For this reason, we opened this chapter with an explanation of both exchange and governance corruption. The purpose of this book is to introduce and investigate the way in which public administration becomes corrupt and which reforms are best suited to restoring the ideal of public service. To do this we will examine corruption with a focus on democracy and sustainable public integrity and the danger to both of these critical values posed by governance corruption.

Our approach to corruption is a point of entry to understanding the deep institutional and systemic problems that surround corruption and to exploring broader questions about participation, justice, and accountability, and the social and political costs of corruption. It is important to remember that some instances of governance corruption may not be formally illegal, but still directly violate democratic values. In these situations, a deterrence approach based on criminal and civil sanctions will miss the target. What are needed in instances of "legal" governance corruption are values-based measures aimed at the personal and public ethics of officials, alongside regulations that require inclusive policy-making.

Plan of the Book

What Corruption Was, Is, and Is Not: Chapter 2

Etymologically the word "corruption" is derived from Latin denoting a degenerated condition—a condition of decay. Dictionary definitions of official corruption tend to center on bribery and immorality. In the online Oxford Dictionaries (2016), for example, corruption is defined as "Dishonest or fraudulent conduct by those in power, typically involving bribery." Social science definitions also have a similar take with a focus on how public roles or resources are violated for private or personal benefit. Historically they additionally underline the negative effects of corruption on the political system and society (Friedrich, 1989, p. 16).

In Chapter 2 we discuss what corruption is and present our argument for a broad definition of corruption in order to embrace important social problems. We discuss this in terms of a two-legged concept where *exchange corruption* concerns the relation of corruption to the effectiveness of government, which is closer to a formal public-office-related, legalistic, and narrower take. *Governance corruption* concerns the quality and effect of social control, and looks at broader structures as well as political exclusion, bias, and the obstruction of voice and vote. In deriving this outlook on corruption, Chapter 2 takes as a starting point what corruption is not and what characterizes good democratic governance. It looks at the role of bureaucratic routines, administrative culture, and mechanisms of exclusion in terms of generating corruption. An important conclusion is that public integrity concerns more than compliance with legal rules and that corruption is not only about officials who break rules but that it may also concern official and legal behavior such as exclusionary and duplicitous policies and systemic interest conflicts.

Can We Know How Much Corruption There Is? On the Measurement of Corruption: Chapter 3

In Chapter 3 we consider how corruption might be measured, and take a closer look at current techniques for assessing corruption. The overarching argument in the chapter is that how we approach corruption measurement is not just a technical issue but is closely connected to issues about what corruption is and how to control and prevent it.

Measuring corruption is not an easy matter due to its hidden nature, the many forms it takes, and how it varies over time and in different contexts. And critically, how we define corruption has a direct impact of what sort of actions and phenomena are included in a given measurement. These problems lead to questions about the feasibility of comparing corruption across localities, and if corruption over time has become less or more common.

Corruption Control in Public Administration: Chapter 4

In Chapter 4 we turn to how public organizations try to ensure public integrity and prevent corruption. We show that finding the right approach and balance between various control measures, such as those relying on law and rule enforcement and those relying on the values of individual government employees, is easier said than done. We provide examples from both national and international organizations and how they approach this issue. In this exploration of integrity and control approaches we refer to changes in public administration, especially those which have shifted public functions to the private sector by applying market values to governance.

The Connection between Public Integrity and Democratic Governance: Four Case Studies—Chapter 5

In Chapter 5 we take a deeper look at four individual cases ranging from clear-cut manifestations of corruption to a journey into the gray zone. We analyze and discuss each case in terms of our definitions of exchange and governance corruption and by looking at factors contributing to corruption at three levels of analysis: individual, organizational, and systemic. This approach is introduced in Chapters 2 and 3 but is further developed in this chapter. For each case we ask:

- What caused the corruption in question?
- Who was involved and what motivated them?
- What environmental factors enabled the misconduct?

Finally, we consider the linkage between corrupt acts, societal-level values, and the organizational routines that influence ethical decision making.

Is Corruption Inevitable? Can It Be Controlled? Chapter 6

Given that corruption can be found everywhere across the world, in various forms, it is reasonable to ask whether it is inevitable and whether it can be controlled. In Chapter 6 we build on Chapters 4 and 5 to address these questions using the case of New York City to study in depth how corruption and the control of corruption develop over time in a particular place. We take a long view, starting with the founding of the Dutch settlement, in what is now New York City, in the 17th century. The city's history, political culture, and reform tradition form the core of the chapter.

The history of corruption and corruption control in New York City provides us with a good illustration of corruption vulnerabilities, how corruption is generated in public organizations including cycles of governance corruption, and corruption control. Nearly every type of corruption is found in the history of the city and virtually every modern method of corruption control has been applied to them at one time or another.

The Future of Public Integrity: Chapter 7

In this chapter we sum up our main points. After a summary discussion of the ideas and concepts we have used to build our argument, we return to the four case studies in Chapter 5 and the case of New York City in Chapter 6 to explain the theoretical and practical significance of each case. A second section is concerned with the broader applicability of our theoretical and practical conclusions to an alternative, cooperative model of public ethics management.

Notes

1 An organization that can raise unlimited funds from individuals and organizations, and can engage in unlimited political spending as long it is done independently of the campaigns of the parties or candidates (e.g. Adams & Wells, 2012).
2 This famous part is also followed by "Great men are almost always bad men, even when they exercise influence and not authority; still more when you superadd the tendency of the certainty of corruption by authority."
3 The correlation between corruption and growth seems to be less robust (i.e. there are countries where growth has been fast despite widespread corruption; for example, Vietnam and China).

References

Acton Institute. (2016). *Lord Acton Quote Archive.* Retrieved from www.acton.org/research/lord-acton-quote-archive.

Adams, R., & Wells, M. (2012, February 21). Super Pacs explained. *The Guardian.* Retrieved from www.theguardian.com/world/interactive/2012/feb/21/super-pacs-campaign-finance-explained.

Andersson, S., & Anechiarico, F. (2015). The political economy of conflicts of interest in an era of public private governance. In P. M. Heywood (Ed.), *Routledge handbook of political corruption* (pp. 253–269). Abingdon, UK: Routledge.

Anechiarico, F., & Jacobs, J. B. (1994). Panopticism and financial controls. *Crime, Law and Social Change, 22*(4), 361–379.

Anechiarico, F., & Jacobs, J. B. (1996). *The pursuit of absolute integrity: How corruption control makes government ineffective.* Chicago, IL: University of Chicago Press.

Armitage, J. (2014, March 1). Exclusive: "Ukrainian assets owned or used by ousted President Viktor Yanukovych hidden behind trail of firms with links to UK". *The Independent.* Retrieved from www.independent.co.uk/news/uk/crime/exclusive-ukrainian-assets-owned-or-used-by-ousted-president-viktor-yanukovych-hidden-behind-trail-9161504.html.

Associated Press. (2017, October 26). Michel Temer, Brazil's unpopular president, avoids corruption trial. *The Guardian.* Retrieved from www.theguardian.com/world/2017/oct/26/michel-temer-brazils-unpopular-president-avoids-corruption-trial.

BBC News. (2010, September 14). Catholic Church sex abuse scandals around the world. Retrieved from www.bbc.com/news/10407559.

BBC News. (2018a, May 18). All Chile's 34 bishops offer resignation to Pope over sex abuse scandals. Retrieved from www.bbc.com/news/world-latin-america-44169484.

BBC News. (2018b, May 22). Australian archbishop Philip Wilson guilty of concealing child sex abuses. Retrieved from www.bbc.com/news/world-australia-44205985.

Bump, P. (2016, April 18). Bernie Sanders keeps saying his average donation is $27, but his own numbers contradict that. *Washington Post.* Retrieved from www.washingtonpost.com/news/the-fix/wp/2016/04/18/bernie-sanders-keeps-saying-his-average-donation-is-27-but-it-really-isnt/?noredirect=on&utm_term=.f994d1fb404c.

Cassin, R. L. (2015, July 8, 2015). Norway jails four ex Yara execs for India, Libya bribes. *FCPA Blog.* Retrieved from www.fcpablog.com/blog/2015/7/8/norway-jails-four-ex-yara-execs-for-india-libya-bribes.html.

Cowie, S. (2018, April 5). Brazil's Lula faces jail for corruption after supreme court ruling. *The Guardian.* Retrieved from www.theguardian.com/world/2018/apr/05/brazil-former-president-lula-jail-corruption-supreme-court-ruling.

Denhardt, R. B., & Denhardt, J. V. (2000). The New Public Service: Serving rather than steering. *Public Administration Review, 60*(6), 549–559.

Friedrich, C. J. (1989). Corruption concepts in historical perspective. In A. Heidenheimer, M. Johnston, & V. LeVine (Eds.), *Political corruption: A handbook* (pp. 15–24). New Brunswick: Transaction Publishers.

Garside, J. (2017, November 5, 2017). Paradise Papers leak reveals secrets of the world elite's hidden wealth. *The Guardian.* Retrieved from www.theguardian.com/news/2017/nov/05/paradise-papers-leak-reveals-secrets-of-world-elites-hidden-wealth.

Garside, J., Watt, H., & Pegg, D. (2016, April 3). The Panama Papers: How the world's rich and famous hide their money offshore. *The Guardian.* Retrieved from www.theguardian.com/news/2016/apr/03/the-panama-papers-how-the-worlds-rich-and-famous-hide-their-money-offshore.

Gersh, N. (2017, February 6). The role of corruption in the Syrian civil war. *Global Anticorruption Blog.* Retrieved from https://globalanticorruptionblog.com/2017/02/06/the-role-of-corruption-in-the-syrian-civil-war/.

Harding, L. (2016, April 5). What are the Panama Papers? A guide to history's biggest data leak. *The Guardian.* Retrieved from www.theguardian.com/news/2016/apr/03/what-you-need-to-know-about-the-panama-papers.

Hatton, C. (2013, January 28). How serious is China on corruption? *BBC News*. Retrieved from www.bbc.com/news/world-asia-china-21231198.

Hood, C. (1991). A public management for all seasons. *Public Administration, 69*(1), 3–19.

Hood, C., & Dixon, R. (2015). *A government that worked better and cost less? Evaluating three decades of reform and change in UK central government*. Oxford: Oxford University Press.

Hopkins, N., & Bengtsson, H. (2017, November 5). What are the Paradise Papers and what do they tell us? *The Guardian*. Retrieved from www.theguardian.com/news/2017/nov/05/what-are-the-paradise-papers-and-what-do-they-tell-us.

Huberts, L. (2014). *The integrity of governance: What it is, what we know, what is done, and where to go*. Basingstoke, UK: Palgrave Macmillan.

Human Rights Watch. (2017). *"Kill the chicken to scare the monkeys": Suppression of free expression and assembly in Singapore*. Retrieved from www.hrw.org/report/2017/12/12/kill-chicken-scare-monkeys/suppression-free-expression-and-assembly-singapore.

Hume, D. (1889). *The natural history of religion*. London: A. and H. Bradlaugh Bonner.

Huntington, S. P. (1968). *Political order in changing societies*. New Haven, CT and London: Yale University Press.

Ingram, H., & Schneider, A. L. (2008). Policy analysis for democracy. In M. Moran, M. Rein, & R. E. Goodin (Eds.), *The Oxford handbook of public policy*. Oxford: Oxford University Press.

Johnston, M. (2005). *Syndromes of corruption: Wealth, power, and democracy*. Cambridge: Cambridge University Press.

Kaplan, S. (2017, November 13). Trump raised more dollars from small donations. PolitiFact. Retrieved from www.politifact.com/truth-o-meter/statements/2017/nov/13/kayleigh-mcenany/trump-raised-more-dollars-small-donations/.

Kettl, D. F. (2005). *The global public management revolution* (2nd ed.). Washington, D.C.: Brookings Institution Press.

Kim, J. Y. (2014). *World Bank Group President Jim Yong Kim's remarks at the International Corruption Hunters Alliance*. Retrieved from www.worldbank.org/en/news/speech/2014/12/08/world-bank-group-president-jim-yong-kims-remarks-international-corruption-hunters-alliance.

Klitgaard, R. E. (1988). *Controlling corruption*. Berkeley, CA: University of California Press.

Leff, N. (1964). Economic development through bureaucratic corruption. *American Behavioral Scientist, 8*(3), 8–14.

Leonhardt, D., & Philbrick, I. P. (2018, October 28). Trump's corruption: The definitive list. The many ways that the president, his family and his aides are lining their own pockets. *New York Times*. Retrieved from www.nytimes.com/2018/10/28/opinion/trump-administration-corruption-conflicts.html?action=click&module=Opinion&pgtype=Homepage.

Lockett, H. (2016, October 9). China anti-corruption campaign backfires. *Financial Times*. Retrieved from www.ft.com/content/02f712b4-8ab8-11e6-8aa5-f79f5696c731.

Machiavelli, N. (1526/1990). *Florentine histories*. Laura F. Banfield and Harvey C. Mansfield, Jr. (Trans.). Princeton, NJ: Princeton University Press.

Marquette, H. (2004). The creeping politicisation of the World Bank: The case of corruption. *Political Studies, 52*, 413–430.

Mauro, P. (1995). Corruption and growth. *Quarterly Journal of Economics, 110*(3), 681–712.

Merton, R. K. (1940). Bureaucratic structure and personality. *Social Forces, 18*(4), 560–568.

Narayanswamy, A., Cameron, D., & Gold, M. (n.d.). Election 2016. Money raised as of Dec. 31. *Washington Post.* Retrieved from www.washingtonpost.com/graphics/politics/2016-election/campaign-finance/.

Nye, J. S. (1967). Corruption and political development: A cost-benefit analysis. *American Political Science Review, 61*(2), 417–427.

OECD. (2016). *OECD Convention on Combating Bribery of Foreign Public Officials in International Business Transactions.* Retrieved from www.oecd.org/corruption/oecdan tibriberyconvention.htm.

Osborne, D., & Gaebler, T. (1993). *Reinventing government: How the entrepreneurial spirit is transforming the public sector.* New York: Plume.

Oxford Dictionaries. (2016). *Corruption.* Retrieved from www.oxforddictionaries.com/definition/english/corruption.

Phillips, D. (2018, January 24). Brazilian court upholds corruption conviction for ex-president Lula. *The Guardian.* Retrieved from www.theguardian.com/world/2018/jan/24/brazilian-court-upholds-corruption-conviction-for-ex-president-lula.

Prince, R. (2009, May 12). MPs' expenses: Clearing the moat at Douglas Hogg's manor. *The Telegraph.* Retrieved from www.telegraph.co.uk/news/newstopics/mps-expenses/5310069/MPs-expenses-Clearing-the-moat-at-Douglas-Hoggs-manor.html.

Rhodes, R. A. W. (1996). The new governance: Governing without government. *Political Studies, 44*(4), 652–667.

Rousseau, J.-J. (1913). *Social contract & discourses.* G. D. H. Cole (Trans.). New York: E. P. Dutton & Co., 1913; Bartleby.com, 2010.

Teachout, Z. (2017, December 11). I'm not convinced Franken should quit. *New York Times.* Retrieved from www.nytimes.com/2017/12/11/opinion/franken-resignation-harassment-democrats.html.

The Economist. (2018, June 28). The future of Syria: How a victorious Bashar al-Assad is changing Syria. Retrieved from www.economist.com/middle-east-and-africa/2018/06/28/how-a-victorious-bashar-al-assad-is-changing-syria.

Transparency International. (2018). Corruption Perceptions Index 2017. Retrieved from www.transparency.org/news/feature/corruption_perceptions_index_2017.

U.S. Securities and Exchange Commission. (2008). *SEC charges Siemens AG for engaging in worldwide bribery.* Retrieved from www.sec.gov/news/press/2008/2008-294.htm.

Warren, M. E. (2015). The meaning of corruption in democracies. In P. M. Heywood (Ed.), *Routledge handbook of political corruption* (pp. 42–55). Abingdon, UK: Routledge.

Watts, J. (2016, August 31). Dilma Rousseff impeachment: What you need to know – the Guardian briefing. *The Guardian.* Retrieved from www.theguardian.com/news/2016/aug/31/dilma-rousseff-impeachment-brazil-what-you-need-to-know.

World Bank (2016). Anti-corruption. Retrieved from www.worldbank.org/en/topic/governance/brief/anti-corruption.

Vaughan, D. (1996). *The Challenger launch decision: Risky technology, culture, and deviance at NASA.* Chicago, IL: University of Chicago Press.

Vaughan, D. (1999). The dark side of organizations: Mistake, misconduct, and disaster. *Annual Review of Sociology, 25,* 271–305.

Weber, M. (1946). *From Max Weber: Essays in sociology.* H. H. Gerth and C. Wright Mills (Trans. and Eds.). New York: Oxford University Press.

Wilson, W. (1887/2007). The study of administration. In J. M. Shafritz & A. C. Hyde (Eds.), *Classics of public administration* (6th ed., pp. 16–27). Boston, MA: Thomson Wadsworth.

Wolfowitz, P. (2006). Good governance and development: A time for action, speech in Jakarta 11 April, 2006. Retrieved from http://documents.worldbank.org/curated/en/938181467987875500/pdf/101339-WP-Box393261B-PUBLIC-2006-04-11-PW-Good-Governance-and-Development.pdf.

Zaba, F. (2016, October 28, 2016). Corruption: Mugabe should walk the talk. *Zimbabwe Independent*. Retrieved from www.theindependent.co.zw/2016/10/28/corruption-mugabe-walk-talk/.

Zúñiga, N. (2018). *China: Overview of corruption and anticorruption*. Retrieved from https://knowledgehub.transparency.org/helpdesk/china-overview-of-corruption-and-anti-corruption-1.

2

WHAT CORRUPTION WAS, IS, AND IS NOT

What It Isn't

"I know it when I see it," you might answer when I ask you to define corruption. You will probably be thinking about crooked politicians, greedy public contractors, and plain old bribery and extortion. But the follow-up question I would have to ask is, "Just *what* are you seeing, when you see *it?*" This is not just a snarky retort. The tough part about defining, studying, or preventing corruption is that it is very hard to see. Most corruption, like other objectionable behavior that "benefits" both parties, takes place out of public view, between consenting adults. Very few people other than parties to corrupt deals have actually "seen" corruption. What we see is the result of investigations, arrests, and adjudication, not the actual fact of the matter.

So, what do we mean by we know it when we see it and when we use the word "corruption"? We think it has more to do with what corruption is not than what it is. We are willing to bet that the readers of this book share with its authors a pretty clear idea of what corruption is *not*. It is not: good, public-spirited governance administered by dedicated, energetic people who use their knowledge and experience for the benefit of those who pay their salaries or fund their contracts. In short, corruption is *not* honest, democratic government. That's vague, but it's the right place to start.

Knowing what we think about the right way to do something gives us a good idea of what the wrong way is. It also gives us an idea of how to recognize error and failure. The clearer our idea is of what is right, the better able we will be to understand what went wrong, how it got that way, and how to avoid going wrong again. But "what is wrong" is also complex. Beyond error and failure is a subtle and more dangerous "wrong way"—a kind of subversion that eats away at or rots what is right. This kind of subversion of "what is right" is called corruption. Think of it as the rot of public values and the decay of democracy.

The following discussion includes both practical and philosophical issues related to the definition of corruption and the problem of public integrity.

What Is Right?

Nikolai Gogol's 1836 comedy *The Inspector-General* begins with a warning received by a provincial governor:

> I hasten to let you know, among other things, that an official has arrived here with instructions to inspect the whole government, and your district especially. ... I advise you to take precautions, as he may arrive any hour, if he hasn't already, and is not staying somewhere incognito.
>
> *(Gogol, 1836/1916, Act 1, Scene 1)*

This sets local officialdom in motion. Comfortable routines that have lined the pockets of bureaucrats and petty tyrants are threatened. It is imperative that the inspector be found and neutralized. But this is a satire, and in their haste those most threatened try to neutralize the wrong visitor. The bite of Gogol's humor was not lost on its audience in Czarist Russia. The thoroughness of corruption in the fictional province had rendered the governor and his minions not only stupid and careless, but incapable of changing or even thinking about their own behavior. Their corrupt world is under attack and has to be defended at any cost. The hysteria and bad judgment that pervade the play are both hilarious and an excellent example of what we call a "cover-up".

The importance of this story for us is the difference in expectations between the local officials, who had come to rely on a steady stream of bribes and privileges, and officials in the Czar's administration, who had modern ideas about efficient government. The remarkable thing about corruption—and Gogol hits it right on the nose—is the extent to which it continues and becomes part of routine, official culture, to the point that those engaging in it no longer think it is wrong. It is simply the way things are done. It is, in fact, just and correct. As Gogol's governor says, when he thinks he's been found out, "I swear to you, it was nothing but my inexperience and insufficient means. Judge for yourself. The salary I get is not enough for tea and sugar" (Act 2, Scene 8). Thus, the governor "deserves" what he's been stealing.

We can pause here to define the key elements in the play that will help us understand the complexity of defining and detecting corruption:

Bureaucratic Routine

Sociologist Max Weber recognized routine and "routinization" as the elemental dynamic of the modern world. All matters, public and private, would over time be shaped by routines set out in well-understood rules, and administered by qualified, dispassionate personnel. The interesting thing about Weber's delineation of this "ideal-type" is that it is value-neutral. A bureaucracy can be efficient and effective in the pursuit of charitable goals or in the administration of evil. The International Red Cross is organized as a bureaucracy, but so was the German Nazi Party. The other characteristics of the ideal-type bureaucracy identified by Weber (1946, pp. 196–198) are:

- Hierarchical authority
- Specialization of function
- Written rules and procedures
- Reliance on credentialed technicians
- Efficiency as primary evaluation criterion

The value neutrality of bureaucracy leads to three, important observations.

First—and here we can return to Gogol's story—efficient, rule-bound routine can be found in the way that the inspector and his superiors in St. Petersburg carry out the search for corruption and other misconduct in their survey of local governments. Though they are off-stage, we are given to understand that those in charge have planned a systematic review of local government finances across Russia.

Second, the corrupt local officials, who are the butt of Gogol's satire, are also part of a routine. Their corrupt behavior is necessarily less formal, but nevertheless carefully structured and efficient. Each official knows how much he is due and from which merchants and land-owners. The merchants and land-owners are part of the routine as well. "Misconduct", in this system, means not paying what is required, when it is required, and to whom it must go. Because there is no real value basis for distinguishing one routine from another, it is possible, and not unusual, for a corrupt system to be more efficiently run than the system that is supposed to root it out.

Third, as routines mature, whether they are corrupt or not, they tend to drift from their original goals. The balance of responsibilities, rewards, incentives, and sanctions in an organization is hard to maintain over time and personal goals and the basic need to keep the routine going (organizational survival) displace the original mission. This can happen in agencies charged with protecting public integrity as well as among the corrupt themselves. Inspectors and other types of officials may hear from their superiors that those even higher up want to see more arrests. More arrests will ensure the future of the agency and each inspector's job. The resulting frenzy of investigation and prosecution makes it more than likely that the innocent will suffer. Likewise, Gogol's governor and his crew will look for more and larger sources of bribes. Whatever logic there may have been to the initial understanding between the local community and the local government will be undercut by greed. Since routines are operated by human beings, they are dynamic and tend over time to dissolve into self-interest and organizational survival. What are the mechanisms and elements of bureaucratic wrongdoing and pathology?

Administrative Culture

We live our lives in several cultures, simultaneously, as students, faculty, or employees of business or government; as family members; as members of religious communities; and as volunteers or hobbyists. "Culture" may be even more difficult to define than corruption. For our purposes, it is a transmissible set of values and expectations that structure behavior and a sense of reality. Those values include what is considered right, wrong, and corrupt.

Over time, the displacement of goals described above can warp the culture of an organization, so that behavior which from other perspectives appears wrong or corrupt is validated as necessary and good. But wouldn't a rational person notice that bad behavior has become acceptable and is encouraged and rewarded by superiors? Some do and either quit or fight, maybe as whistleblowers. But most of us will follow the values embedded in everyday communication with peers, directives from the hierarchy, and what evidently will help us keep our jobs and get ahead. "You have to go along to get along" is perhaps the best way to summarize the strong influence that administrative culture has on personal behavior.

But sometimes the culture shift that allows corruption is the result of a conscious choice on the part of leaders. Some of the greatest tragedies in history, including the Holocaust, result from such choices. Administrative culture makes sense out of our work lives and, just as it can support and encourage honesty and integrity, it can validate lies and evil.

Case: Administrative Culture and Routine at NASA

On January 28, 1986, just minutes after the launch, the space shuttle *Challenger* caught fire, killing seven crew members. The night before, engineers at Morton Thiokol, the company that designed the rocket carrying the shuttle, expressed serious concerns that the "O" rings that joined parts of the rocket would fail if the rocket was launched in a temperature under 53°F. The predicted temperature at the scheduled, morning launch time in Florida was at least 20 degrees below that.

All this was debated the night before the launch in teleconferences between the Morton Thiokol engineers in Utah, the NASA flight center in Alabama, and the launch directors in Florida. After several engineers presented their arguments against launching in cold weather, one official at NASA responded that he was "appalled" and another asked, "My God, when do you want me to launch— April?" (quoted in *Los Angeles Times*, 1986). The Presidential Commission on the disaster included an exchange about the pre-launch teleconference between a member of the Commission, Arthur Walker, a Stanford University physicist, and Roger Boisjoly, a mechanical engineer on the rocket design team at Morton Thiokol. Here, Walker is asking Boisjoly what happened after he and others had voiced their objections and NASA officials had pushed back:

Dr. Walker: At this point did anyone else speak up in favor of the launch?

Mr. Boisjoly: No, sir. No one said anything, in my recollection, nobody said a word. It was then being discussed amongst the management folks. After Arnie and I had our last say, Mr. Mason said we have to make a management decision. He turned to Bob Lund and asked him to take off his engineering hat and put on his management hat. From this point on, management formulated the points to base their decision on. There was never one comment in favor, as I have said, of launching by any engineer or other non-management person in the room before or after the caucus. I was not even asked to participate in giving any input to the final decision charts. ... I did not agree with some of the statements that were being made to support the decision. I was never asked nor polled, and it was clearly a management decision from that point.

(Presidential Commission, 1986)

A *Los Angeles Times* (1986) summary of the events leading up to the launch is entitled "The 24 hours of pre-launch debate that could have prevented a tragedy." It is tempting to blame the management team for the disaster, in light of the objections raised by the engineers before the launch. But, if we stop with the management team and the pre-launch teleconference, we miss the more complex, persistent organizational elements of the disaster. The way that NASA had come to accept a much wider margin of error for the performance of the "O" rings is called "normalized deviance" by Diane Vaughan. Because of time and political pressure and a culture of accomplishment that included landing humans on the moon, the failures or erosions of the "O" rings in un-manned launches slowly became acceptable and normal (Vaughan, 1996).

Reciprocal Expectations

At this point, it is worth pointing out the obvious: corruption can be understood from several perspectives. Let's start with one of the most prominent approaches, which is based on micro-economic theory. When we think about the reciprocity in many corrupt dealings, we tend to think of market exchange. I give you something in exchange for something you give me. This exchange is also embedded in culture, is surrounded by routine, and relies on agreement that the exchange is fair and equal. The legal term for this kind of reciprocity is "quid pro quo", literally "something for something".

But there is a dark side to this kind of reciprocity. According to the micro-economic, rational-actor model, the assessment of costs and benefits is purely subjective. That is, I might decide that I no longer care for my new Rolls-Royce; in fact, I hate it and want it gone as quickly as possible. As a rational actor, I then decide to sell it for five dollars. The micro-economic model does not allow anyone to call me irrational. I have valued the car according to my preferences. They may be odd, but they are mine. But what if someone persuades me to sell the Rolls for five dollars by threatening me? We would like to think that coercion and fear put this transaction in another category, but my decision to sell it to my persecutor for five dollars is still rational. My preference is to comply, in light of the likely costs. The reciprocity involved in corruption includes this kind of persuasion quite often.

Case: Reciprocal Expectations in Building Inspection

I might understand that in order to start leasing the apartments in a new building I borrowed heavily to build, I must pay off two or three municipal inspectors, but how reciprocal is such a transaction? I would not try to "find" someone to pay, if the inspection process was fair and efficient. The idea that bribes are an efficient way of indicating who most wants a good or service neglects the possibility of honest government, where bribery is not acceptable. Bribery as reciprocity must be examined in light of honest government, which is what corruption is not.

We will discuss building and construction regulation in New York City in Chapter 6. But the chronic corruption in the city's Department of Buildings is an object lesson in the way reciprocal, corrupt relationships become part of administrative culture, so that the mission of guaranteeing safe, legal construction is displaced by personal preference for money. Goals are displaced and deviance is normalized. These pathologies are particularly noticeable in the history of the Department of Buildings, but, we argue, they are part of the history of all large, bureaucratic organizations.

Official Misconduct

There is an unfortunate amount of official behavior that we might classify as misconduct but that may not be corrupt. There is neglect of standard operating procedures, rudeness to the public, inefficiency, and laziness. A state court defined official misconduct, often called "malfeasance", as:

> a wrongful act which the actor has no legal right to do; as any wrongful conduct which affects, interrupts or interferes with the performance of official duty; as an act for which there is no authority or warrant of law; as an act which a person ought not to do; as an act which is wholly wrongful and

unlawful; as that which an officer has no authority to do and is positively wrong or unlawful; and as the unjust performance of some act which the party performing it has no right, or has contracted not, to do.

(Daugherty v. Ellis, *1956)*

What is interesting about this definition is how it shifts back and forth between the law ("legal right", "warrant of law") and morality ("wholly wrongful", "ought not to do"). This is a critical aspect of misconduct. It is shaped by moral values as well as statutes and court decisions. Of course, the law is also shaped by morality. But, as the state court indicates, our definition of misconduct is broader than most legal definitions.

Most organizations, including public agencies, have codes of conduct that punish behavior that is not criminal and for which there is no civil liability. These codes and expectations are a function of administrative culture and an assessment of what it takes to maintain bureaucratic routine. These can look strange to outsiders.

Case: Defining Official Misconduct at West Point

In the late 1960s, a number of colleges in the United States accepted several mid-year transfers from the U.S. Military Academy at West Point. The transfers had been caught up in a cheating scandal that resulted in the expulsion of more than a dozen cadets. Most of them had not actually cheated, but had failed to turn in those who had. This seemed draconian, but was quickly recognized as misconduct by anyone who understood moral values at West Point.

The idea behind the West Point honor code is to establish and enforce a very high level of moral behavior among future Army officers. If the value of honesty in all things becomes part of your rational calculations and, indeed, one of your personal preferences, it will be unnecessary to monitor you in the future. The idea behind the tough treatment of those expelled from the Academy for not turning in their fellow cadets was to make "West Point graduate" synonymous with "honesty and integrity". In this way, the tendency of bureaucratic organizations to drift toward corruption might be avoided in the Army—the largest bureaucratic organization in the United States.

Good Governance

Good governance is what corruption is not. The quality of governance is determined by the very broadest values that are identified and propagated in a society. Those values range from security and order to liberty and rights. In fact, we can array what might be called prime governing values between the poles of *security* and *liberty*. That puts authoritarian systems, where state and official security is the prime value, at one end, and anarchy at the other. In between, we find fascism, corporatism, democratic socialism, pluralist democracy, and many hybrids.

A deeper, more thorough discussion of the quality of governance would have to take classical and Enlightenment philosophy into account. At the risk of insulting our colleagues in the fields of political theory and philosophy, we would like to point out three important, theoretical markers that underlie good governance in a democratic society: participation, duty, and inclusion.

a. **Civic participation**, according to Aristotle

Aristotle argued that human potential could only be realized by a life lived in the political arena. Active, civic participation, with all of its frustrations and possibilities, is a necessary part of the "good life". As he put it, "[T]he active life will be the best, both for every city collectively, and for individuals" (*Politics*, Book VII, p. 3).

However, Aristotle's acceptance of slavery, social hierarchy, and a political class system has been enough to alienate many modern readers. We can agree that what he says on these topics in *Politics* ranges from the despicable to the ridiculous. We can also agree with Michael Sandel that his reasoning on these matters is relatively unconvincing, perhaps even to himself (Sandel, 2009, pp. 200–203). So, it is possible to move on to Aristotle's notion of democracy.

It can be argued that good governance can be found in non-democratic systems. There may be less inequality and better infrastructure and public service in some authoritarian systems than in many democracies. But this is a book about corruption. Whatever virtues authoritarian systems may have, they lack the notion of popular consent that underlies decision making in democracies. Without popular consent and participation, it is impossible to know whether government is honest. In China, Cuba, North Korea, Venezuela, Russia, Saudi Arabia, and Iran, among other countries, corruption is prosecuted in defense of the state, as defined by those in power. But the political use of corruption charges is not unknown in democratic systems either. What distinguishes democracies from other systems is the definition of good governance as the consent of the governed. Thus a violation of that consent must be considered corrupt. Here we return to Aristotle for a simple and powerful defense of democracy:

> [I]t is obviously necessary on many grounds that all the citizens alike should take their turn of governing and being governed. Equality consists in the same treatment of similar persons, and no government can stand which is not founded upon justice.
>
> *(Politics, Book VII, p. 14)*

The importance of this statement is in the way that Aristotle links and combines democracy, equality, and justice. All three are necessary to the good life and good governance.

b.   **Duty to humanity**, according to Immanuel Kant

Kant's moral philosophy argues that we each have a rational and necessary duty to the truth and to each other. It is rational, Kant says, to adopt and act on principles that you would like everyone else to follow. He calls this the "categorical imperative". The categorical imperative reflects a regard for humanity that Kant ranks as our first duty. It follows, then, that we should be honest. If we are all acting according to universalized principles, those principles should be known and the degree to which we comply with them in our daily behavior should also be evident. Such a system cannot work without careful regard for the truth. If I would like you to follow the principles that I have adopted for myself, but which I do not follow myself, I am both a hypocrite and a liar and the imperative has no moral basis: "From such crooked wood, nothing straight can be fashioned" (Kant, 1798, p. 421).

The categorical imperative and the humanity principle help us understand why we should worry about corruption. Corruption is based on lies and hypocrisy; it undermines morality and neglects humanity. As Kant puts it, "Act so as to use humanity—yourself and others—always as an end, and never as a means to an end" (1785/1964, p. 429). As representatives and employees of the state and the people, public officials should consider the value and condition of humanity—of those they serve—as an end. Any official's use of humanity as a means to other ends—like personal financial gain—is a violation of his or her duty (and the duty of everyone, Kant says) and may be considered corrupt.

But what does this mean in practical terms? We can return to the building owner seeking final approval from a building inspector for an answer. The inspector acts with the power of the state, granted with the consent of the people. The inspector's duty is to use that power in the interest of the people (humanity). That interest is the "end" Kant talks about. However, if the inspector asks the developer for a bribe or accepts one that is offered, humanity embodied in the people's power—the authority to withhold final approval—is used as a means to personal enrichment. The other effect of the bribe is to establish a principle of behavior about which it is necessary to lie. We grant public officials coercive power for specific purposes related to our needs as humans. We need an orderly, safe physical environment. That need requires the use of sanctions by trained specialists, who will carefully and honestly assess each change in that environment. This is not just part of the job description of building inspectors; it is their duty as human beings.

c.   **Democratic inclusion**, according to Mark Warren

The value of democratic inclusion can be understood as a combination of Aristotle's linked values of justice, equality, and democracy and Kant's principles. In the same vein, political theorist Mark Warren (2004) pointed out that the prevailing definition of corruption as private gain from public office doesn't consider other critical values, like democratic participation and moral duty. A further problem with the prevailing definition is its neglect of new, more complex forms of governance. The most prominent of these is the use of state power by private entities and individuals. What is known as New Public Management (NPM) is a dominant, administrative perspective in the United States, United Kingdom, Australia, New Zealand, Sweden, other OECD countries, and beyond. The central tenet of NPM is that public goods and services can be more efficiently and effectively produced and provided by the private sector. Everything from diplomatic security in war zones, nursing home care, primary and secondary education, and mail delivery is currently being provided in one country or another by private companies, acting with state authority. But does NPM guarantee duty, justice, and equality? We hope so, but the foundation of the private sector is profit and, while privatization and contracting-out are often effective and popular, recent history is rife with examples of profit displacing other, public values. Whether popular and effective or not, the use of public power by private, profit-oriented actors requires us to broaden the definition of corruption beyond conduct in "public office". There are a great many private entities like churches, international non-governmental organizations, and media corporations that exercise such substantial influence over people's lives that their behavior also must be considered part of governance.

Corruption

The discussion of *routine, culture, reciprocity, misconduct*, and the *quality of governance* sets the stage for a definition of corruption. Up to this point, we have argued that the conventional definition of corruption as private gain from public position is an important starting point, but it is only a starting point. What we gain from an examination of the political thought of Aristotle, Kant, and Warren is an appreciation of the necessity of inclusion and engagement in the democratic ideal of governance, which is what corruption is not. It follows, then, that *corruption of the democratic ideal includes not only the self-dealing of the conventional definition, but also policy, routine, and administrative culture that excludes and disengages citizens from the business of their own governance.*

Most of the terms in this definition have been examined already. But what do we mean by "the business of their own governance"? If governance is the essence of human potential, the business of it would be very broad. It might include most of what humans do in a lifetime. If governance is the duty we have to each other, then a strict moral code, based on the humanity principle, would control and confine the behavior of public officials. But politics is the art of the possible, inspired by ideals but never actually attaining them.

Without losing sight of moral imperatives, corruption of the democratic ideal must be brought down to earth and defined in terms of ordinary policies and official actions that are most important to those affected by them. Therefore, *not everything that displeases me or with which I disagree is corrupt, but anything that keeps me from engaging in the formulation or reform of official action that materially affects my circumstances or life chances can and should be considered corrupt.* This will include bribery and corruption, which effectively short-circuit the democratic process, by giving preference in the use of official authority to those willing to pay for it. But it must also extend to abusive policies, the effects of which are unauthorized by those they harm. It must extend, further, to official action that disregards or denies the rights of those without the resources to assert and protect them. Often those excluded are marginal or minority populations, but sometimes corruption of democratic ideas is generalized and harms rich and poor, minority and majority alike. Examples of such pervasive corruption are found in environmental policies that result in foul water, polluted air, and unsustainable development. Unfortunately, there are so many specific examples of this kind of corruption that it is often accepted as an inevitable part of modern life. But that is only true if—and here we find Kant looking over our shoulder—it is truly inevitable, and not the product of human decisions and actions that might have gone in a different direction.

In some instances, exclusion and disengagement is a clear, stated goal of those in power. But in other cases it is difficult to attribute to specific actors, and is the product of goal displacement and administrative culture that is blind to the harm it causes. One of the key indicators of conscious exclusion and disengagement is "unnaming", or labeling a person or group, so as to set them apart and treat them differently from other members of the community. Unnaming, along with stereotyping and labeling, is a technique of exclusion and control.

The idea that all of the ancient cultures of North America could be labeled "Indians" because of the mistaken belief by European settlers that India was on the other side of the Atlantic is one example. But perhaps the most comprehensive and insidious example of unnaming and labeling is the construction of racial groups.

It is clear that the historical proliferation, enforcement, and embeddedness of broad racial distinctions—Caucasian, black, Asian—have no basis in genetics or biology (Livingstone & Dobzhansky, 1962). Unnaming of individuals occurs when skin color and ancestry are repurposed to erase individual identity and place everyone in an artificial political and social hierarchy, so that some are on the inside and others on the outside; some are higher and some are lower. But, while racial categorization is the more significant and damaging example of unnaming and labeling, there is the long, nasty list of racial, ethnic, and gender epithets to remind us of the power of exclusionary labeling. Anyone who has been on the receiving end of such an epithet understands what unnaming means.

Organizational Effectiveness and Democratic Governance

So, we have emphasized the moral influence of organizations as they pursue efficient, effective results. We have also emphasized the components of good, fair government. Figure 2.1 is a graphical description of how these two parts of the integrity puzzle fit together.

The point of the overlapping ovals is the complex connection between effective governance, democratic governance, and the definition of corruption. The ovals should help us keep both parts of the definition in mind, but, like all definitions, they are a starting point. Two other elements of the governance/corruption problem should be addressed to move us toward specific examples and case studies. They are the formal functions of government designed to protect public administration from corruption: inspection and oversight.

Inspection

Like the rest of us, public officials are guided by values that are integral to their character and personality. In a perfect (perfectly honest) world, those values would include effective and democratic governance. But the world is far less

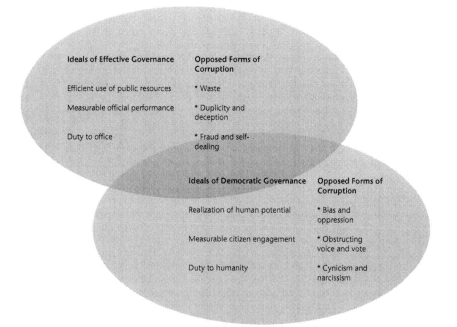

FIGURE 2.1 Corruption Conceptualized as the Violation of Nested Values in Two Categories

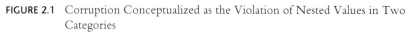

Source: Figure created by authors

than perfect, so, for our own good, we need to watch and correct the behavior of those in power. This need is the basis of checks and balances and countervailing power. As James Madison put it,

> Ambition must be made to counteract ambition … It may be a reflection on human nature, that such devices should be necessary to control the abuses of government. But what is government itself, but the greatest of all reflections on human nature? If men were angels, no government would be necessary.
>
> *(Madison, 1788, Federalist 51)*

Establishing an independent, official function to watch and correct official behavior is in line with Madison's advice. Inspectors and auditors, like the elusive emissary in Gogol's play, are empowered to investigate and identify waste, fraud, and abuse in the public sector and among private actors doing business with the public. The expectation is that inspectional agencies will recover stolen and diverted resources and, if they are thorough enough, deter further wrongdoing. But inspectors are also human and imperfect. How do we ensure that they are effective enough to keep things honest, but not so zealous that they intimidate service providers to the point of ineffectiveness?

Inspection, then, is a problem of balance. Independence of inspectors from political interference would appear necessary. Complete independence, however, can and has led to a displacement of the service mission of government with Inquisition-like zealotry. The other critical problem of balance is between the two categories in Figure 2.1, between the preservation of government effectiveness, which is a big job with high visibility, and the protection of democratic values, which is hard to see but without which government effectiveness is meaningless. The examples in later chapters will illustrate the difficulty and maintaining the balance in inspection.

Oversight

In addition to the administrative function of inspection, which is supposed to be independent of politics, there is oversight, which must be political. The way that the integrity standards are defined, communicated, and enforced in public administration is a matter for political decision making by legislative committees, executive budget officers, and personnel management officials. *Integrity standards* should include careful *scrutiny* of *administrative culture* and an awareness of the various ways that the *democratic service mission* of any government function can be *displaced or perverted*. But the way that each term in the previous sentence is defined is a political decision.

With oversight, as with inspection, balance is critical. The charge of corruption by those responsible for oversight is a time-honored way to attack and discredit political opponents. When it is used by those in power, it can ruin careers and send people to jail. In short, corruption can become a political crime, resulting in those convicted becoming political prisoners. On the other hand, neglect of political oversight can result in a free-wheeling disregard of effective, democratic governance, which is often called "official impunity".

The balance will be maintained first by adherence to best practices and second by transparency. The standards that are used to identify administrative corruption and make accusations should be available for public scrutiny and any and all proceedings against public officials should also be open to the public and the media. Ultimately, though, it is public opinion and popular judgment through the electoral process that must strike the right balance of inspection and oversight.

Chapters 4 to 6 explain the ways in which oversight and inspection form part of corruption control and what are considered best practices.

Summary and Conclusion

When we work backwards from long-standing ideals of good governance, we get a view of what corruption is. As we have argued, there are two parts to the definition:

- *Exchange corruption*: The use of official/public position for private gain.
- *Governance corruption*: Official action or neglect that keeps individuals or groups from engaging in the formulation or reform of public policies that materially change their circumstances or life chances.

If we understand organizations as factories producing both policies and values, we see that understanding what goes on inside them is crucial to knowing how exchange corruption begins and how governance corruption becomes not only tolerated but often defended and preferred. This process is often called *organizational pathology*, that is, the displacement of goals and normalization of deviance that make harmful errors routine and which can, over time, turn exchange corruption into governance corruption.

In the most prominent scandals, all these aspects of the definition are apparent. Though they may not be significant historically, most cases of corruption that come to public attention are exchange corruption and, by themselves, may not damage democratic values. This is not to say that one-off corruption is not bad, but that it may not mean much to the political system more generally. In other cases, there may be little evidence of exchange corruption, but clear evidence of governance corruption. In these cases, the pathologies of organization play an important role. These are cases, which we referred to earlier, in which exclusion, oppression, and worse are considered "good". These are cases in which deviance like ethnic cleansing or gender violence is normalized and the governance mission of justice and humanity is displaced or discarded.

Chapters 5 and 6 provide detailed examples of the interplay between these aspects of the definition.

References

Daugherty v. Ellis (142 W. Va. 340, 357–8, 97 S.E.2d 33, 42–3 (W. Va. 1956) 1956).

Gogol, N. V. (1836/1916). *The Inspector-General* (Vol. 4). New York: AA Knopf.

Kant, I. (1785/1964). *Groundwork for the metaphysics of morals.* H. J. Paton (Trans.). New York: Harper Torchbooks.

Kant, I. (1798). *Essays and treatises on moral, political, and various philosophical subjects* (Vol. 1). London: William Richardson.

Livingstone, F. B., & Dobzhansky, T. (1962). On the non-existence of human races. *Current Anthropology, 3*(3), 279–281.

Los Angeles Times. (1986, June 10). Challenger disaster: The 24 hours of pre-launch debate that could have prevented a tragedy. Retrieved from www.latimes.com.

Madison, J. (1788). Federalist Paper No. 51. The structure of the government must furnish the proper checks and balances between the different departments. In A. Hamilton, J. Madison, & J. Jay (Eds.), *The federalist papers.* Various publishers.

Presidential Commission. (1986). *Report to the President by the Presidential Commission on the Space Shuttle Challenger Accident.* Retrieved from https://spaceflight.nasa.gov/out reach/SignificantIncidents/assets/rogers_commission_report.pdf.

Sandel, M. J. (2009). *Justice: What's the right thing to do?* New York: Farrar, Straus and Giroux.

Warren, M. E. (2004). What does corruption mean in a democracy? *American Journal of Political Science, 48*(2), 328–343.

Vaughan, D. (1996). *The Challenger launch decision: Risky technology, culture, and deviance at NASA.* Chicago, IL: University of Chicago Press.

Weber, M. (1946). *From Max Weber: Essays in sociology.* H. H. Gerth and C. Wright Mills (Trans. and Eds.). New York: Oxford University Press.

3

CAN WE KNOW HOW MUCH CORRUPTION THERE IS? ON THE MEASUREMENT OF CORRUPTION

In this chapter we take a closer look at the measurement of corruption. An overarching argument that influences how we approach corruption measurement in this book and in this chapter is that we should not deal with it simply as a technical issue or as isolated from issues about what corruption is and how to pursue corruption. Instead we argue that these issues are very closely related. The broad definition of corruption that we are using—the violation of democratic governance, as well as private gain from public office—has important implications. Not only does it require analysts to revise their thinking about official misconduct, it also changes the nature of corruption investigation and control. More immediately, though, the broader definition affects how corruption is measured.

Corruption is very difficult to measure for three reasons: it is hidden, the line between corrupt and acceptable official behavior is not always clear, and it is expensive and time-consuming to investigate and detect. That corruption is usually hidden might seem obvious. If we take the example of bribery, a common form of corruption, where cash is exchanged for official favors, those taking part in such exchanges have a strong interest in secrecy. But, using the broader democratic governance definition, we find that deceitful, harmful behavior that distorts institutional goals also happens in the shadows.

Both kinds of corruption damage society. In the case of bribery and extortion, which we call *exchange corruption*, the official taking or demanding a bribe will often feel vindicated: he or she is defeating the delay and obstruction of bureaucracy-as-usual and actually getting something done. The bribe taker is often convinced that the extra money is appropriate compensation for underpaid, unappreciated service to the public. On the other side of the deal, the bribe giver is happy to get the favor for which he or she is paying. If it is a case of extortion, however, the bribe giver is likely to think of the bribe as a kind of tax—coercive, annoying, but unavoidable.

In the case of the broader perspective on corruption, which we call *governance corruption*, the perversion of policy making and implementation may be a conscious choice by public administrators of politicians, or it can happen slowly and be reinforced by neglect and passivity. In either case, the shift in policy and practice is generally accepted within the public organization, as necessary. Governance corruption, then, presents a double challenge to anyone seeking to measure corruption. First, identifying governance corruption is often contentious. Those in charge of agencies accused of this kind of corruption will often counter-charge that the accusation is politically motivated or based on a misunderstanding of the agency's work and environment. Second, unless there is evidence that the undemocratic shift in agency policy was caused by specific administrators, it will be hard to find a particular party to accuse. There are ways to redress governance corruption other than the indictment of individuals, like court-ordered and supervised reforms, but this kind of redress is expensive and time-consuming.

In sum, both exchange and governance corruption are hard to detect and investigate, and, therefore, hard to measure. Suppose we want to aggregate and compare how much corruption there is in two different localities. This brings out several of the aspects of how difficult corruption measurement is, for example: should we measure the absolute number of corruption incidents in each locality? Or the aggregate monetary value of these incidents? What forms of corruption should be included? Should we also include corruption that takes place within the private sector? Our take on these types of questions will affect the result and benchmarks for comparison.

No matter what answers we get to these questions, we also need to consider what kind of data to use and how to collect such data. Should we stick to indicators that are based on hard facts like the number of offenses reported within the legal system, or the amount of money missing (e.g. Reinikka & Svensson, 2001), or take into account public or expert assessments of the amount of corruption? When surveying groups, citizens, and investors, should we stick to asking them about their own experiences with public officials or should we ask for their opinions and perceptions? If, on the other hand, experts are surveyed, how should they be selected? These are important issues that we will discuss further.

Given that we argue for a broad take on corruption including democratic governance, we will use a three-part approach to the measurement of corruption.

- First, no single measure will do the trick for all purposes and all research questions, so we need to combine more than one method and use various data sources.
- Second, although country rankings with scores for aggregate corruption are useful in highlighting the problem and putting it on the agenda,

careful interpretation is needed together with an understanding of what these scores and rankings stand for and what type of conclusions they support. If we are interested in preventing corruption this country-level focus does not help much.

- Third, we argue that the dominant approaches to corruption measurement in the last 20 years or so have given too little attention to both the various types of corruption and how they vary across and within countries and too much attention to bribes. Governance corruption is an important aspect to consider in corruption measurement.

We do not believe that corruption takes the same form across countries (see Alam, 1995; Heidenheimer, 1970/1989; Johnston, 2005). This means that it is not only important to consider how to define corruption but also how a given definition determines the typologies of corruption we use to understand it empirically. The dominant approach is related to a common view that corruption in developing countries is the result of too little economic liberalization (i.e. too many tariffs, heavily regulated markets, too much state intervention). From this perspective, corruption reinforces illiberal economic policies and prevents the open trade and deregulation that underlie economic liberalization. Economic liberalization, it is argued, will reduce incentives for corruption by reducing the barriers to market exchange.

The balance of this chapter explains how corruption is measured, including the pros and cons of different approaches. We start with the challenge of measurability. Then, we consider conventional and other measures. Finally, we illustrate some of the difficulties in measuring corruption with two case studies: one of the well-known Corruption Perceptions Index (CPI; Transparency International, 2015b) and the other, the case study of Sweden.

Why Measure Corruption?

In many places (just ask your friends and neighbors) there is a widespread feeling that corruption is common and "getting worse" (Gallup News, 2015; Pring, 2015, 2016, 2017a, 2017b), that business has an inside track in public policy making, and that public policy is made to benefit certain interests and wealthy individuals at the expense of the public. Frequent scandals in established democracies can be seen as giving credence to corruption as a growing problem. But another influence on the sense that corruption is growing is the continuing, feverish attention given to corruption since the 1970s by citizens, media, governments, and international organizations, all of which have anti-corruption agendas.

In democratic countries the media have played a key role in uncovering corruption. This raises the public profile of corruption and puts it high on the agenda of political and economic issues both domestically and internationally. Moreover, in relation to questions of measurement, media attention raises the question of whether the perceived increase of corruption is due to increased attention and exposure or to a "real" increase in corruption and, if so, what constitutes a real increase?

So why then, given such difficulties, should we bother measuring corruption? Measuring corruption is not an end in itself. There are several reasons for trying to measure corruption as accurately as possible:

- First, adequate measurement will indicate the scale of the problem. For example, what is the level of corruption in a certain locality, to what extent and why is corruption tolerated by citizens, and what is the impact and cost of corruption?
- Second, measurement allows us to find patterns of corruption by identifying explanatory variables and corruption vulnerabilities. It may not be the amount of corruption that is crucial, but rather the form that corruption takes. Measurement can also ask "who" (perpetrators and victims), "where" (vulnerable areas and activities), and "why" (dynamics and mechanisms).
- Third, effective methods for counteracting corruption require knowledge about where to take action, and what that action should be. The context and environment of governance corruption is particularly important and entails consideration of broad social and economic problems.

Moreover, how corruption is defined and how it is measured are directly related. It is useful to remember that the definition of corruption changes over time. Anechiarico and Jacobs (1996, p. 14) noted in their study of New York City over a 100-year period that what was formally defined as corruption widened (more types of behavior were included), making it difficult to know both whether corruption increased and how to assess whether particular anti-corruption measures were effective.

How corruption is defined influences what we look for when we measure it. When measurement is for the purpose of assessing risk and vulnerability, corruption measures should combine broad, generic definitions with typologies that capture the full range of corruption in light of the operational environment of the service area in question.

Types of corruption, *other than* bribery and extortion, include favoritism (abuse of authority to the benefit of family, party, or friends), embezzlement and fraud (misleading others or disregarding professional responsibilities for private gain from the organization or citizens), conflict of interest (situations where an official has self-interest that conflicts with the obligations to carrying out duties for the public good; this could be due to outside interests such as jobs or gifts from third parties) (Andersson, 2017, p. 62), and the exclusionary policies and practices that constitute governance corruption.

Patterns and forms of corruption vary among societies and communities, with particular corruption syndromes being characteristic of specific societal types. The nature, magnitude, and mechanism of corruption differs between rich and poor countries, and established democracies and countries under political-economic development or transition. We can expect that some forms of corruption are relatively more common in some places than others. High-level bribery, for example, would be expected to be relatively less common in rich democracies than developing countries (Graycar, 2015, p. 88; Graycar & Monaghan, 2015, p. 587; Heidenheimer, 1970/1989; Johnston, 2005, 2014).

We will elaborate on this later in the chapter. But let's first look at various measurement methods used in research on corruption.

Ways of Measuring Corruption

We begin with several conventional methods of measuring corruption (Table 3.1). The information about corruption collected with these methods is divided between "soft data" and "hard data". Soft data on corruption are perceptions and attitudes related to corruption and relative levels of honesty in government. Hard data indicate empirically observed instances of corruption—corruption which is seen, reported, or discovered.

Different measurements are suitable for different tasks. For example, using arrests or prosecutions gives access to hard and accessible data and is useful for

TABLE 3.1 Methods of Measuring Corruption

A. *Formal accounts of corruption* such as arrests, prosecutions, convictions, cases reported to authorities concerning corrupt/unethical conduct as specified by constitutional acts and national statutes, local ordinances and statutes, administrative regulations, or judicial precedent.

B. *Public expenditure tracking.* By following the money allocated for a certain purpose through the government system to the receiver and implementer, one can tell how much is lost along the way. The observation here is of the results of corrupt behavior but such a measurement would find it difficult to distinguish waste and inefficiency due to corruption or incompetence.

C. *Cases reported in media.* Media investigations and reports enable us to see what alleged corruption cases are about and what actors and policies are involved. Using the number of media reports over time to assess the level of corruption will be affected by surges in interest and capacity in media for investigative journalism.

D. *Perception surveys:* Surveys of expert perception and broad, public perception. Using surveys where respondents provide views on corruption in various governments' activities and institutions.

E. *Experiences of corruption:* Experience of citizens, e.g. surveys of crime and victimization, users of public services, providers of public services, and surveys of companies, where respondents are asked about their own experiences of corruption.

F. *Experimental research:* Experimental situations in which various scenarios are evaluated by public officials and others; for example, concerning propensity to act corruptly or tolerance and acceptance of corrupt actions in specific situations.

Source: Created by authors

seeing the development of corruption and the response to it over time in a locality. But if we want to compare different systems or countries, what does a different number of arrests or prosecutions mean? Is a higher number of cases in one country an indicator of more corruption or rather a measurement of a more aggressive and efficient legal system, which looks harder and therefore catches and prosecutes more offenders? Say we are interested in whether police corruption is more widespread in country A than country B. We get access to statistics on the number of police officers charged with offenses related to bribery in both countries. In country B, there is a much higher number of officers reported for such violations. What does this say? Is it a result of cases of police corruption being *de facto* more common in country B? Or is the higher number of violations a result of low tolerance for such behavior by the justice system in country B and by the police themselves? Beyond tolerance, it may be that country B is simply more efficient in dealing with such offenses. In real situations, other information about the police force, the legitimacy it has among the public, how it is organized, what kind of internal and external oversight mechanisms there are to detect integrity violations, and the culture within the department will help to interpret the data. One way of contextualizing such data would be to survey experts and citizens in general in the two countries about their views of the police and police integrity.

The Use of Corruption Data

Once they have been collected, data fall into three categories or three levels of study. All of the data collection methods just mentioned can be used in all three categories.

A. *Individual integrity studies* focus on the behavior and performance of individual actors (micro level). They seek to understand how corruption works: what are the motivations, incentives, personal circumstances, and other environmental factors that either enable or obstruct official misconduct. These studies collect data at the level of the individual or small, connected group of individuals involved in corrupt acts, and could encompass interviews with such individuals, material from criminal and civil legal proceedings, expenditure tracking, and experimental research.

B. *Systemic integrity studies* focus on structures, behavior, performance, and decision making of governments and societies, at regional, national, and global levels (macro level). Such studies often use aggregate data to reveal factors causing corruption and the effect of corruption on democratic stability, wealth, and economic growth, e.g. the CPI or World Bank Worldwide Governance Indicators (WGI, one variable being Control of Corruption; World Bank, 2015).

C. *Organizational integrity* studies look at corruption that develops and is embedded in both official and private organizations (and their structures, policies, or culture) responsible for providing important goods and services to the public (meso level). Studies at this level link the individual actors who inter-pret and carry out policies that may be corrupt (including bribery/extortion and governance corruption) with the systemic-level values and routines that reinforce and guide organizational behavior.

Painting a complete picture of public integrity in any location requires atten-tion to all three levels. Let's take an unfortunately common example.

Suppose there have been reports of kickbacks from paving contractors to officials in the public works department in your town. Your first instinct would probably be to stop it and then to recover the money that's been kicked-back and bring the culprits to justice. Your local prosecutor would have to be per-suaded to investigate and charge the public works officials and contractors who were parties to the scheme. It could end there, but if you want to understand how and why the kickback scheme developed and how further corruption of this type can be prevented, you need to know more—you need to collect data in the three categories.

The prosecutor would start at the individual level and so should you: who are the individuals involved, and why did they jeopardize their jobs, reputations, and even freedom to line their pockets by defrauding the public? Here, court records will be useful. What does the testimonial and material evidence introduced in the trial indicate about motives of those involved? It is possible that those charged and convicted will agree to talk with you. If they won't, others involved in the prosecution may agree to discuss it, including the lawyers on both sides, wit-nesses, and those who reported on the case in the media.

At the organizational level, you would raise questions about how those respon-sible got away with it. What, if any, oversight and review is in place to check on the way funds are allocated and used in the public works department? Is it reasonable to suppose that those in charge should have known about the corrupt bargain between the contractor and public works officials? If not, is there some aspect of the organization—its culture, pattern of communication, or morale—that allowed or enabled kickbacks? Some of this may be in court records, but understanding organizational communication and culture requires considerable time and effort. A study at this level would include interviews with personnel at all levels of the organization and review of internal reports and directives.

The systemic-level analysis of this instance of corruption is challenging, but important. What is the cultural and political context of the fraud in this case? You would start by looking at the political jurisdiction in which it took place. If it occurred in New York State, it would be useful to know that kickbacks of this kind have been endemic for generations and that, while state law is clear about their illegality, oversight is relatively weak. If it occurred in the prov-ince of Blekinge, Sweden, the context would indicate that kickbacks, although

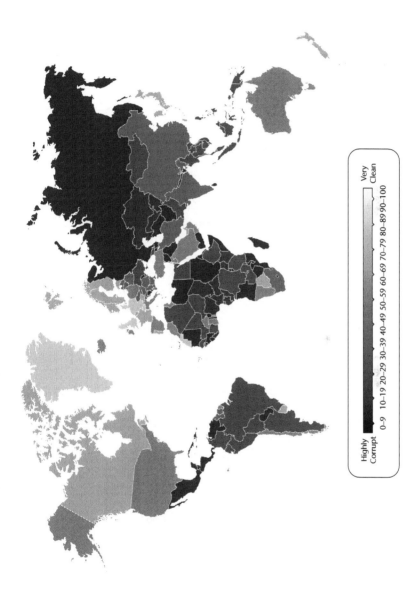

FIGURE 3.1 The Corruption Perceptions Index 2017

Source: Transparency International (2018)

less frequent but not unheard of, run counter to settled expectations about the behavior of public officials. In either case, the incidence of corruption at the local level is put in the frame of expectations and political culture. Economic factors, like median income, indices of inequality, and unemployment, are also considered at this level.

Perceptions as Data and Country Comparisons[1]

Doing the work to understand the kickbacks, thoroughly, will involve the collection and analysis of both qualitative data (interviews, observations, review of evidence and testimony) and quantitative data (kickback trends in the jurisdiction, attitude and experience surveys of personnel and the public, related demographic and economic factors). If qualitative approaches tend to be more common historically, since the 1990s quantitative approaches have become more prominent, especially in comparative research across countries. This development goes hand in hand with the development of cross-country integrity research, especially easily accessed rankings of countries by level of corruption (e.g. the CPI and WGI).

Transparency International (TI), established in 1993, has emerged as a key anti-corruption non-governmental organization (NGO), and a leader in identifying corruption as an important international economic and political issue. TI succeeded in putting corruption on the international policy agenda (Andersson & Heywood, 2009). Its annual publication, beginning in the 1990s, of the CPI, a cross-country ranking of countries in terms of "how corrupt their public sectors are seen to be" (Transparency International, 2017b) has been widely influential, and is probably the most well-known corruption measurement. Rankings of countries in terms of how corrupt they are perceived to be (Transparency International, 2017c) provide a powerful image, Figure 3.1 (the CPI is presented either in a list or as a map with different colors categorizing countries from totally corrupt, 0, to free from corruption, 100). The CPI became a benchmark indicator of cross-country corruption widely used by media, government, and NGOs.

Other organizations, like the World Bank, followed. The World Bank's governance indicators emphasize corruption control (see Box 3.1). In addition, regional development banks also rank countries on a corruption scale. Some rankings are supposed to provide businesses and investors with risk assessment. This type of ranking, presenting individual scores for most of the countries of the world, spurred research on whether other factors—wealth, democracy, governance quality, and social organization—were more or less associated with corruption levels, and what effect corruption has on the values that society strives for (for one of the earlier, classical examples, using data from Business International, see Mauro, 1995). These rankings and this research placed corruption and anti-corruption higher on the international agenda.

BOX 3.1   THE WORLD BANK WORLDWIDE GOVERNANCE INDICATORS

The WGI are available for over 200 countries and territories for six governance dimensions between 1996 and 2016:

- Voice and Accountability
- Political Stability and Absence of Violence
- Government Effectiveness
- Regulatory Quality
- Rule of Law
- Control of Corruption

These six indicators aggregate results from surveys of citizens, experts, and corporate representatives in industrial and developing countries. More than 30 individual data sources are used from survey institutes, think tanks, NGOs, and international organizations.

Source: World Bank (2018)

Some rankings were based on questions tapping perceptions among citizens or experts, others on their experience of corruption, and others on views or experience of businesses and other organizations. Surveys, which are a common tool in ranking studies, are composed of questions about which sectors and institutions are perceived as corrupt, what respondents think about the development of corruption over time, and whether respondents have ever been asked to pay bribes (Global Corruption Barometer, Transparency International, 2015a). In other cases, surveys ask business executives and administrators for an estimate of what firms like theirs must pay in informal fees or gifts, as a percentage of total annual sales, to get things done (World Bank, 2016). Other examples are studies and surveys aiming to determine the variation in quality of government and corruption nationally and sub-nationally, or the extent to which citizens believe public officials are engaged in corruption and whether accepting bribes is thought to be justifiable (World Values Survey, Inglehart et al., 2014; Quality of Government Institute, 2016). Data on corruption are also available from other organizations, NGOs, and academic projects, like the Sustainable Governance Indicators (Bertelsmann Foundation), Varieties of Democracy (co-hosted by the Department of Political Science, University of Gothenburg, Sweden, and the Kellogg Institute, University of Notre Dame, United States), International Crime Victim Survey, and World Justice Project.

As we mentioned, the rapid acceleration of data collection beginning in the 1990s made measurements based on country scores standard for cross-national research on corruption (e.g. the CPI and the Control of Corruption variable in the WGI; Kaufmann, Kraay, & Mastruzzi, 2010). It contributed to knowledge about the relationship between corruption and democracy, institutional strength, and economic growth and development (e.g. Collier, 2002; Kaufmann et al., 2010; Lambsdorf, 2007; Mauro, 1995; Treisman, 2000).

But there are also problems and caveats that must be taken into account concerning empirical validity and interpretation of these cross-country data. For example, what exactly do these surveys measure and how should they be understood? Even more fundamentally, aren't there serious problems in using perceptions of corruption as a measure of actual corruption levels, and how should we interpret differences between perceptions of corruption and experience of it? (Andersson & Heywood, 2009; Andvig, 2005; Groop, 2013; Heywood & Rose, 2014; Miller, Grødeland, & Koshechkina, 2001; Søreide, 2006; Weber Abramo, 2007). Additionally, corruption may also vary within a country, among levels of government and different policy sectors, and not just between countries, something that will not be captured by data at the country level (see Alam, 1995). This can be illustrated by the findings of Linde and Erlingsson (2013) concerning the reduced capacity of country measures to catch the scope and forms of corruption in countries where it occurs mainly at the local level when local self-government is strong. In a Europe-wide study, Charron, Lapuente, and Rothstein (2013) find sub-national variation of quality of government and corruption to be important in some countries and minor in others (Charron, 2013). Similarly, corruption incidence has been shown to vary between states in the United States (Liu & Mikesell, 2014).

Another problem with using a single-score measure of corruption for a country is that it assumes corruption to be a one-dimensional phenomenon, which shows itself and is recognized in exactly the same way across countries and continents and thus only varies in amount but not in form. This has potential effects on accuracy as we would expect forms of corruption and its manifestation to vary across societies as a reflection of the strength of institutions and political participation and how wealth and power are accumulated (Heidenheimer, 1970/1989; Johnston, 2005, 2014). Finally, such single-score measures tend to be more focused on bribery than other forms of corruption. There is a risk corruption will be underestimated by using bribery as a proxy for overall corruption in rich established democracies where bribery is relatively less common (Andersson, 2017). A focus on bribery may also allow us to ignore other official behavior that damages democratic values—what we call governance corruption (see Chapter 2).

In later sections, the case studies of the CPI, Iceland, and Sweden are used to illustrate and discuss the problem of perception-based measures in more detail. But let us here first look at some of these issues.

As you can see, many modern indicators rely on perceptions of corruption. Perception and real corruption may not be the same and may depend on whose perception is tapped—whether we ask citizens about their opinion or target groups with expertise in areas of interest. Here Erlingsson and Kristinsson (2016) argue that expert opinion is more reliable than public perceptions, but they also add that it matters who the experts are, because accuracy of results increases when domestic experts with local knowledge of governance and public administration in the country at hand are consulted, rather than, say, foreign business leaders. This argument is based on the case of Iceland and how corruption in Iceland was underestimated when measured by the CPI, as opposed to overestimation if instead relying on perceptions of the general public.[2] (More on Iceland later.)

Another alternative is to ask respondents about their experiences with government and whether any of them have involved extortion or other kinds of corruption. The distinction between surveys focused on perception and experiences is important. The general difference between the two is whether respondents/interviewees are expected to report only their own experience or perceptions of the situation based on their views in general (which could be based on experience or knowledge of official corruption, media reports, what you hear from friends, general view of public services, etc.). To illustrate the difference let's assume that we are interested in levels of corruption in policing in a particular country. Using a perception-based method we could ask citizens to evaluate police integrity, for example using a 1 to 10 scale. Using a big enough sample to be representative, we can produce an assessment of police integrity, as perceived by residents. In contrast, an experience-based approach would first ask whether the respondent has had contact with the police. In the case of such contacts, the interviewer would then ask if the respondent had experienced any police misconduct, including any integrity violations (for examples of experience- or perception-based questions see, for instance, the Global Corruption Barometer, Transparency International, 2015a).

But does it matter which measurement is used? It can. Each will provide a different picture of the situation. In some countries citizens' perceptions of high corruption correspond to the experience of citizens who have experienced corruption, while in others, perceptions of corruption may be high even though there is relatively little experience of integrity violations. This was, for example, the result found by Miller et al. (2001) in Ukraine and the Czech Republic. The first situation was found to be the case in Ukraine, while the latter situation was illustrative of the Czech Republic. Sweden is another case of high perception and low experience, as is the case in many other rich countries with established democracy. Almost half of Swedish respondents (44 per cent) perceived corruption as widespread (European Commission, 2014) while very few had experienced being asked to pay bribes, most surveys pointing to around or less than 1 per cent. One possible reason for this is that few have experienced bribery but have an inflated perception of the pervasiveness of corruption due to media reports or the most prominent scandals or because they are dissatisfied in general with politics and public services. Alternatively, it could be argued that the two questions are measuring different forms of corruption. It is possible that respondents when answering questions about the pervasiveness of corruption interpret corruption more broadly than bribery, by including in their answers recognition of interest conflicts and favoritism in the public sector, and that such behavior is assessed as more common than bribery. It could also be a combination of these two possibilities.

Other Alternatives for Comparison of Societies and Countries

If we want a deeper understanding of corruption problems and vulnerability in a specific country, so we know what reforms are likely to be effective, data based on country scores will not be of much help. To develop a deeper understanding, several types of in-depth studies have been developed.

One prominent example of in-depth analysis of corruption is the World Bank governance and anti-corruption diagnostic surveys that include questions about both respondents' experience of corruption and their perception, using a triangulation method with three target groups of respondents: households, businesses, and public employees. Another example that is qualitative in its approach is the National Integrity Systems (NIS) study. This methodology focuses on how strong and well-functioning institutions are that are important in upholding integrity and preventing corruption rather than measuring corruption per se. Institutions are evaluated for service capacity and strength of governance, and an assessment is made based on 13 indicators. Scores are based on questions that are answered by researchers mainly based on interviews with key actors, previous research, and data available, and then summarized on a standardized scale (0, 25, 50, 75, 100). This methodology was used in the European NIS, a comparative project of 25 EU states and some more non-member states (Transparency International, 2010).[3]

Overall, the frequent and perhaps strongest critique of country-wide corruption rankings is their one-dimensionality, since a single score is used to indicate the overall corruption level for a country. Single-score rankings emphasize variations in quantity rather than the form and patterns of corruption. Further, single scores of corruption are more apt to pick up bribery than other types of corruption. But, as we argue here, corruption takes many forms that vary depending on the type of society, its political and economic development, and the way wealth and power are accumulated (Heidenheimer, 1970/1989; Johnston, 2005, 2014). Also, which institutions are viewed as corrupt differs between rich democratic countries and developing countries, due to trust and personal engagement with various institutions, particularly the police.

If corruption takes many forms, do some forms have enough in common to group them into categories? The famous categories developed by Arnold Heidenheimer (1970/1989), which label corruption "black, grey or white", provide us with an example. The focus of this categorization is to develop a basis for comparing corruption in one society to corruption in another. The fundamental idea is that across societies there are different forms of corruption, and variation in incidence, in seriousness of corruption, and in the tolerance among the public and elite for various kinds of official misconduct.

The typology developed by Heidenheimer is based on a categorization of societies into four archetypes: family, patron–client, modern boss–follower (political machines), and civic–culture-based systems.[4] Several questions are used to distinguish the categories:

- How are political exchange obligations organized? How is the level of socio-economic development related to political exchange relations? (That is, does money equal access?)
- How often do specific corrupt acts occur?
- What is the tolerance for these acts in terms of how they are viewed by the public and the elites and how this varies across the four systems (the basis for distinguishing between black, gray, and white corruption)?

For example, a bribe typically specifies compensation in exchange for a specific action, while other corrupt political exchanges are vaguer, with less exact amounts. The more developed the economy becomes the more likely that benefits are less specific, and the more likely that exchanges look more like ordinary social transactions than like direct economic exchanges. So in developed economies the less formal, more social nature of corruption makes it harder to identify. Corrupt exchanges, like bribery, in less developed societies often are more direct, which makes them more easily identified (pp. 149–150).[5]

The Heidenheimer typology sees corruption as multifaceted, consisting of various behaviors, with varying patterns across societies. Corrupt acts between individuals and tolerance of them by the public increase in frequency when moving from the civic-culture-based category to the family-based category (pp. 156–157). It is important to remember that the Heidenheimer categories are ideal types or models and that empirically we could expect to find some traits from a particular category dominating in a society and also some traits from other categories, and that these traits change over time (this is illustrated empirically as we describe the development of corruption historically in New York City in Chapter 6).

Building on Heidenheimer's work, Michael Johnston (2005, and followed up in 2014) explores how corruption syndromes differ across societies and relates the differences to the level of political participation and the strength of social and political institutions. Johnston, like Heidenheimer, asks what types of corruption are found in each society but also broadens the systemic questions, including:

- What are the links between economic and political liberalization (between markets and rights)?
- How strong are the state and key political and social institutions?
- What is the role of economic wealth and political power for the nature of corruption?

The key issue in Johnston's analysis is how wealth and power are sought, used, and exchanged, and how the state, social, and political structures tolerate or curb corrupt activities (Johnston, 2005, p. 39).

In answering these questions, Johnston develops categories—he calls them "syndromes"—of corruption that parallel Heidenheimer's. It is a typology of four broad categories of corruption patterns: official moguls (country examples used: China, Kenya, Indonesia), oligarchs and clans (examples: Russia, Mexico, the Philippines), elite cartels (Italy, South Korea, Botswana), and influence markets (United States, Germany, Japan) (Johnston, 2005, p. 59). These various syndromes are the result of variation across societies regarding the use of wealth and power and connections between the two and to what extent this weakens open, competitive participation and/or economic and political institutions or prevents the development of such institutions (Johnston, 2005, p. 12).

In the *official moguls syndrome*, power is personal and used to rob state resources. The regime is undemocratic, political competition is very weak, institutions are also weak, and economic opportunities are limited (Johnston, 2005, p. 3).

The syndrome dominated by *oligarchs and clans* is found in states that display weak institutions within a risky setting of rapidly expanding economic and political opportunities, as the system transitions to open markets. It is thus difficult to identify who is in power and who is an entrepreneur or politician, and it might be difficult to separate private and public functions. Power struggles between groups may be fierce. Corruption is pervasive, so it is difficult to protect profits and enforce contracts. This goes hand in hand with violence, organized crime and protection rackets being essential parts of this syndrome (Johnston, 2014, p. 24).

Elite cartel corruption is found where politics and markets are becoming more competitive but key institutions are not very strong. Power and wealth are changing, which creates risks. Networks (political, bureaucratic, business, military, other) of power and privilege stay in control by sharing corrupt returns through collusion between top figures in various spheres of society. Civil society in situations of post-conflict or post-dictatorial regimes are weak or manipulated from above (Johnston, 2014, pp. 22–23).[6]

Influence market corruption is found in rich, established democratic states with mature, open market economies and strong political institutions, legitimate constitutional frameworks, political competition, free news media, and strong civil societies that help to safeguard against abuses, but when these societies developed these characteristics they adapted to powerful wealth interests (Johnston, 2005, pp. 42–57). Wealth is used for political influence, and private interests rent access by using public officials as enablers and intermediaries, often within the legal framework but still hindering institutions and pre-empting the participation of others. This is in line with the systemic or governance corruption identified in Chapter 2.

From a measurement perspective, the influence market syndrome is particularly interesting and helps locate and explain governance corruption in these countries. This is because corruption of strong, well-established institutions requires complicated forms of influence and access, rather than deals and connections used to bypass established institutions (Johnston, 2005, pp. 39, 42). Corruption therefore tends to be "invisible". This is the case in many established market democracies (like the United States, Australia, and France). That this corruption is systemic and invisible is a contributing factor to most influence market countries coming out well in standard corruption rankings. The interwoven nature of public and private interests in influence markets makes corruption more difficult to pick up. Given that corruption measurement is better at picking up bribery, the risk is that corruption is underestimated in influence market countries (Andersson, 2017).

The first two syndromes, oligarchs and clans and official moguls, are associated with corruption in states that are developing politically and economically and those that are in transition from one system to another. The latter two syndromes, influence markets and elite cartels, are associated with the rich and relatively rich democracies (cf. Graycar & Monaghan, 2015, p. 588). Another important point is that the four syndromes indicate different qualities of corruption, rather than different levels of corruption (Johnston, 2014, p. 17). The purpose of Johnston's syndromes is to highlight various patterns and forms of corruption. This allows reform to be more effective. You might imagine attempting to reform an official moguls system using the tools of oversight and transparency developed for a system with strong, democratic institutions. Such reforms would either be ignored and ineffectual or they would present an opportunity for even more corruption (Johnston, 2014, p. 53).

If we turn to the influence market examples of the United States and Sweden, corruption would be expected to take place within public institutions with officials granting access in exchange for favors (Johnston, 2005, pp. 39–42). While bribery has been the focus of corruption since the 1990s, other forms of corruption than high-level bribery can be expected to be relatively prevalent in influence markets like Sweden, such as various forms of interest conflicts (Andersson & Anechiarico, 2015). This point was made by Dennis Thompson (1995) and Lawrence Lessig (2013) in relation to the U.S. Congress. Thompson found that institutional corruption in the Congress includes improper use of office for private gain (i.e. exchange corruption) but also "conduct that under certain conditions is a necessary or even a desirable part of institutional duties" (1995, p. 7). Lessig (2013, p. 2) makes a similar point by defining institutional corruption as an outcome of "influence within an economy of influence that illegitimately weakens the effectiveness of an institution especially by weakening the public trust of the institution". One illustration of this influence is congressional campaign financing by wealthy donors so that these donors will have preferred access to policy making. Such actions are corrupt in spite of not breaking any formal legal rules. This systemic/governance corruption is also in line with what studies have found in other rich countries (e.g. Graycar & Monaghan, 2015). Iceland (see below) is another example of an influence market where subtle, largely hidden favoritism is the most common form of corruption (Erlingsson & Kristinsson, 2016).

Capturing Corruption with the Right Measurements: A Case Study of the CPI

There are important reasons to take an extra look at the CPI when discussing measurement. First it has been widely used both in the political debate and in research and is well known. As expressed by TI (2017b) itself, the CPI "sends a powerful message and governments have been forced to take notice and act". Indeed, the CPI is used for both political and economic ends and does have real impact on the behaviors of governments and organizations. This would include the CPI's impact on investment decisions by companies, its influence on government anti-corruption policy, and decision-making about foreign aid (Andersson & Heywood, 2009). One reason for its wide use is its simplicity and accessibility. Let's look further at the pros and cons of the CPI.

The CPI has been published annually since 1995. It measures corruption in the public sector and ranks countries in terms of the perception of such corruption on a scale from 0–100 (before 2012, the scale was 0–10 with one decimal point) where 0 indicates the highest level of perceived corruption and 100 the lowest level. As mentioned above, it is a measure based on perceptions of corruption, mainly by country experts and business people with knowledge of each country. The index is a composite, based on many underlying surveys, i.e. TI uses other available surveys to form the index (e.g. the 2017 CPI was based on 13 different data sources from the past two years, provided by 12 institutions; see Box 3.2). The composite makes sure that each country score relies on several sources to avoid the impact of extreme, outlier perceptions. These data sources are standardized, where the standardized scores (z-scores) are adjusted to fit the 0–100 scale. The year 2012 is used as a baseline year, to set the mean and standard deviation, which allows the adjusted values to be compared over time against the baseline year. For a country to be included, at least three sources assessing it must be available (Transparency International, 2016).

BOX 3.2 CORRUPTION PERCEPTIONS INDEX 2017: FULL SOURCE DESCRIPTION

Thirteen data sources were used to construct the 2017 CPI:

1. African Development Bank Governance Ratings 2016
2. Bertelsmann Foundation Sustainable Gov. Indicators 2017
3. Bertelsmann Foundation Transformation Index 2017–2018
4. Economist Intelligence Unit Country Risk Service 2017
5. Freedom House Nations in Transit 2017
6. Global Insight Country Risk Ratings 2016
7. IMD World Competitiveness Yearbook Executive Opinion Survey 2017
8. Political and Economic Risk Consultancy Asian Intelligence 2017
9. Political Risk Services International Group Country Risk Guide 2017
10. World Bank Country Policy and Institutional Assessment 2017
11. World Economic Forum Executive Opinion Survey 2017
12. World Justice Project Rule of Law Index Expert Survey 2017
13. Varieties of Democracy (V-Dem) Project 2017

Source: Transparency International (2017a)

The value of the index for comparative study of corruption has already been mentioned. The index provides easy access to empirical data that can be used for statistical analysis and cross-country comparisons. "Desk studies" (that don't require field research) can be done, using the country scores to investigate patterns and find correlations with other variables on the country level. For example, how the number of years that a country has had a democratic governance structure influences the corruption score, or the influence on corruption levels of other variables like per capita GDP, size of the public sector, etc., to provide new empirical insights.

But there are also downside and potential pitfalls. Because the CPI is a composite index that draws on various data sources and asks a wide variety of questions of different respondents and experts, what is measured by these sources also varies. Given the aim of these cross-country surveys to say something about overall levels of corruption, many measurements use expert opinion as the preferred alternative in order to get as close to the real situation as possible. But it matters who the experts are. To what extent does the CPI emphasize the views of business leaders and market and finance actors from the developed West? This is critical, because the perspective of the experts determines what forms of corruption are focused on and included in the CPI. Western business leaders will be more likely to focus on public officers demanding bribes than on how company officers buy political influence. Indeed, several of the underlying surveys in the CPI are conducted for the purpose of providing corruption-risk analysis for businesses—rather than on the risk of corruption perpetrated by those same businesses.

We should also ask if the CPI interval scale 0–100 (or previously 0–10) gives a false sense of precision and whether such crude estimates of corruption and its prevalence can be converted into such exact estimates. The CPI scale might be compared with Johnston's analysis that replaces a composite scale with four over-arching syndromes of corruption.

Another issue concerns how results over time relate to short-term variation. Over time the index has improved the possibility of tracking long-term trends and of comparing levels of corruption over several years (at least since 2012), but it is still difficult to know how to relate long-term findings to shorter-term fluctuations.

The risk of circularity is another issue. We have to be concerned about the role of the CPI in shaping the perceptions that it measures. To what extent are the views of analysts/experts who are consulted in underlying surveys shaped by the CPI? This is of course difficult to know but it is also something that has been noted by some of the surveyors in the field. The Bertelsmann Foundation, which conducted two of the surveys that were included in the 2017 CPI, specifically addressed this in its questionnaires by telling respondents that:

> Note: Please be aware that the Corruption Perceptions Index (CPI) of Transparency International uses the data and information given in response to question D4.4 for their assessments. To avoid circularity of assessments, please do not base your evaluation on the CPI.
>
> *(example from QD4.4, Bertelsmann Stiftung, n.d.)*

Another aspect of circularity is reflected in how the index is constructed. Suppose that we are interested in the strength of anti-corruption regulation of conflicts of interest and how such regulation affects levels of corruption. If we use the CPI as a proxy for corruption levels across countries, we must be aware that some of the underlying surveys include such regulations as proxies for corruption levels. So to some extent we might be using the existence of regulations to determine the effect of regulations.

A final problem is that the CPI is better at picking up corruption taking place in central governments than in regional or local governments, and is more likely to find corruption when it takes the form of bribery.

The Rise and Fall of Iceland in the CPI

The collapse of Iceland's economy, after the financial crisis of 2006–2008, is an example of the difficulty of measuring and interpreting the measurement of corruption. Before the crisis, Iceland was perceived as nearly corruption-free, with the highest scores on the CPI, 9.6 (out of 10), which ranked it first, in the world, along with Finland and New Zealand. But revelations during and after the financial crisis of corrupt deals and conflicts of interest in closed political and economic influence networks affected post-crisis perceptions of corruption in Iceland and the score deteriorated to 8.3, with a rank of 13th in the world.

How should we interpret the drop in Iceland's score? One explanation would be that after 2006 Iceland became more corrupt and that corrupt behavior in Iceland began after 2006. However, that does not seem very likely, because the behavior and processes that were laid bare by the crisis had been in place for years. But even if we argue that the economic policies of deregulation, privatization, and the increased role of the finance sector in Iceland lead to more serious conflicts of interest, it is clear that these changes were planned and developed over time. A reasonable conclusion is that conflicts of interest and corrupt influence in Icelandic politics were present before the crisis erupted, but were just not picked up by the CPI (Erlingsson, Linde, & Öhrvall, 2016, p. 575). In this respect, "being wise after the event", the experts who lowered the score after the crisis benefitting from hindsight are clearly Monday morning quarterbacks.

Details of the Icelandic collapse illustrate the problems of measurement and interpretation raised by perception-based indices. The banking sector collapsed within three days in 2008 when the crisis hit Iceland, the stock market lost about 80 per cent of its value, and borrowers (individuals and companies) and mortgage holders could not pay their debts (BBC, 2016). Public protests erupted, followed by calls for the prime minister and government to resign.

The year before the collapse, the biggest commercial banks in Iceland held foreign debt worth more than five times Iceland's GDP, with assets valued at eight times Iceland's GDP. The financial sector had grown rapidly in the 1990s and 2000s, using opportunities that had opened up for them when Iceland joined the European Economic Area, which gave Icelandic banks access to Europe, while lax local oversight, safety, and crisis measures stayed in place, along with the influence networks that supported the laxity (Gudmundsson, 2010). Banks and their profits grew exponentially, and were supported by government policy allowing big bank mergers, privatization, and the purchase of foreign assets (Wade & Sigurgeirsdottir, 2012, p. 129). The Icelandic banking boom, backed by a closed economic and political network, is a classic example of what is called state capture, i.e. the purchase and control of legislation and government regulation by powerful economic interests: politics and finance in Iceland was controlled by a small network of people. In sum, the financial industry controlled government policy (Wade & Sigurgeirsdottir, 2012, p. 135), and public administration was shot through with conflicts of interest.

Effects of Corruption Measurement: A Case Study of Sweden

Another case that will help us understand the problems of corruption measurement is Sweden. In particular, Sweden illustrates the effect of country scores on the definition of corruption and even on what we think of public integrity. Given that Sweden is a rich established democracy, or an influence market, to use Johnston's term, we might expect forms of corruption other than bribery to be common. Further, Sweden is a country with strong local government, which serious research on corruption in Sweden must take into account.

In general, Sweden is regarded as one of the world's least corrupt countries. Various measurements contribute to this assessment. Sweden's score on the 2017 CPI was 84, placing it 6th in the world (a score of 88 and 4th place in 2016). Likewise, measurements of corruption that are experience-based also place Sweden among the least corrupt. Surveys asking citizens about their experience of bribery in contacts with the public sector find that 1 per cent or fewer of respondents in Sweden have had any experience of bribery (Bergh, Erlingsson, Sjölin, & Öhrvall, 2016; Charron et al., 2013; European Commission, 2014). Thus, both experience and perception country measurements give us a picture of Sweden with very minor problems of exchange corruption.

But, as we know, the CPI does not enable us to look at variation in types of corruption between countries as well as variation among localities within countries. We also know that the CPI tends to be better at picking up bribery than the kind of governance corruption common in influence markets.

Moreover, the picture of Sweden changes if we use different measurements. If we turn to citizens for their view of corruption in the public sector, the result is very different from their experience of bribery. Forty-four per cent of those surveyed in Sweden perceive corruption to be rather common in the public sector (which is still lower than the EU average of 74 per cent), even though the CPI score says Sweden is nearly the least corrupt country in the world (European Commission, 2014, p. 6). How should we understand the difference? One explanation might be that citizen perceptions are not as well informed as the experts who are surveyed for the CPI. Citizens, it may be argued, are often affected by a general dissatisfaction with government performance. But another explanation is that citizens interpret corruption more broadly than bribery and view other forms of corruption as being more common. There are data that support the second explanation.

Research has found that Swedes are skeptical about the impartiality of public servants. About 40 per cent of respondents said that the service they receive from civil servants definitely depends on personal contacts, a number that is higher than in other neighboring Nordic countries (Linde & Erlingsson, 2013, pp. 591–592).

Citizens also point to forms of governance corruption as being more common than bribery, as measured by their experience of favoritism and nepotism (Andersson & Babajan, 2014). Similarly, politicians in local government point to corruption in job recruitment as a more common form of corruption than bribery in public services and government contracting (Dahlström & Sundell, 2013). So measures focused on bribery might lead us to underestimate corruption in Sweden.

The problem of underestimation becomes even more significant when we discover that Sweden's local governments are more prone to corruption than national government institutions. Most government services in Sweden are produced and provided at the local level, where compared with the national level internal and external integrity controls are limited, as are the available punishments for corrupt officials. This picture complements the view of citizens who perceive local government institutions as more prone to corruption than national institutions. Measurements like the CPI, that tend not to pick up on corruption at the local level, risk missing the most important corruption problems in a country like Sweden.

But if, instead of relying on either citizen or expert surveys, we use actual cases of corruption reported to the Anti-Corruption Unit at the Swedish Prosecution Authority as an indicator (Table 3.2),[7] we find corruption to be evenly distributed between the national government (27 per cent), local and regional governments (26 per cent), and the private sector (34 per cent).

And if we narrow our analysis to convictions for corruption, the picture changes considerably. The share at the national level (41 per cent) increases while that at the local and regional government level decreases (10 per cent). Again, we have a problem of measurement interpretation. First of all, convictions are overwhelmingly for crimes involving bribery. We simply do not know whether governance corruption follows the same pattern. Secondly, "selection effects" are also likely. Bribery at the national level may be more difficult to hide and more important to prosecute than other kinds of corruption at any level of government. The Swedish Public Employment Act of 1994 (sec. 22) requires state agencies to report employees for prosecution if they are suspected of offenses, including bribery and misuse of office[8] when such offenses might result in sanctions other than fines. However, the same requirement does not apply to county councils and municipalities, thereby increasing the likelihood

TABLE 3.2 Reported Cases of Corruption 2003–2011 by Sector (Per Cent)

	State Government	Local & Regional Govt	Private Sector	Other
Alleged Offenders (n=1211)	27	26	34	13
Convicted Persons* (n=267)	41	10	34	16

*The sum of the per cent scores is not equal to 100 due to rounding.

Note: Other includes private persons and associations not belonging to the other categories.

Source: based on corruption cases reported to the Anti-Corruption Unit 2003–2011 (Salén & Korsell, 2013, pp. 26–27). These data are also published in Andersson (2017, p. 65)

that local cases will be dealt with internally and not reported to the Prosecution Authority, which means that corruption in the largest arenas of official activity are less likely to appear in Table 3.2.

Summary and Conclusion

All corruption measurements have positive and negative aspects, which the cases of Iceland and Sweden illustrate. Governance corruption at the systemic level (Chapter 2, and further elaborated on in depth in Chapter 6) is not a direct offense included in the official Swedish Penal Code definition of corruption, which is more narrowly focused on bribery and other aspects of corruption charged under various labels (e.g. breach of trust, embezzlement, misconduct), but aspects of it may fall under the offenses of breach of trust or misuse of office. If "bribery" is used as a synonym for "corruption", as is often the case, other types of corruption are hidden under other labels or tend to be completely ignored. But favoritism and conflicts of interest are clearly important issues in Iceland (with severe consequences), Sweden, and in other influence markets. These crucial aspects of corruption are not sufficiently accounted for by the most widely used measurements and indices, but they can be. Research in Sweden demonstrates that digging deeper into citizen perceptions, prosecutorial priorities, and conviction rates will provide a much more complete measurement of corruption.

In sum, we argue for a combination of measures; there is no single measurement suitable to explain the state of public integrity in a given society. Moreover, we argue that the current emphasis on aggregate country-level measures does not provide the type of information necessary for knowing what action to take against corruption, where, and when. For this we need estimates more concentrated on assessing, for example, sub-units of government or specific agencies over time and across locations, and estimates that take into account what type(s) of corruption we are dealing with. The development of new measures for various types of corruption, particularly governance corruption at the systemic level, will also require qualitative case studies that aim to uncover vulnerabilities to corruption. This will lead to a broader discussion of corruption that includes changes in governance caused by large-scale contracting-out and privatization of public services. Corruption measurement is critical to the study of public integrity, but needs further development to provide us with more meaningful comparative and analytic tools.

Notes

1 Some parts of the following sections have similarly been discussed in Andersson (2016, 2017).
2 They use three different groups in their survey: the public, domestic experts of public administrations, and practitioners (elected officials and officers in local government). They point to three aspects that are important to consider when choosing expert groups

(p. 233): can experts make evaluations that are based on wide knowledge and understanding of concepts, whether they have direct corruption experience that can compensate for lack of knowledge, and whether they are likely to be affected by emotive factors (such as self-justification or ideology).

3 The same questions and aspects were applied to each institution but with the research teams in charge for the particular country having the ultimate say about scores rather than the central coordinating instance.

4 In the traditional family-based system, family obligation is typical for political exchange relations as the only loyalty is to the family, the protector being the family head. In the traditional patron–client-based system ties with powerful protectors, patrons, are strong while the general identification with the community is weak. In contrast to the family-based system patron–client relations are voluntary but create a strong feeling of reciprocal commitment. Clients need the patron to approach and deal with public officials. The modern boss–follower-based system is exemplified by American big-city political machines during the early 20th century. The political boss is the protector and services and favors are traded for votes and contracts. A difference with the previous two archetypes is that a modern boss–follower system consists of open, modern urban centers with diversified economies. The political machine is the decider, giving traditional social and bureaucratic elites little influence. Political exchange is mainly in the form of the economic exchange model, which is adaptable to various situations (in the traditional patron–client-based category social exchange instead is the main form). Finally, in the civic-culture-based system, in contrast to the other archetypes, citizens do not have to go through middlemen to benefit from laws or administrative programs. Strong community-regarding norms are developed and supported via voluntary organizations, where members are paid not with money but instead with moral satisfaction (Heidenheimer, 1970/1989, p. 155).

5 Concerning the variation of corrupt practices and toleration toward them, see also, for example, Graycar and Monaghan (2015).

6 Johnston notes how several countries have gone on to build democratic states (e.g. South Korea, Israel, Spain, South Africa, and some former communist European states); others hold regular but less competitive elections.

7 All in all, there were 684 investigated cases and 1,248 alleged offenders from 2003 to 2011 (Salén & Korsell, 2013).

8 When a person "in the exercise of public authority by act or by omission, intentionally or through carelessness, disregards the duties of his office" (Swedish Penal Code, 1962, p. 700).

References

Alam, M. S. (1995). A theory of limits on corruption and some applications. *Kyklos, 48*(3), 419–435.

Andersson, S. (2016). Corruption. In A. Farazmand (Ed.), *Global encyclopedia of public administration, public policy, and governance* (pp. 1–10). Cham: Springer International Publishing.

Andersson, S. (2017). Beyond unidimensional measurement of corruption. *Public Integrity, 19*(1), 58–76.

Andersson, S., & Anechiarico, F. (2015). The political economy of conflicts of interest in an era of public private governance. In P. M. Heywood (Ed.), *Routledge handbook of political corruption* (pp. 253–269). Abingdon, UK: Routledge.

Andersson, S., & Babajan, T. (2014). Korruptionen i det svenska folkstyret: vad säger medborgarna? *Surveyjournalen, 1*(2), 103–121.

Andersson, S., & Heywood, P. M. (2009). The politics of perception: Use and abuse of Transparency International's approach to measuring corruption. *Political Studies, 57*(4), 746–767.

Andvig, J. C. (2005). *A house of straw, sticks or bricks? Some notes on corruption empirics.* Norks Utenrikspolitisk Institutt. Retrieved from https://brage.bibsys.no/xmlui/han dle/11250/2395390.

Anechiarico, F., & Jacobs, J. B. (1996). *The pursuit of absolute integrity: How corruption control makes government ineffective.* Chicago, IL: University of Chicago Press.

BBC. (2016). *How did Iceland clean up its banks?* Retrieved from www.bbc.com/news/ business-35485876.

Bergh, A., Erlingsson, G. Ó., Sjölin, M., & Öhrvall, R. (2016). *A clean house? Studies of corruption in Sweden.* Lund: Nordic Academic Press.

Bertelsmann Stiftung. (n.d.). *Codebook: Sustainable governance indicators 2017.* Retrieved from www.sgi-network.org/docs/2017/basics/SGI2017_Codebook.pdf.

Charron, N. (2013). QoG at the sub-national level and the EQI. In N. Charron, V. Lapuente, & B. Rothstein (Eds.), *Quality of government and corruption from a European perspective: A comparative study of good government in EU regions* (pp. 70–138). Northampton, UK: Edward Elgar.

Charron, N., Lapuente, V., & Rothstein, B. (2013). *Quality of government and corruption from a European perspective: A comparative study of good government in EU regions.* Northampton, UK: Edward Elgar.

Collier, M. W. (2002). Explaining corruption: An institutional choice approach. *Crime, Law and Social Change, 38,* 1–32.

Dahlström, C., & Sundell, A. (2013). Impartiality and corruption in Sweden. *QoG Working Paper Series, 2013*(14), 14.

Erlingsson, G. Ó., & Kristinsson, G. H. (2016). Measuring corruption: Whose perceptions should we rely on? Evidence from Iceland. *Stjórnmál og Stjórnsýsla, 12*(2), 215–236.

Erlingsson, G. Ó., Linde, J., & Öhrvall, R. (2016). Distrust in Utopia? Public perceptions of corruption and political support in Iceland before and after the financial crisis of 2008. *Government and Opposition, 51*(4), 553–579.

European Commission. (2014). *EU anti-corruption report. Report from the Commission to the Council and the European Parliament.* Retrieved from http://ec.europa.eu/dgs/ home-affairs/e-library/documents/policies/organized-crime-and-human-trafficking/ corruption/docs/acr_2014_en.pdf.

Gallup News. (2015). 75% in U.S. see widespread government corruption. Retrieved from http://news.gallup.com/poll/185759/widespread-government-corruption.aspx.

Graycar, A. (2015). Corruption: Classification and analysis. *Policy and Society, 34*(2), 87–96.

Graycar, A., & Monaghan, O. (2015). Rich country corruption. *International Journal of Public Administration, 38*(8), 586–595.

Groop, C. (2013). *Accountability and corruption: A study into political institutions as referees between principals and agents* (PhD diss.). Åbo: Åbo akademi University Press.

Gudmundsson, M. (2010). Lessons from the financial crisis in Iceland (presentation by the Governor of the Central Bank of Iceland, December 2, 2010). Retrieved from www.imfs-frankfurt.de/fileadmin/user_upload/Events_Presentations_Programs_ Flyer/101202_MG_IMFS_Presentation_Gudmundsson.pdf.

Heidenheimer, A. J. (1970/1989). Perspectives on the perception of corruption. In A. J. Heidenheimer, M. Johnston, & V. T. LeVine (Eds.), *Political corruption: A handbook* (pp. 149–163). New Brunswick: Transaction Publishers.

Heywood, P. M., & Rose, J. (2014). "Close but no cigar": The measurement of corruption. *Journal of Public Policy, 34*(3), 507–529.

Inglehart, R., Haerpfer, C., Moreno, A., Welzel, C., Kizilova, K., Diez-Medrano, J., ... Puranen, B. (2014). World Values Survey: Round Six – Country-Pooled Datafile Version. Retrieved from www.worldvaluessurvey.org/WVSDocumentationWV6.jsp.

Johnston, M. (2005). *Syndromes of corruption: Wealth, power, and democracy.* Cambridge: Cambridge University Press.

Johnston, M. (2014). *Corruption, contention and reform: The power of deep democratization.* Cambridge: Cambridge University Press.

Kaufmann, D., Kraay, A., & Mastruzzi, M. (2010). The Worldwide Governance Indicators: Methodology and analytical issues. Retrieved from www.brookings.edu/~/media/research/files/reports/2010/9/wgi%20kaufmann/09_wgi_kaufmann.pdf.

Lambsdorf, J. G. (2007). *The institutional economics of corruption and reform.* New York: Cambridge University Press.

Lessig, L. (2013). Institutional corruptions. Edmond J. Safra Working Papers, No. 1. Retrieved from https://papers.ssrn.com/sol3/papers.cfm?abstract_id=2233582.

Linde, J., & Erlingsson, G. Ó. (2013). The eroding effect of corruption on system support in Sweden. *Governance, 26*(4), 585–603.

Liu, C., & Mikesell, J. L. (2014). The impact of public officials' corruption on the size and allocation of U.S. state spending. *Public Administration Review, 74*(3), 346–359.

Mauro, P. (1995). Corruption and growth. *Quarterly Journal of Economics, 110*(3), 681–712.

Miller, W. L., Grødeland, Å. B., & Koshechkina, T. Y. (2001). *A culture of corruption? Coping with government in post-communist Europe.* Budapest: Central European University Press.

Pring, C. (2015). People and corruption: Africa Survey 2015. Global Corruption Barometer. Retrieved from www.transparency.org/whatwedo/publication/people_and_corruption_africa_survey_2015.

Pring, C. (2016). People and corruption: Europe and Central Asia. Global Corruption Barometer. Retrieved from www.transparency.org/whatwedo/publication/people_and_corruption_europe_and_central_asia_2016.

Pring, C. (2017a). People and corruption: Asia Pacific. Global Corruption Barometer. Retrieved from www.transparency.org/whatwedo/publication/people_and_corruption_asia_pacific_global_corruption_barometer.

Pring, C. (2017b). People and corruption: Latin America and the Caribbean. Global Corruption Barometer. Retrieved from www.transparency.org/whatwedo/publication/global_corruption_barometer_people_and_corruption_latin_america_and_the_car.

Quality of Government Institute. (2016). Downloads. Retrieved from http://qog.pol.gu.se/data/datadownloads.

Reinikka, R., & Svensson, J. (2001). Explaining leakage of public funds. Retrieved from www.wider.unu.edu/conference/conference-2001-2/plenary%20papers/Reinikka_03_08.pdf.

Salén, L. H., & Korsell, L. E. (2013). *Den anmälda korruptionen i Sverige: struktur, riskfaktorer och motåtgärder.* Stockholm: Brottsförebyggande rådet.

Søreide, T. (2006). *Is it wrong to rank? A critical assessment of corruption indices* (8280621342). Retrieved from www.cmi.no/pdf/?file=publications/2006/wp/wp2006-1.pdf.

Swedish Penal Code (1962:700). Translation (DS 1999:36).

Thompson, D. F. (1995). *Ethics in Congress: From individual to institutional corruption.* Washington, D.C.: Brookings Institution Press.

Transparency International. (2010). NIS Assessment Toolkit for EU Member States 2010–11. Retrieved from www.transparency-se.org/ENIS-Toolkit-Final-January-2011.pdf.

Transparency International. (2015a). Global Corruption Barometer. Retrieved from www.transparency.org/research/gcb/.

Transparency International. (2015b). What is the Corruption Perceptions Index? Retrieved from www.transparency.org/cpi2012/in_detail.

Transparency International. (2016). Corruption Perceptions Index 2016: Short methodology note. Retrieved from http://files.transparency.org/content/download/2054/13228/file/CPI_2016_ShortMethodologyNote_EN.pdf.

Transparency International. (2017a). Corruption Perceptions Index 2017: Full source description. Retrieved from http://files.transparency.org/content/download/2181/13740/file/CPI_2017_SourceDescription%20Document_EN.pdf.

Transparency International. (2017b). Corruption Perceptions Index: Overview. Retrieved from www.transparency.org/research/cpi/overview.

Transparency International. (2017c). News: Corruption Perceptions Index 2016. Retrieved from www.transparency.org/news/feature/corruption_perceptions_index_2016.

Transparency International. (2018). Corruption Perceptions Index 2017. Retrieved from www.transparency.org/news/feature/corruption_perceptions_index_2017.

Treisman, D. (2000). The causes of corruption: A cross-national study. *Journal of Public Economics*, 76(3), 399–457.

Wade, R. H., & Sigurgeirsdottir, S. (2012). Iceland's rise, fall, stabilisation and beyond. *Cambridge Journal of Economics*, 36(1), 127–144.

Weber Abramo, C. (2007). How much do perceptions of corruption really tell us? Retrieved from www.economics-ejournal.org/economics/discussionpapers.

World Bank. (2015). Worldwide Governance Indicators. Retrieved from http://info.worldbank.org/governance/wgi/index.aspx#home.

World Bank. (2016). Enterprise surveys indicator descriptions (International Finance Corporation). Retrieved from www.enterprisesurveys.org/data/exploretopics/~/media/GIAWB/EnterpriseSurveys/Documents/Misc/Indicator-Descriptions.pdf.

World Bank. (2018). Worldwide Governance Indicators. Retrieved from http://info.worldbank.org/governance/wgi/#home.

4

CORRUPTION CONTROL IN PUBLIC ADMINISTRATION

Introduction

This chapter builds on the discussion in previous chapters about what corruption is and how corruption can be measured. We now turn to the tough job of controlling corruption. Which approaches work and which don't? Are some applicable to either exchange or governance corruption or to both? What are the costs and benefits of corruption control? Our examination of control strategies will include examples from local, national, and international government. Further, the effect of our broad, two-part definition of corruption is a concern with legal as well as illegal activity that violates norms of democratic inclusion.

Despite the focus on power and democracy in political science, ethics and integrity are not mainstream issues in the discipline (Huberts, 2014, p. 200). Given how central integrity is for trust and legitimacy of government, we argue corruption control should cover a broad range of *integrity violations*, defined as behaviors that violate "relevant moral values and norms" (Huberts, 2014, p. 4), including conflict of interest, fraud, discrimination, and improper use of authority, which includes both exchange and governance corruption.

In the following sections we return to the contrast introduced in Chapter 1, between corruption control strategies based on punitive external controls (law enforcement strategies) and others based on the personal and public ethics of officials (values-based strategies). We also ask whether there might be a third approach. This chapter illustrates how approaches vary across sectors and countries, and how controls have developed over time.

Approaches to Integrity in Public Administration

Of particular interest to those studying ethics management and corruption control is whether ethics management should rely on compliance with rules to foster

FIGURE 4.1   Two Ideal Types of Ethics Management

Source: Figure created by authors

expected behavior within an organization or whether it is possible to rely on personal values and self-regulation by government employees (Heywood & Rose, 2014, p. 152). Corruption control approaches are often described in the public administration literature by where they fall in relation to two ideal types.

At one end of the continuum we find *law-enforcement-based* (or rules-based) ethics management and at the other *values-based* ethics management (Figure 4.1). These two approaches and their emphasis on internal versus external control go back to the classical discussion in the 1930s and 1940s between Carl Friedrich, who put his faith in internal control because of his belief that politics could not easily be removed from administration, and Herman Finer, who had no such faith in internal control and argued that power relations in administration required external political and institutional controls (Finer, 1941). Central to the debate was administrative discretion, the autonomy of an official to use his or her professional judgement to choose between alternatives (cf. Wallander & Molander, 2014, p. 1). Friedrich emphasized the need for discretion in carrying out a professional role and regarded internalized standards and sensitivities as the only effective guide, while Finer did not trust internal controls to effectively guide administrators' discretion, and saw the need for external controls to constrain and monitor it (Cooper, 2006, p. 156).

Law enforcement approaches center on constraints on the conduct of individual public servants "that originate from outside themselves" (Cooper, 2006, p. 149), such as codes of ethics, laws, formal rules and procedures, monitoring, and sanctions (Tremblay, Martineau, & Pauchant, 2017, p. 221). The law enforcement approach is based on compliance with rules and deterrence of illegal behavior since, it is argued, we should not expect self-regulation and professional standards to guarantee ethical behavior (Cooper, 2006, p. 149). Clearly, the law enforcement approach is a top-down integrity management strategy.

Values-based approaches on the other hand focus on internal controls that presume self-regulation. Values-based approaches set out organizational values and standards and encourage understanding of and commitment to them by administrative staff. The emphasis is on the development of an ethical culture via internal controls that consist of values, beliefs, knowledge, and ethical standards nurtured by each individual public servant to encourage ethical conduct in the absence of numerous rules and intensive monitoring. Kant's moral philosophy is in line with this perspective. These internal (and internalized) controls reflect the value consensus in the organization, but are anchored in the judgement of each public servant. Thus internal control presumes that personnel in an organization will use moral values to make decisions motivated by what is right rather than by fear of punishment for doing what is wrong. Education, ethical dilemma exercises, experience exchange, and rewards for exemplary and ethical conduct are methods used to develop internal control (Cooper, 2006, p. 150; Lawton, Rayner, & Lasthuizen, 2013, pp. 117–120).

The advantage of values-based approaches is that they define and encourage good behavior; the downside is the difficulty of implementing and measuring personal ethics. Law-enforcement-based approaches on the other hand are easier to implement and monitor. However, tough enforcement of ethics laws often leads to inefficiency and goal displacement by encouraging avoidance of illegality rather than providing employees with incentives to develop ethical thinking and act according to shared values. Most obviously, formal rules cannot cover all eventualities or anticipate the creative ways that those so inclined will invent to defraud the government (Lawton et al., 2013, pp. 103–104, 116–118).

The two approaches should be seen as ideal types that help us understand how organizations try to protect integrity and avoid corruption. In actual practice the two types are often mixed in various ways, though it is often argued that once law enforcement takes hold (usually in the aftermath of a scandal) values-based tactics get much less attention and may be ignored completely. The approach of organizations is also influenced by factors at the systemic level. For example, in the United Kingdom, ethics management has historically leaned toward values-based internal control, informal codes, and trust in the professionalism and moral integrity of civil servants, with less reliance on external controls. However, beginning in the 1990s the United Kingdom shifted toward law enforcement in response to scandals and to the New Public Management (NPM) reforms that changed the structure of public administration by moving more and more public service provision into the private sector. As part of its response to contracting, privatization, and scandal, the British government introduced independent bodies for ethical oversight and imposed centralized, detailed, ethical codes. In contrast, the United States has a long history of quickly resorting to legislation and law enforcement to deal with ethical problems (Cooper, 2006, p. 160). The law enforcement approach in the United States emphasizes external control of conflicts of interest, second jobs, post-public employment, gifts, financial disclosure, and, above all, monitoring public servants using investigative agencies charged with conducting surveillance and undercover operations to detect corruption.

Hong Kong is often referred to as one of the best examples of a political system that has reduced corruption from high levels, so that by the time the British returned the Crown Colony of Hong Kong to the Chinese government in 1997 it had a reputation for honest government and as a good place to do business. Otherwise the success of anti-corruption programs in most countries has been modest.

But, a note of caution: there is little evidence of the impact and effectiveness of most anti-corruption reforms, other than those relying on surveys of public opinion (Chên, 2015, p. 2). Still, it was hard for residents and outsiders with experience in Hong Kong to avoid noticing how it changed into a place where starting a business, getting a restaurant license, or export certification did not require paying off public officials. Because it is one place where the effects of corruption control strategies are so obvious, the Hong Kong model has been widely discussed and adopted elsewhere. The centerpiece of the model is the Independent Commission Against Corruption (ICAC) established in 1974, in the wake of a corruption scandal in the British colonial police (Box 4.1). The ICAC is based on a law enforcement approach including broad investigative powers and tough sanctions. However, values-based aspects such as preventive education were also part of the Hong Kong model. Neighborhood walk-in booths, a TV show featuring the ICAC's exploits, and intensive ethics training for civil servants have given the agency a very high profile locally.

BOX 4.1 THE HONG KONG APPROACH TO ANTI-CORRUPTION

The Independent Commission Against Corruption (ICAC) has from its inception in 1974 used a three-pronged approach of law enforcement, prevention, and community education to fight corruption. These parts are also reflected in its organizational divisions, with departments for corruption prevention, community relations, and operations. Some of the main traits of the model include a single organization with monopoly on corruption control with strong independence from the government, and secure funding even in times when public expenditure in other areas are cut. The success in bringing corruption down is often attributed to the ICAC's extensive powers in several areas, including rights of arrest and detention (Scott, 2011, p. 401).

To understand its success, it is also important to acknowledge the special circumstances under which it was set up, with unique political and cultural factors at the individual, organizational, and systemic levels. Its staff is known for its high moral standards. Systemic factors are also important. The ICAC has experienced wide public support (it is recurrently regarded as the most trusted organization in Hong Kong), which is often not the case in other country contexts, and acceptance for very strong investigative and prosecutorial powers that in many democracies would be questioned. It has been regarded by the public as a guarantor of a corruption-free relationship between the public and the government. Moreover, it has been backed by a strong political will to combat corruption.

The model has developed over time and adapted to many changes, especially the resumption of Chinese sovereignty in 1997 (and fears of increased corruption), challenges by new and sophisticated forms of corruption—think conflict of interest rather than bribery, but also note the change in legislation in 1970 from a previous focus on bribery to defining the offense as to "'offer, solicit or accept' an advantage" without mentioning the word "bribe" or "corruption" (Scott, 2011, p. 403). The approach has moved toward values-based integrity management, in order to better cope with conflict of interest in relation to contracting out and post-public employment. New legal instruments have been added to cope with new areas of corruption or unethical behavior (the offense of misconduct in public office). Organizationally the ICAC also collaborates with other government departments through integrity management programs and forms partnerships with private sector organizations (Scott, 2011).

However, the key question in the field of public ethics is not about whether to rely on external or internal control, but about finding a balance between these approaches or some third way that respects both the law and also the intelligence and judgement of civil servants. The "right" approach hinges not only on the organization itself but also on the surrounding ethical framework, including national culture, statues, laws, and tolerance of ethical failure (Tremblay et al., 2017, p. 219). As Terry Cooper (2006, p. 182) puts it, there should be enough external control to avoid self-interest and enough internal control to encourage socially constructive and altruistic and creative behavior. They should also reinforce each other in order to effectively encourage appropriate, ethical behavior. This is a worthy, but difficult, quest.

Searching for Balance … Or an Alternative

Before 1980, integrity in both public and private organizations was considered to be something personal: either you had it or you didn't. The overwhelming concern of public and private organizations was efficiency, not public integrity. The idea of managing organizational ethics emerged in the early in 1980s (see Bowman, 1983). One of the questions framing organizational ethics was "If corruption cannot be prevented, how can it be responsibly controlled?" (Bowman, 1983, p. 75). In approaching this question, James Bowman argued that democracy depends on individual integrity and trust between citizens and public officials, and that citizens have been able to depend on the professional self-discipline of those hired to do the public's work. However, Bowman recognized, an exclusive focus on individual ethics is not enough given the inevitable discretion involved in all government service (1983, pp. 73–74). To maintain ethics in a discretionary environment, Bowman suggested a three-pronged approach:

- Training programs
- Codes of conduct
- Protection of administrative dissent (i.e. whistleblowing)

Interest in dealing with integrity and ethics issues increased after the Watergate scandal in the 1970s in the United States and ethics scandals elsewhere in the 1980s, in both the public sector and the corporate sphere in established democracies. At the time, the ethics strategies employed were mostly law-enforcement-oriented, based on deterrence and punishment. However, academic work on ethics programs indicated that the law enforcement approach alone could not deal with complex ethical problems in organizations (Tremblay et al., 2017, p. 220). Moreover, as organizations in the public sector adopted principles of NPM and were less constrained by rules and regulation and increasingly focused on performance, ethics management moved toward broad guidance and values-based internal control. NPM and performance management gave even more discretion to managers, so the values of these now more powerful managers became critical. The ethical grounding of public administration was shifting as government started to rely increasingly on market-based, profit-oriented public service provision. However, the leap into the brave new world of NPM was premised on removing rules and regulations, at the very time when administrators faced the ethical challenge of allowing private companies to define the public good. Basically, by 1990 public service managers were navigating ethics without a rulebook. This required agency managers to emphasize and rely on the subjective responsibility[1] of officials charged with letting and monitoring the contracts and privatizations that NPM entails (Mulgan & Wanna, 2011, p. 417). Examples of the shift toward values-based ethics management in the era of NPM are found in the World Bank, the OECD, and Transparency International (TI).

By the 1990s, the law-enforcement-based and values-based approaches began to be mixed within frameworks. Two examples of the new mix are TI's National Integrity Systems (NIS) scheme (Figure 4.2) and the OECD's Ethics Infrastructure strategy (Figure 4.3). The NIS scheme focuses on the strength of institutions regarded as pillars of integrity.

The OECD's Ethics Infrastructure model emphasized three elements (control, guidance, and management) and their constituent parts, and the commitment of the political leadership.

In 2009, the OECD elaborated its model by introducing the Integrity Management Framework, which has become one of the most influential and widely used tools for public ethics management. The Framework includes both law enforcement and values-based components in an attempt to balance external and internal controls (Tremblay et al., 2017, p. 221). The OECD emphasizes

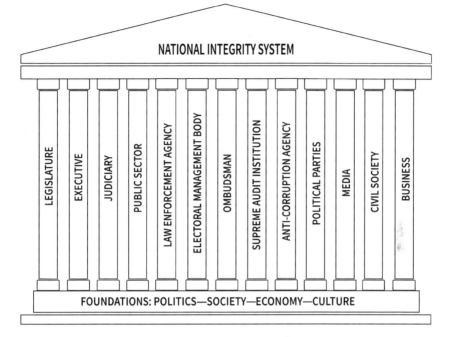

FIGURE 4.2 Pillars of Transparency International's National Integrity System

Source: Transparency International (2012, p. 4)

how integrity management is based on instruments, processes, and structures and how the integrity instruments applied serve four main functions (Figure 4.4).

The Integrity Management Framework and other approaches that mix law enforcement and values-based approaches have been criticized because of the difficulty of implementing a mix of what are very different strategies. In addition, there are no established methods for evaluating the balance between the two approaches, which leaves organizations to implement the mix without knowing its effects or its cost (Hoekstra, 2016; Huberts, 2014). A further criticism is that an individual's compliance with the elements of the Framework is determined by the level of his or her commitment and motivation, which is also very difficult to verify (Tremblay et al., 2017, p. 224). Take, for example, Fran, a college student who is driven to study because she finds it exciting and it provides her with greater understanding (intrinsic motivation), or another student, Fred, who works hard because the car his parents have given him will be confiscated if he does not achieve an A average that term (extrinsic motivation).

The two students may seem to have incompatible perspectives, but the contrast between intrinsic and extrinsic motivation is not as simple as it first appears. If Fred gets the A average he will certainly be relieved that he still has a car, but

ETHICS INFRASTRUCTURE

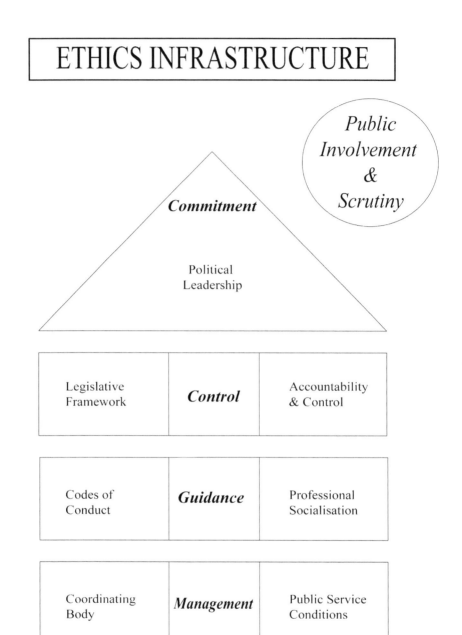

FIGURE 4.3   Elements and Functions of the OECD Ethical Infrastructure Model

Source: OECD (1996, p. 26)

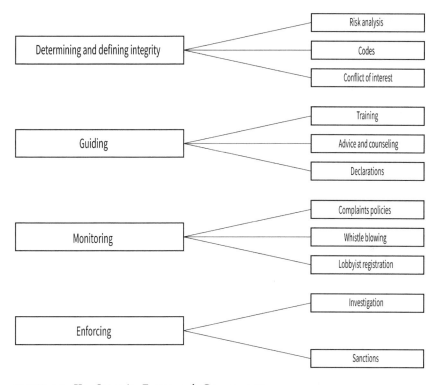

FIGURE 4.4 Key Integrity Framework Components
Source: OECD, n.d.

he may also recognize and appreciate the understanding he has gained from his courses in doing so. The following term, even though his car is secure, Fred may have the motivation to study for the intrinsic reward of understanding. If the external origin of the law enforcement approach is internalized by an individual, it will become intrinsic motivation.

So, a control measure may take many forms depending on how it is internalized by the receiver and what motivation it triggers. The impact of controls cannot be predicted by researchers or organizational leaders but depends on the degree to which individuals internalize them. Public organizations cannot ensure how effective controls will be implemented in relation to the balance of internal and external controls (Tremblay et al., 2017, pp. 224–226). An additional problem is that controls are often implemented as an ad hoc response to scandals rather than as parts of a comprehensively developed framework (Heywood, 2012).

We should also remember that external and internal controls mainly target individual behavior, while many of the problems of public ethics, including governance corruption, may result from organizational pathologies or systemic dysfunction. Further, the term "control" and the institutionalization of control reduces individual autonomy and limits the ability of employees to manage ethical ambiguity using their own moral values (Tremblay et al., 2017, pp. 223–224).

To deal with these and other shortcomings of the Integrity Management Framework, Maryse Tremblay, Joé T. Martineau, and Thierry C. Pauchant (2017) propose a "pluralistic contingency approach" which includes a variety of ethic methods and procedures. The basic idea is to include not only the individual level but also the organizational and systemic (which they call "strategic") levels. This is a bottom-up approach, starting with evaluating individual ethical needs and preferences in contrast to the top-down Integrity Management Framework, which is based on the perception by management of the ethical needs of the organization. The difference between the two approaches is summarized by the authors in Figure 4.5.

The difference between the Framework and the pluralistic approach is evident. Most starkly, the "Approaches" section in the comparison chart lists "Compliance (external controls)" under the Integrity Management Framework and "Normative practices" under the pluralist framework.

The pluralist approach is indicative of a trend in public administration. Overall, ethics management has shifted from law enforcement toward values-based strategies and a recognition of the toxic effect on public integrity of organizational and systemic malfunction. This shift is supported by research showing that cultural values and informal expectations are at least as important to corruption control as legal regulation (Mulgan & Wanna, 2011, pp. 416–417).

	Integrity management framework	*Pluralist ethics management framework*
Aim	• Prevent corruption and other integrity violations	• Manage ethics in complex environment through implementation of ethics practices representative of people and ethical issues • Promote ethical reflection and ethical behavior
Approaches	• Stimulate and enforce integrity • Compliance (external controls) • Integrity (internal controls)	• Normative practices • Detection practices • Structural practices • Social and environmental responsibility practices • Consultation and participation practices • Experiential ethical development practices
Levels Covered	• Individual	• Individual • Collective • Strategic
Outcome	Management of unethical behavior	Management of individual and organizational
Basis	Perception of management (top-down)	perceptions and needs in terms of ethics (bottom-up)

FIGURE 4.5 Comparison of Integrity Frameworks

Source: Tremblay et al. (2017, p. 229)

Anti-corruption strategies reflect the interplay of culture and law and increasingly focus on developing cultural norms of integrity, without which the law changes from a behavioral framework to a weapon. Integrity culture is defined as "endorsed social understandings, behaviors and practices that affect how people think and act" when confronted with ethical choices (Mulgan & Wanna, 2011, p. 417). What the discussion up to this point makes plain is that integrity culture often differs from or is in opposition to formal organizational structures and rules.

But, as we have noted, the thinking about what to do to prevent and detect corruption is often driven not by integrity culture, but by reaction to scandal, which is usually accompanied by media attention and public demand for stronger law enforcement. The impact of tougher law enforcement measures on the quality of public integrity is not often evaluated. Therefore, the next scandal may be taken to mean that law enforcement must be even tougher. On the other hand, the *absence* of scandal will be taken as proof that tough measures are working and must be kept in place. There is very seldom an incentive to weaken or remove law enforcement measures—anyone trying to do so may well be labeled "soft" on corruption.

Variation of Approaches to Integrity across Sectors: The Example of Ethics Codes

The relationship between national political culture and organizational norms is important to corruption control since national culture influences what is considered acceptable ethical behavior and what is regarded as corrupt (Mulgan & Wanna, 2011).

But within a given country, culture and values will vary among public sector organizations. Those working in public agencies must manage values that are shaped by the unique needs of their clients, the professional values of agency staff, historical agency norms, and their own ethical values (Lawton et al., 2013, p. 4). Because of the specific ethical challenges of their environment, public organizations have come to rely on ethics codes or codes of conduct designed to deal with those challenges. Codes set out the values that officers and staff are expected to follow, provide guidelines for official decision making, and lay down sanctions for ethical violations. Formally, codes are an external form of control. However, they can also have an impact on the intrinsic motivation and sense of subjective responsibility of officers and staff of public organizations. To begin, formulating these codes can raise awareness about ethical issues and require discussion about what ethical values should guide the organization. If the formulation process engages individuals at all levels of the organization, it will anchor organizational ethics in consensus and become what we might call *cooperative* ethics management.

Ethics codes in public organizations are usually related to general values in the public sector like impartiality, integrity, accountability, and acting in the public interest. In several countries and in international organizations broad principles have been codified that should apply to public officials across agencies and organizations in the public sector. One famous example is the "seven principles of public life" formulated by the Committee on Standards in Public Life in the United Kingdom in 1995 (Box 4.2).

BOX 4.2 THE SEVEN PRINCIPLES OF PUBLIC LIFE (UK)

1. **Selflessness**. Holders of public office should act solely in terms of the public interest.
2. **Integrity**. Holders of public office must avoid placing themselves under any obligation to people or organisations that might try inappropriately to influence them in their work. They should not act or take decisions in order to gain financial or other material benefits for themselves, their family, or their friends. They must declare and resolve any interests and relationships.
3. **Objectivity**. Holders of public office must act and take decisions impartially, fairly and on merit, using the best evidence and without discrimination or bias.
4. **Accountability**. Holders of public office are accountable to the public for their decisions and actions and must submit themselves to the scrutiny necessary to ensure this.
5. **Openness**. Holders of public office should act and take decisions in an open and transparent manner. Information should not be withheld from the public unless there are clear and lawful reasons for so doing.
6. **Honesty**. Holders of public office should be truthful.
7. **Leadership**. Holders of public office should exhibit these principles in their own behaviour. They should actively promote and robustly support the principles and be willing to challenge poor behaviour wherever it occurs.

Source: Committee on Standards in Public Life (1995)

Principles like these are based in the history of the jurisdiction in question. In the case of the United Kingdom, a long tradition of an independent, professional civil service is the basis of the seven principles. The quite different administrative history of the United States is reflected by the addition of "loyalty" to a comparable list (Lawton et al., 2013, p. 99).

Organization-specific codes often relate to broader principles. The OECD (2017, p. 4) code of conduct sets out to ensure that officials within the organization live up to ethical standards of professional international civil servants. It includes independence, impartiality, and confidentiality, and prohibitions on interest conflicts, outside jobs, and post-employment obligations. This is followed by instructions on how to seek advice in difficult, ambiguous situations and what to do if one is witness to or the victim of misconduct. Finally, the OECD code provides examples of situations and responses to them.

A country-level example of a code combining general, public sector principles with agency-specific guidelines is the code (ethical guidelines) developed by the Swedish Tax Agency. Like all revenue collection agencies, the Agency's paramount concern is upholding trust in its operations, avoiding conflicts of interest,[2] and remaining above party politics (Box 4.3). The code is related to six general principles for employees of state agencies in Sweden: democracy; legality; objectivity; freedom of expression; respect; and effectiveness, efficiency, and service. Box 4.3 details the way these principles are applied to the job of tax collection.

BOX 4.3   THE ETHICAL GUIDELINES OF THE SWEDISH TAX AGENCY

Trust. The question here is how your action would stand up if you told family, friends, colleagues and the media about it (much in line with Cooper's (2006, p. 37) advice that public officers could avoid scandals if they first consider how their action would be seen by the others).

The objectivity of the civil servant. All taxpayers must be treated equally under the law. The importance of impartiality and professionalism, in an agency with power over citizens' finances, includes the importance of ensuring there is no possibility of personal or other irrelevant interests influencing the application of the Swedish revenue law. There is a clear and imperative prohibition on accepting bribes and on having conflictual second jobs. The code also explains how to avoid unethical situations and what to do when one occurs.

Openness. The importance of appropriate and correct handling of taxpayer information is discussed in relation to the strong constitutional guarantee of citizen access to official records, the protection and anonymity of whistleblowers, and the ban on the interrogation of employees to plug "leaks". However, the Agency code at the same time exempts a large portion of data from public access and reinforces the centrality of confidentiality.

An inclusive tax agency. Here the emphasis is on inclusiveness and zero tolerance of any form of discrimination, either within the authority or against citizens.

(continued)

(continued)

To be efficient with state resources. This point emphasizes financial restraint and careful use of Agency resources. This includes guidelines concerning employee travel, environmental responsibility, and prohibition of personal use of Agency resources and facilities.

A culture that countervails corruption. Dialogue and an ongoing discussion about ethics and values in the Agency is highlighted in the interest of embedding a high level of ethical responsibility in Agency personnel and in Agency culture.

Source: Skatteverket (2018)

Important to the contribution of ethics codes to good governance is consideration of context, consent, implementation, and enforcement (Lawton et al., 2013, p. 98). In essence, the goal of codes and the way they are constructed and implemented is cooperative development and internalization of organizational ethics. However, it must be noted that there is unfortunately little research about the impact and effectiveness of ethics codes in preventing unethical behavior and corruption (Cooper, 2012, p. 146).

Anti-corruption over Time and the Case of the United States in Comparison

Approaches to preventing corruption have changed dramatically over time (Chapter 6 will illustrate this further). There have been major shifts in how much emphasis is placed on corruption control compared to other issues in public administration, in what is considered as the main cause of the problem, in tactics and strategies of corruption detection and deterrence, and in what punishment for corrupt behavior is appropriate.

Using the U.S. example, we can see that anti-corruption efforts have an important impact on how government units are organized and operated. Over time, more and more corruption control measures have been added in reaction to scandals at all levels of American government. This has had an impact not just on corruption control per se but also on government effectiveness.

Ethics management in the United States at the end of the 19th century and start of the 20th leaned toward the values-based approach, internal controls, and a belief in the public spiritedness of professional public administrators. During this period, which overlaps with the reforms of the Progressive Era, government employees thought of themselves as trustees for the interests of the people they served. But beginning with the New Deal in the 1930s, as bureaucratic organizations expanded and became more complex, corruption

controls became increasingly external, moving from trust in the virtue of officers and internal control in public administration to emphasis on surveillance
and law enforcement.

The integrity reforms following the Watergate scandal in the 1970s shifted
corruption control so far toward law enforcement that they were compared by
Anechiarico and Jacobs (1996) to Bentham's all-seeing Panopticon (Wikipedia,
2018):[3] in this period of administration history, the civil service was seen as fer-
tile ground for corruption with ample opportunities magnified by inadequate
monitoring. Reform proposals in the decades following Watergate built on prior
reforms, but were more expansive and intense. Reforms were also based on a
longer list of individual behavior that was considered corrupt. However, the
focus during the Panoptic period was still on exchange corruption, with very little
attention to the organizational or systemic dysfunctions that comprise governance
corruption. Moreover, as noted by Bowman (1983, p. 69) these measures did not
stem the tide of corruption and scandal in government.

Panoptic controls include more surveillance, expanded capacity for investigative agencies, a wider role for ethics management, and tighter fiscal controls.
Whistleblower protection for those who reported irregularities in an organization
also became a common part of the ethics framework. The aspiration of Panoptic
controls is to collect complete information about resource use and performance.
As Michel Foucault (1977/1995) argues, Panoptic controls persuade those being
"watched" that whatever they do can and will be observed and so they come
to control themselves, not because they have public values at heart, but because
their ability to make personal choices has been suppressed. The Panopticon has
never characterized all ethics management in the United States, but it became a
very popular model and ushered in an era of stringent law enforcement in the
design of corruption controls.

But by the 1990s, bureaucratic government came under attack for its inefficiency and burdensome rules, including those designed to prevent corruption.
In many places, critics argued, law enforcement ethics management had not
only paralyzed public service provision with paranoia-inducing surveillance,
but it had failed to prevent corruption. The squeeze on administrative discretion of Panoptic controls reduced the ability of agency managers to use their
professionalism to do good by identifying new and creative approaches to old
problems. If, for example, the solution to after-school violence requires cooperation between agencies, churches, and private businesses, a closely-watched school
board employee would likely shy away from the complex mix of profit motives
and public goals involved in an innovative program of prevention; it is just safer
to stick with crossing-guards and letters to parents. This sort of suppressed initia-
tive was the target of anti-bureaucracy reformers.

In the 1990s, administration reform in the United States was inspired by ideas
about reinventing government and dismantling bureaucracy (Osborne, 1993),
which came to be known as New Public Management. NPM was inspired

by market-based public policy in the United Kingdom and New Zealand particularly. These reforms used the market to undercut bureaucracy, in the hope of making government businesslike, entrepreneurial, and cost effective. In general, these ideas were a response to the critique of high taxes and big government, the decreasing trust in government institutions, and the need to find a way to reshape government to work more effectively as globalization became increasingly important (Kettl, 2005, p. 65). Reform proposals included decentralization, deregulation, business methods, entrepreneurship, and market privatization (Anechiarico & Jacobs, 1994, pp. 468, 471). But here as well, the view of corruption, when it was mentioned at all, focused on exchange rather than governance corruption.

As NPM has evolved, it has been criticized in several important ways:

- First, because governance structures were mixed with market mechanisms (contracting out of juvenile detention or even police service), corruption vulnerability increased.
- Second, there was little evidence that performance improved or costs dropped (Hood & Dixon, 2015, pp. 180–183).
- Third, fairness as measured by service users' perceptions seemed to worsen (Hood & Dixon, 2015, pp. 180–183).
- Fourth, the democratic nature of public administration was strained as the role of citizen was replaced by the role of public service consumer (Denhardt & Denhardt, 2000, p. 557).

Public administration, in the age of NPM, is characterized by "market intervention, technical efficiency and the private value of public things", and not by public values[4] (Bozeman, 2002, p. 157). Economic individualism and the stress on economic criteria, efficiency, and effectiveness may be good in certain circumstances but bad when crowding out collective interests, which results in "public value failures" (Bozeman, 2002, p. 150).

Take the situation where a private equity firm buys a company providing elder care on a local government contract. The private equity firm lends money to buy the company and puts the cost for the loan on the balance sheet of the elderly care company. The idea is then to quickly make the elder care company profitable. To do so, the elder care company needs to cut costs drastically, which among other things means staff and programming cuts. There is then less time for staff to care for patients, which causes complaints from patients and their families. A couple of years and even more cuts later, the company has paid the loans and breaks even, and now the private equity firm that owns it sells it for a considerable profit. What does this case mean for the public value of caring for vulnerable, elderly citizens? Who is responsible for the drop in service quality here? Just the company, or the company and the public officials that let and oversee the contract?

In cases where public services are contracted out it may seem obvious that contracts should cover oversight and service quality, but in many cases these issues are neglected in order to give the contractor creative flexibility and because the contracting agency has been hollowed out by shifts of its functions to the market and does not have the resources required for effective oversight. It has been shown in cases similar to this illustrative one (Anechiarico & Andersson, 2016) that in the absence of agency oversight it is difficult for media and the public to get access to information about the owners of such companies and hold them accountable. The lesson of NPM to date is that in market-based services transparency is low and lines of accountability are blurred.

It is difficult to say whether NPM has led to more corruption. But if the hope was that shrinking the public sector would lead to less exchange corruption, it has not been realized. Transparency rules designed to enhance accountability generally apply to public officials and agencies but not to the same extent to private providers of outsourced services. Less accountability and less transparency mean more risk of corruption. But not just the risk of more exchange corruption, but also the risk of private entities excluding critical public interests and marginalizing vulnerable, less influential individuals in their quest for profit, which adds up to governance corruption. The preeminence of NPM in public administration has been followed by a critique that calls for moving public values up the agenda and finding ways of getting citizens and communities more deeply involved in their own governance.

Since corruption controls and ethics management influence organizational behavior and therefore the quality and effectiveness of public services, it is worth considering a more inclusive model, not only in policy making but in ethics management. We have noted that some more recent models of ethics management mix law-enforcement-based and values-based strategies. A good example is the cooperative way some organizations have written codes of conduct and in doing so have made it possible for government employees to internalize ethical controls. But if the critics of NPM think participatory models are good for policy making, why not go beyond codes of conduct to participatory models for ethics management itself? There are prominent examples, mostly in local government, of agencies that surface and discuss ethics on a regular basis and in which agency employees have a role in protecting the integrity of their operation. The popular model of Q (quality) Circles gives members of an organization a forum for questioning operations and decisions from a variety of perspectives, including ethics and integrity (Ishikawa, 1985).

In the 1990s, a charter reform in Santa Rosa, California, changed city council elections from district-based to at-large and, at the same time, required that city administrators engage the public in the design and implementation of public goods and services. To comply with the charter's engagement provisions, municipal officials mandated and inspected regular interaction of all program and agency managers with relevant constituencies in the community. This meant, for example, multiple meetings with residents of an area where a new park was planned, with consensus rules about its structure and use. But engagement was not just between administrators and the public, but also among administrators themselves. As program managers explained, these meetings assessed the quality of the agency's work, but also how successful the agency was at maintaining high ethical standards for professional conduct. This was a mechanism to reinforce value internalization and lessen the need for external controls. Perhaps the model of both citizen and peer engagement in public service agencies is the kernel of an alternative, cooperative approach to ethics management.

Globalizing Corruption Control

The OECD was one of the earliest advocates of putting more focus on fighting corruption globally to protect fair competition in foreign trade. In 1997 the OECD (2016) adopted rules against the use of bribery of foreign public officials in international business deals (Box 4.4). The convention has played an important role in harmonizing the way countries deal with bribery and extortion committed by their citizens abroad. The aim is to treat foreign bribes the same way in all member countries in order to create a level playing field for companies, no matter their country of origin.

BOX 4.4 THE OECD CONVENTION ON COMBATING BRIBERY OF FOREIGN PUBLIC OFFICIALS IN INTERNATIONAL BUSINESS TRANSACTIONS

Previously the American Foreign Corrupt Practices Act (FCPA, 1977) was quite alone in being tough on bribing foreign officials for a trade advantage. However, U.S. companies argued that the new law created an uneven playing field in relation to its competitors. The United States pressed for harmonization within the framework of the OECD.

The OECD convention requires signatory countries to make it illegal and a criminal offense to bribe foreign officials. It requires prosecution and punishment of both individuals and companies similar to how they would be treated for similar offenses committed in their home countries (Davids & Schubert, 2011). If we take the UK bribery act as an example, we find that it includes the offense of "failure to prevent bribery". To avoid punishment under this provision, companies doing business in foreign countries must perform due diligence in hiring, education of staff, and supervision of staff interactions abroad. In the United States, the FCPA has been effective in using civil suits to reach big settlements from companies (Davids & Schubert, 2011, p. 337).

For example, in 2008 the engineering company Siemens paid USD1.34 billion in fines, including USD900 million to U.S. authorities, for long-term bribery of foreign officials (Lichtblau & Dougherty, 2008). In 2016 the Brazil-based construction company Odebrecht and its affiliated petrochemical company Braskem paid about USD3.5 billion in an international case that included corrupt contracts with the state-owned Brazilian Petrobas, with most of the fines going to Brazilian authorities (Rosenberg & Raymond, 2016).

The United Nations (United Nations, 2016) similarly worked to increase cooperation internationally and harmonized treatment of corruption. Its Convention against Corruption (UNCAC) was adopted in 2003 and entered into force in 2005. It builds on previous UN work concerning the international drug trade and organized crime. Increased travel, improved communications, and new technology had made crime ever more international, indicating the need for international instruments of corruption control (Joutsen, 2011).

The UNCAC requires member countries to criminalize domestic and foreign bribery, influence trading, embezzlement, and money laundering, and provides for asset recovery. Preventive measures include transparency of political financing, establishing anti-corruption bodies, promoting efficiency in public services, and merit-based civil service recruitment. The convention obliges public servants to be subject to codes of conduct, financial disclosure, and possible sanctions. It calls for transparent and accountable public finance and the establishment of requirements for corruption prevention in public procurement and the judiciary. It also emphasizes the importance of active involvement of citizens and non-governmental organizations (NGOs) in domestic ethics management.

The UNCAC is a detailed framework for cooperation but an important issue concerns its implementation and how it is enforced within states. Effective enforcement requires investigators, prosecutors, and judges to be given the instruments to carry out their work (Joutsen, 2011). The underfunded UN has made some progress in this regard, but the goal of international enforcement of public integrity standards remains aspirational.

TI (Transparency International) is the most prominent example of an NGO's influence on domestic and international public integrity protection. Established in 1993, it has played an important role in placing corruption high on the international political and economic agenda, and in the shift of the World Bank toward issues of public integrity and anti-corruption policy. As we have discussed in Chapter 3, its annual publication of the Corruption Perceptions Index that provides cross-country corruption data was important for this outcome.

However, corruption is difficult to fight, and many countries have struggled while others have given up. Although comparative research on the effectiveness of anti-corruption reforms is limited, we can point to two important reasons for this struggle and failure. First, it is difficult to combat corruption that is entrenched in the ruling elite—an elite will not be easily persuaded to investigate itself. Second, the use of a one-size-fits-all approach like law enforcement ethics management does not consider local variation in the causes and intensity of corruption. The World Bank (2016) and other foreign aid and investment donors have begun to give these two factors more attention.

Conclusion

Upholding integrity and controlling corruption is easier said than done. In this chapter we have looked at the most common approaches, their costs and benefits, and how the approaches vary depending on the country context and the public service area we are concerned with. We looked at examples of corruption in organizations at the local, national, and international level, and how control is approached at each. An important part of the discussion concerned the difficulty in finding the right balance between law-enforcement-based and values-based approaches, with reference to the classical debate between Friedrich and Finer. Friedrich's argument at that time was about how complex government organizations were making it very difficult to ensure accountability of administration. His solution, to emphasize internal standards and values as the best way to uphold integrity, is even more valid today. We noted, though, how the anti-corruption movement concentrates on bribery and exchange corruption, which leads to a law enforcement strategy. This, we argue, neglects governance corruption problems that may be more widespread and damaging. We also noted how the balance in public administration has tipped toward values-based corruption controls in reaction to the ethical shortcomings of NPM, which indicates the possible alternative ethics management approach of cooperative engagement at the agency work-group level.

A final take-away from the discussion of corruption controls is the need to include organizational pathology and systemic dysfunction and bias in designing corruption controls, as Tremblay and colleagues argue in their pluralist contingency approach. Doing so empowers ethics management to reduce vulnerability to both exchange and governance corruption. This is perhaps the most significant reason for defining government corruption as we do here to include damage to democratic governance by exclusion and neglect. If bias and misconduct at the organizational and systemic level must be considered in designing corruption controls, then the definition of corruption must comprehend them as well.

Notes

1 Subjective responsibility concerns how actions of officials are guided by their own beliefs about loyalty, conscience, and identification, while objective responsibility concerns how administrative behavior of officials is guided by external accountability to superiors or elected officials through the law; responsibility for tasks, goal achievement, and subordinate staff; and responsibility to citizens and to serve the public (Cooper, 2006, pp. 81–90).

2 In 2017 investigative journalists revealed that the two most senior executives at the Agency had given heads-up to a former Government Office colleague and friend about an upcoming investigation of alleged tax avoidance (Bergman & Dyfvermark, 2016).

3 The U.S. Congress adopted the 1978 Ethics in Government Act with stringent disclosure of income and employment practice. It also established the Office of Government Ethics to implement these measures (Cooper, 2006, p. 149).

4 Bozeman (2007, p. 13) defines public values of a society as "those providing normative consensus about (a) the rights, benefits, and prerogatives to which citizens should (and should not) be entitled; (b) the obligations of citizens to society, the state, and one another; and (c) the principles on which governments and policies should be based" (p. 13).

References

Anechiarico, F., & Andersson, S. (2016). Shaping the state to private purposes: A comparison of conflicts of interest in the United States and Sweden. In F. Anechiarico (Ed.), *Legal but corrupt: A new perspective on public ethics* (pp. 29–53). Lanham, MD: Lexington Books.

Anechiarico, F., & Jacobs, J. B. (1994). Visions of corruption control and the evolution of American public administration. *Public Administration Review, 54*(5), 465–473.

Anechiarico, F., & Jacobs, J. B. (1996). *The pursuit of absolute integrity: How corruption control makes government ineffective.* Chicago, IL: University of Chicago Press.

Bergman, S., & Dyfvermark, J. (2016, April 6). Skatteverkets överdirektör försökte varna för granskning. *SVT Nyheter.* Retrieved from www.svt.se/nyheter/granskning/ug/ skatteverkets-overdirektor-forsokte-varna-bekant-for-granskning.

Bowman, J. S. (1983). Ethical issues for the public manager. In W. B. Eddy (Ed.), *Handbook of organization management* (pp. 69–102). New York: Marcel Dekker.

Bozeman, B. (2002). Public-value failure: When efficient markets may not do. *Public Administration Review, 62*(2), 145–161.

Bozeman, B. (2007). *Public values and public interest: Counterbalancing economic individualism.* Washington, D.C.: Georgetown University Press.

Chên, M. (2015). Successful anti-corruption reforms. Transparency International. Retrieved from www.transparency.org/whatwedo/answer/successful_anti_corruption_reforms.

Committee on Standards in Public Life. (1995). The seven principles of public life. Retrieved from www.gov.uk/government/publications/the-7-principles-of-public-life/the-7-principles-of-public-life--2#selflessness.

Cooper, T. L. (2006). *The responsible administrator: An approach to ethics for the administrative role* (5th ed.). San Francisco, CA: Jossey-Bass.

Cooper, T. L. (2012). *The responsible administrator: An approach to ethics for the administrative role* (6th ed.). San Francisco, CA: Jossey-Bass Wiley.

Davids, C., & Schubert, G. (2011). The global architecture of foreign bribery control: Applying the OECD Bribery Convention. In A. Graycar & R. G. Smith (Eds.), *Handbook of global research and practice in corruption* (pp. 319–339). Cheltenham, UK: Edward Elgar Publishing.

Denhardt, R. B., & Denhardt, J. V. (2000). The new public service: Serving rather than steering. *Public Administration Review, 60*(6), 549–559.

Finer, H. (1941). Administrative responsibility in democratic government. *Public Administration Review, 1*(4), 335–350.

Foucault, M. (1977/1995). *Discipline and punish: The birth of the prison* (Vintage Books 2nd ed.). New York: Vintage Books.

Heywood, P. M. (2012). Integrity management and the public service ethos in the UK: Patchwork quilt or threadbare blanket? *International Review of Administrative Sciences,* 78(3), 474–493.

Heywood, P. M., & Rose, J. (2014). "Close but no cigar": The measurement of corruption. *Journal of Public Policy, 34*(3), 507–529.

Hoekstra, A. (2016). Institutionalizing integrity management: Challenges and solutions in times of financial crises and austerity measures. In A. Lawton, Z. Van der Wal, & L. Huberts (Eds.), *Ethics in public policy and management: A global research companion.* Abingdon, UK: Routledge.

Hood, C., & Dixon, R. (2015). *A government that worked better and cost less? Evaluating three decades of reform and change in UK central government.* Oxford: Oxford University Press.

Huberts, L. (2014). *The integrity of governance: What it is, what we know, what is done, and where to go.* Basingstoke, UK: Palgrave Macmillan.

Independent Commission Against Corruption. (2018). About ICAC. Retrieved from www.icac.org.hk.

Ishikawa, K. (1985). *What is total quality control? The Japanese way.* Englewood Cliffs, NJ: Prentice Hall.

Joutsen, M. (2011). The United Nations Convention Against Corruption. In A. Graycar & R. G. Smith (Eds.), *Handbook of global research and practice in corruption* (pp. 303–318). Cheltenham, UK: Edward Elgar Publishing.

Kettl, D. F. (2005). *The global public management revolution* (2nd ed.). Washington, D.C.: Brookings Institution Press.

Lawton, A., Rayner, J., & Lasthuizen, K. (2013). *Ethics and management in the public sector.* Abingdon, UK: Routledge.

Lichtblau, E., & Dougherty, C. (2008, December 15). Siemens to pay $1.34 billion in fines. *New York Times.* Retrieved from www.nytimes.com/2008/12/16/business/worldbusiness/16siemens.html.

Mulgan, R., & Wanna, J. (2011). Developing cultures of integrity in the public and private sectors. In A. Graycar & R. G. Smith (Eds.), *Handbook of global research and practice in corruption* (pp. 416–428). Cheltenham, UK: Edward Elgar Publishing.

OECD. (1996). Ethics in the public service: Current issues and practice. Public Management Occasional Papers No. 14. Retrieved from http://citeseerx.ist.psu.edu/viewdoc/download?doi=10.1.1.194.8759&rep=rep1&type=pdf.

OECD. (2016). OECD Convention on Combating Bribery of Foreign Public Officials in International Business Transactions. Retrieved from www.oecd.org/corruption/oecdantibriberyconvention.htm.

OECD. (2017). Code of Conduct for OECD Officials. Retrieved from www.oecd.org/legal/Code_of_Conduct_OECD_2017.pdf.

OECD. (n.d.). Integrity framework. Retrieved from www.oecd.org/gov/44462729.pdf.

Osborne, D. (1993). Reinventing government. *Leadership Abstracts, 6*(1), n.p.

Rosenberg, M., & Raymond, N. (2016, December 21). Brazilian firms to pay record $3.5 billion penalty in corruption case. Reuters. Retrieved from www.reuters.com/article/us-brazil-corruption-usa/brazilian-firms-to-pay-record-3-5-billion-penalty-in-corruption-case-idUSKBN14A1QE.

Scott, I. (2011). The Hong Kong ICAC's approach to corruption control. In A. Graycar & R. G. Smith (Eds.), *Handbook of global research and practice in corruption* (pp. 401–415). Cheltenham, UK: Edward Elgar Publishing.

Skatteverket. (2018). *Statstjänstemannarollen och etik inom Skatteverket.* Retrieved from www.statskontoret.se/globalassets/forvaltningskultur/etiska-koder/statstjanstemann-arollen-och-etik-inom-skatteverket.pdf.

Transparency International. (2012). NIS Assessment Toolkit. Retrieved from www.trans parency.org/files/content/nis/NIS_AssessmentToolkit_EN.pdf.

Tremblay, M., Martineau, J. T., & Pauchant, T. C. (2017). Managing organizational ethics in the public sector: A pluralist contingency approach as an alternative to the Integrity Management Framework. *Public Integrity, 19*(3).

United Nations. (2016). United Nations Convention against Corruption. Retrieved from www.unodc.org/unodc/en/treaties/CAC/.

Wallander, L., & Molander, A. (2014). Disentangling professional discretion: A conceptual and methodological approach. *Professions and Professionalism, 4*(3), 1–19.

Wikipedia. (2018). Panopticon. Retrieved from https://en.wikipedia.org/wiki/Panopticon.

World Bank. (2016). Anti-corruption. Retrieved from www.worldbank.org/en/topic/governance/brief/anti-corruption.

5

THE CONNECTION BETWEEN PUBLIC INTEGRITY AND DEMOCRATIC GOVERNANCE

Four Case Studies

Chapters 1 through 4 have discussed exchange corruption and governance corruption as separate parts of the same phenomenon, both damaging, both important, and both inevitable. Our job in this chapter is to explain how the parts interact and what the nature and consequences of that interaction are. To put it a different way, the case studies in this chapter will demonstrate the relationship between *integrity*, the honest administration of public business; and *democracy*, the control of public business by the people. We will explain this relationship by describing each case at the individual, organizational, and system level.

These three levels include broader governance factors, especially aspects of the public/private divide in governance, agency leadership, and routine, down to the effects of personal experience and psychological disposition on the decisions of public employees. Thus, we include cases that illustrate situations of governance with different types of actors in both public and private organizations that straddle the public/private boundary in different ways but who are in all cases responsible for doing the public's business, no matter who pays their salary. The mission of this chapter is practical illustration of problems, reasons, and effects that may apply to corruption of official behavior in organizations. We are concerned here with organizational and systemic—as well as individual—corruption.

The four cases discussed in this chapter are set in industrial democracies: the United States, Sweden, and the Republic of Ireland. They are all characterized by what Michael Johnston (2005) calls the syndrome of "influence market corruption". Influence markets, as the name suggest, are characterized by the buying and selling of control over public policy. The reason that examples drawn from influence markets are useful is the challenge to democratic governance presented by their heavy use of the private sector to produce and provide public goods.[1]

Critical public decisions are made and implemented through markets or market-like processes, with less restrictive regulations and fewer and weaker means of accountability (Johnston, 2005, p. 12). As we have noted before, using profit-oriented organizations to serve the public may involve their use of power and wealth in ways that hinder or exclude citizen participation, but are still legal. Influence market corruption often involves favoritism, which causes conflicts of interest ("softer" forms of exchange corruption than bribery), or it may be a more systemic bias in the use of wealth and power that causes governance corruption. And this despite influence markets being less associated with high-level bribery, and exchange corruption, in comparison with other corruption syndromes. In short, case studies of influence market corruption illustrate both exchange and governance corruption.

The first of the four cases concerns judicial corruption in 2007 in Pennsylvania in the United States related to private operation of state juvenile detention facilities. The second case concerns revelations in 2016 of favoritism and institutional conflict of interests in the supreme audit institution of Sweden. These first two relate to exchange corruption, primarily and most clearly in the first case, but also imply serious problems of democratic governance. The second two cases involve governance corruption. The first explores the consequences of aggressive street policing in New York City between 2002 and 2014, and the second addresses revelations beginning in 1995 of child sexual abuse in the Irish Catholic Church, and how the Church and the Irish government reacted (Anechiarico, 2016; O'Kelly, 2016).

Approaching Cases at Three Levels of Analysis

These case studies allow an in-depth look at corruption. What were the contributing[2] factors in each corruption scandal and what roles in the scandal were played by individual actors and by public and private institutions? What were the consequences of the scandals and what can we learn from them? The case study of each of the four corruption scandals will consider causes and effect at the individual, organizational, and systemic levels of analysis (Table 5.1). This involves knowing who key individual actors are, discovering their incentives, and understanding how they interpret and carry out corrupt policies. What are the links to system-level values and routines that affect organizational behavior? (We develop this further below.) Next, at the organization level, we consider how bureaucratic routines, administrative culture, and the nature of oversight work in practice. At the systemic level we are concerned with the social values and historical factors that shape each case study.

More specifically, at the *individual level* corruption is understood through questions about motivations, incentives, and other factors concerning individual circumstances. How do these circumstances enable or obstruct official misconduct?

Greed or financial desperation may contribute to involvement in corruption and in relation to financial circumstances. Individuals may take shortcuts or extort bribes; they may distort agency performance measures in the hunt for status and advancement. We often read about corrupt officials arguing that they felt entitled to "compensate" themselves for their hard work and the sacrifices they have made for the benefit of the public; in their view, they have done nothing wrong, although some "unreasonable" rules may have been broken in the process.

To illustrate the role of individual circumstances and how they interact with opportunities for unethical behavior, let us take the example of Terry Cooper's (2006) "responsible administrator". Cooper (pp. 27–28) argues that the more administrators "consciously address and systematically process" the ethical aspects of their decisions the more responsible will they be. He outlines a model for self-conscious, ethical decision making at the individual level in a five-step process (pp. 32–39).

- First, actors identify and describe the situation.
- Second, they define the ethical issue (conflicting values rooted in a practical problem).
- Third, alternative courses of action are distinguished.
- Fourth, plausible consequences (positive and negative) of these alternatives are predicted.
- Fifth, a practical, ethical decision is made.

This last step requires consideration of moral rules in relation to alternatives and their consequences:

- Whether the chosen alternative can be defended in public.
- The balance between duty to ethical principles and the outcome of the decision.
- Whether the alternative enhances the administrator's self-esteem.

Cooper points out that administrators, like the rest of us, have a tendency to trust accounts of situations from people higher up the hierarchy more than from people lower down. This will affect the range and nature of alternatives taken into account. In relation to the fifth, decisional step Cooper (2006, p. 37) argues that many people who have been caught up in corruption scandals could have avoided them had they just thought about how their action would be seen by the public: "Would I do this, if I knew it was going to appear on the front page of the newspaper—or the top of an internet news feed—tomorrow?"

Our personal values, actions, and ethical awareness, Cooper shows, are affected by what our co-workers and others around us think. One of the effects of social pressure is what has been called "group-think", which suppresses the assertion of individual ethics and is a powerful disincentive for whistleblowers. Group-think persuades the individual that he or she has to go along to get along—or, less poetically: career advancement requires conformity.

Unethical behavior is thus related to the social forces present in all organizations.

At the *organization level* we look at corruption that develops and is embedded in the structures, policies, and culture of both official and private organizations that provide goods and services to the public. Studies at this level link the organizational characteristics to corrupt actions and policies with systemic values and routines that reinforce and guide organizational behavior like legal rules about transparency and accountability.

Here factors detailed in Chapter 2 are relevant. The main point to keep in mind is that the ethical nature of organizational actions and routines is determined by the rules, norms, and goals of the organization as they are shaped by administrative culture. That culture is either reinforced or challenged by a given organization's leadership which communicates, directly or indirectly, what behavior is expected and acceptable in the organization.

Other questions raised at the organization level are:

- Is any integrity training provided to staff?
- How ethically aware are organization members?
- What are the organization's policies on integrity?
- Is a certain degree of unethical behavior tolerated?

Both administrative culture and bureaucratic routine are connected to how corruption and ethics are viewed in the organization and how deviance and corrupt behavior may be tolerated and even normalized.

Of particular interest in the four case studies are mechanisms for internal control of individual behavior and policy making like reporting requirements and formal inspection. The purpose of these mechanisms is to identify and investigate waste, fraud, and abuse in public sector agencies and in public–private cooperation. The strength and prominence of oversight and accountability naturally affect organizational behavior. This leads us to the system level and the historical and societal factors that establish the environment in which organizations act.

At the *system level* we search in each case study for broad-scale factors that influence the ethics of organizations and their members. Can organizations recognize the social and historical context in which they operate and so be structured to prevent or reduce the risk of corruption? Our goal in the case studies at this level is to understand social and historical factors as they operate in governance structures at regional, national, and global levels. This includes regional and national ethics legislation and international anti-corruption conventions. Examples of the factors that we discuss in the case studies are the extent of democratic participation; the accountability of political institutions; wealth, racial, and other inequalities; relative economic opportunity; the strength of economic institutions; and the integrity of law enforcement and judicial institutions. Johnston's classification of corruption syndromes is based on several of these factors, including democratic participation and political and economic opportunity.

The four case studies here are drawn from influence markets, where corruption patterns tend to concern access and influence within established institutions rather than attempts to circumvent those institutions. In influence markets it is especially important to understand how state and business relations are regulated, the laws and regulations governing campaign finance and conflicts of interest, and in general how public services are organized and operated. In short, how "public values" are interpreted and protected. The public role of an organization cannot not be assessed only according to ownership or its legal status; we also have to look at the degree of "political authority constraints and endowments" affecting the organization, which means that some institutions, whether governmental or not, are more "public" in their values than others (Bozeman, 2007, p. 8).

Given that we are looking at individual cases that involve specific organizations there will naturally be an extra focus on the organizational level. This level of study enables us to link the individual actors who interpret and carry out policies that may be corrupt with the systemic-level values and routines

TABLE 5.1 Factors at Three Levels of Analysis

Individual

- Individual: character/personality, private financial situation, personal values, emotion, and friendship
- Individual and work-related: type of work, colleagues, operational leadership, relationships and networks, ethical awareness

Organizational

- Bureaucratic routines: rules, norms, and goals of the organization
- Accountability structures: control, supervision, separation of responsibilities, discretion
- Inspection: administrative review and investigation independent of political interference
- Administrative culture: goals/mission, organizational values and norms (formal and informal)
- Policies: integrity policy, reward system (and penalties)
- Leadership and the tone at the top: operational strategies

Systemic

- Economic: wealth and income, competition, openness and trade, inequality
- Political-administrative: state–private sector relations, political–bureaucratic relations, public values versus private-market-based values (including integrity)
- Historical: governance frameworks, tradition of democratic participation and accountability, ethnic–racial–class separation
- Oversight: political accountability of public organizations
- Judicial: relative independence, reliance on the rule of law
- Societal norms: norms and values, feelings of injustice, human rights, crime

Source: adapted from Huberts and De Graaf (2014, p. 164)

that reinforce and guide organizational behavior. Therefore, the cases cover the individual level, in terms of characteristics of individual actors and individual circumstances, and the systemic context of the cases, regarding social norms, state–private sector relations, democratic participation and accountability, and inequality. The cases show how these levels interact and influence each other.

Case One: Juvenile Justice Corruption in Luzerne County, Pennsylvania

This case considers a scandal that took place in Luzerne County's juvenile court (Court of Common Pleas) in Pennsylvania in the United States. The scandal developed in 2007 when parents complained to a non-profit, advocacy group, the Juvenile Law Center, about their children being sentenced for minor offences to harsh, out-of-home placements in (for-profit) youth detention centers without legal representation in hearings that lasted only minutes (Dale, 2009; Juvenile Law Center, n.d.; Schuppe, 2015). In some cases, children were taken from the courtroom in "leg shackles and handcuffs attached to thick leather belts" (Interbranch Commission on Juvenile Justice, 2010, p. 54).

The case involved over 2,500 juveniles and 6,000 cases from 2003 to 2008. Over 50 per cent of children that were sentenced by one of two judges at the center of the case, Mark A. Ciavarella, Jr., had no legal counsel. Over 60 per cent were sent to out-of-home placement and many of them to the privately operated detention centers that were involved in the case (Juvenile Law Center, n.d.).

The Juvenile Law Center petitioned the Pennsylvania Supreme Court in 2008 to vacate all juvenile sentences by Ciavarella and delete the records of them. This was denied at first, but after the U.S. Attorneys charged Ciavarella and the other judge in question, Michael Conahan, with fraud and taking bribes, extraordinary relief[3] was granted. In 2009, all of the juvenile sentences between 2003 and 2008 issued by the two judges were dismissed and their records deleted (Juvenile Law Center, n.d.).

The two judges and two other perpetrators involved in the scheme, a co-owner of the private facilities and the developer who built them, were all found guilty and received prison penalties.[4] The final part of the legal case was a federal class action law suit against the offending parties seeking damages for children and parents (Juvenile Law Center, n.d.). Marsha Levick (quoted in Schuppe, 2015), deputy director of the Juvenile Law Center, said concerning the legal outcome that,

> Justice has been done as much as it can be done through the legal process, but it's an incomplete reckoning. How do you put a price on the kids' constitutional rights, on being removed from their communities and taken from their schools and everything else they suffered?

The Interbranch Commission on Juvenile Justice[5] (2010, p. 17) in Pennsylvania that was established in 2009 in the aftermath of the corruption scandal with the mission of investigating what led to the corruption, rebuilding public confidence in justice, and preventing this from happening again, warned about the consequences for democracy if citizens "cannot trust the honesty and fairness of officials in the legal system".

What Happened and Why

This is a case where at the organizational level we see clear examples of how bureaucratic routines drifted from their original goals and how self-interest and greed became motives at the individual level. Here also normalization of deviance is important in understanding what happened as harsh sentences for infractions were accepted, or at least not opposed by others in the organization, including the police and school authorities. This case is a clear example of exchange corruption but also governance corruption as vulnerable juveniles and their families faced bias and exclusion and were denied voice. The two judges in question created conditions in the court for an increased number of juveniles to be sent to the detention facilities in which they themselves had financial interests, thereby systematically denying the constitutional rights of juveniles (Interbranch Commission on Juvenile Justice, 2010, p. 60; U.S. Department of Justice, 2009a).

Judge Michael T. Conahan was elected to the Court of Common Pleas in 1993 and Judge Ciavarella in 1995. Conahan was president of the court from 2002 through 2006 (then Ciavarella, 2007–2009). The two judges were close friends, partners in business ventures, and neighbors during this period (Interbranch Commission on Juvenile Justice, 2010, p. 13). The financial gain for the involved actors were substantial. All in all the two judges took about USD2.8 million in payments from Robert Powell, one of the owners of the PA Child Care and Western PA Child Care detention centers, and from Robert Mericle of Mericle Construction, a developer who built the two facilities. The payments were for advocating and arranging the closure of the county-run facility and placing juveniles in the two private facilities instead. Robert Powell had a law practice in Luzerne County and was also the lawyer for the county planning commission, which had authority to approve construction of the new facilities. Powell did a lot of legal work for the county and from 1995 through 2002 he donated to the campaigns of county commissioners. However, in the required financial disclosure statements between 2004 and 2007, neither judge reported his financial relationship with Powell and Mericle (Interbranch Commission on Juvenile Justice, 2010, pp. 9, 14, 19; Learn-Andes, 2015; *The Citizens' Voice*, 2011; U.S. Department of Justice, 2009a, 2009b).

Court president Conahan and Powell entered into corrupt agreements to place juveniles at Powell's private facilities, and Conahan helped withdraw funding from the county facility, which resulted in its closure. Juveniles were sometimes sent for detention against the recommendation of juvenile probation officers. Ciavarella also put pressure on staff to shift from the common practice of recommending release to recommending detention more often (Interbranch Commission on Juvenile Justice, 2010, pp. 9, 19; U.S. Department of Justice, 2009a, 2009b).

According to Ciavarella, it had been his idea to shift juvenile detention to private centers. He had asked the county commissioners in 1998/1999 to build a new facility but without result, so he asked Conahan about finding someone who could build them. In June 2000 Conahan then introduced Ciavarella to Robert Powell (Interbranch Commission on Juvenile Justice, 2010, p. 15; *The Citizens' Voice*, 2011). Ciavarella then introduced Powell to Mericle, with whom who he was friendly. Powell and PA Child Care bought land and worked with Mericle to build the centers (Interbranch Commission on Juvenile Justice, 2010, pp. 15, 18).

Mericle was officially the low bidder and so won the construction contract. However, he later admitted paying USD2.1 million to the judges. Powell pre-paid six years of rent on Conahan and Ciavarella's Florida residences to the tune of USD720,000. Ciavarella did not disclose these payments from Powell or recuse himself when Powell appeared in court before him (Allabaugh & Kalinowski, 2014; Dale, 2009; Interbranch Commission on Juvenile Justice, 2010, p. 15).

The judges thus took a series of actions to benefit businesses in which they had undisclosed financial interests. A key action was Conahan's signing in January 2002 of the agreement between the court and PA Child Care to place juvenile offenders at the for-profit facility. The court would pay a rental fee to Powell of USD1.3 million. The commitment between the court and PA Child Care was used by Powell to secure construction financing, but not made public until a reporter identified Powell as a key investor in the proposed center. In October 2002, at the direction of Conahan, the court informed the county that from the beginning of 2003 juveniles would not be sent to county-owned facilities. In February 2003, the county started sending juveniles to Powell's for-profit centers (*The Citizens' Voice*, 2011; U.S. Department of Justice, 2009a).

According to Ciavarella's testimony, Mericle told him that he would pay Ciavarella a finder's fee[6] of about 10 per cent of the contract price when the contract was set. Ciavarella then offered Conahan half the money. Ciavarella's share of the finder's fee was USD440,000. It was paid from Mericle's company to one Robert Matta, then to a company owned by Conahan, and finally to Ciavarella. Ciavarella did not see the money as illegal or as bribes but instead as something he was entitled to. He also said that he thought Conahan had paid taxes on the money (Interbranch Commission on Juvenile Justice, 2010, p. 15).

Further, the indictment against the two judges described how Mericle in January 2003 arranged to pay the two judges USD997,600. Mericle and Powell signed a written "Registration and Commission Agreement" prepared by Mericle. This was backdated to February 19, 2002, in order to make the payment look like a finder's fee, from Mericle to Powell (Interbranch Commission on Juvenile Justice, 2010, p. 18).

In November 2004 Democratic majority leaders of the Luzerne County Commission Todd Vonderheid and Greg Skrepenak approved a USD58 million,

20-year lease with PA Child Care (Allabaugh & Kalinowski, 2014). The minority Republican commissioner Stephen Urban voted no and was very critical of the decision that ignored warnings from state auditors who called it "a bad deal" (Buffer, 2011). Urban argued that repairs and improvements to the public-owned center could be made for between two and four million dollars (Interbranch Commission on Juvenile Justice, 2010, p. 9). Urban also pointed out that Powell, who was doing legal work for the county, did not disclose his interest in PA Child Care, when the court sent the Commission the proposal to lease the for-profit center. Powell also ignored requests from county officers to file required financial disclosure forms for his years of employment with the county (Learn-Andes, 2015). There were rules and integrity policies that were designed to detect the conflicts of interest in this case, but they were not enforced.

On the development and construction side of the scandal, Mericle contributed at least USD35,000 to the joint campaign committee for Skrepenak and Vonderheid, and Vonderheid's personal campaign committee received an additional USD6,000. Vonderheid served as vice-president for economic development and member services at the local business chamber (Greater Wilkes-Barre Chamber of Business and Industry) before he was elected to the Luzerne County Commission in 2003. In 2007 he resigned as county commissioner to become president of the chamber. Mericle, who was a friend of Vonderheid's, served on the chamber board from 2003 through 2008 and was one of Vonderheid's key backers when he sought the president's post (Buffer, 2011).

Payments were made by Powell and Mericle over several years to the judges, who, even after the centers were built, continued to ask for payments from Powell "for their past and anticipated future official actions" (Interbranch Commission on Juvenile Justice, 2010, p. 18).[7] When news about an investigation into these matters broke in the local paper, Powell agreed to sell his interest in the centers to co-owner Greg Zappala (*The Citizens' Voice*, 2011).

Conflict of Interest and Failing Countermeasures

Conflicts of interest are at the heart of this case: conflicts that were unreported and undetected for a very long time. Ethics rules and financial disclosure requirements were either ignored or neglected. In this case, we find exchange corruption in the form of kickbacks and quid pro quo payments that reveal individual motives that led the judges and developers to take advantage of corrupt opportunities. However, there are also systemic aspects of the case that connect to the organizational level of analysis. Many of the people involved had one foot in the judicial or executive branches of government and the other in the private sector. These people used their official authority to shape public services to serve private rather than public interests.

The judges were receiving money from people with an interest in the private juvenile facilities. In the United States the trend of contracting out incarceration service has been strong. From a governance point of view incarceration and prisons used to be seen as core government functions, but since the 1980s they have been increasingly carried out by for-profit companies who are part of what has become a multi-billion-dollar industry. This in itself raises questions about the moral limits of markets. Michael Sandel (1998) points out the risks involved in turning certain government services into commodities, whereby the intrinsic public value of these services is degraded and corrupted. The obvious instances of exchange corruption in this case should not obscure the systemic (cf. Underkuffler, 2005) governance corruption indicated by the subversion of fairness and impartiality by the key actors, whose conflicts of interest were fueled by institutional incentives and a lax, insider administrative culture (cf. Warren, 2015, p. 50).

Let's look more closely at the corrupt networks in this case, at the organizational and systemic levels of analysis. The Supreme Court of Pennsylvania found in its ruling on the scandal that Conahan and Ciavarella had manipulated the Luzerne court system so that they would control the assignment and trial of individual cases. The Interbranch Commission (2010, pp. 13–14) found that conflicts of interest and corruption had been part of the historical culture of Luzerne County, of which both judges were natives. Underlying the culture of corruption in the county was the unchecked authority exercised by court president Conahan, who was described by contemporaries as a feared power broker. Conahan placed friends and relatives on the court staff—the court administrator was his cousin—and personally assigned cases. Further, Conahan consorted with criminals. He had regular breakfast meetings with an organized crime leader, William "Big Billy" D'Elia, with whom he discussed court cases. D'Elia occasionally sent envelopes to Conahan by way of a court security guard with connections to D'Elia (Interbranch Commission on Juvenile Justice, 2010, pp. 13–14).

In a case that did not directly concern the juvenile justice scandal, Conahan and D'Elia conspired to promote a defamation suit against the local newspaper *The Citizens' Voice*. The paper had reported that a businessman who was friendly to D'Elia had company records seized in a federal racketeering investigation that targeted D'Elia. The newspaper quoted sources who implicated the investigation's targets in money laundering, illegal gun sales, and drug dealing. The businessman argued that by publishing the allegations the newspaper defamed his character. He argued further that his business relations with D'Elia were minor and legal, so he sued the paper. Ciavarella heard the case and ruled in favor of the businessman, requiring the newspaper to pay USD3.5 million in damages (Interbranch Commission on Juvenile Justice, 2010, p. 14; Janoski, 2009).

Conahan had directed his cousin, the court administrator, to give the case to Ciavarella, who heard the case without a jury despite not being assigned to handle non-jury cases. The paper appealed the verdict but the appellate court upheld it. However, subsequent testimony described the cozy relationship between the two judges and D'Elia and how the case was prejudged. In a retrial, the State Supreme Court found for the paper and dismissed the judgement and monetary award (Interbranch Commission on Juvenile Justice, 2010, pp. 14–15; Janoski, 2009, 2011c).

But what about oversight and the usual way that governments are supposed to protect themselves against fraud and corruption? According to the Interbranch Commission, the power accumulated by the two judges and the protective network they built defeated law and procedure. Conahan and Ciavarella used fear and intimidation to hide their misconduct from the public and to suppress any opposition. Other institutions did not react until the non-profit Juvenile Law Center started reporting on the case. The exclusionary way that judges were able to act points to the importance of interest and watchfulness by civil society institutions, the media, and concerned citizens. The scandal resulted from breakdowns in all three branches of government both at the county and state level. On the legislative side, the Luzerne County Commission allowed what appeared to be an unnecessary replacement of publicly operated juvenile detention facilities with very expensive private centers. In the executive, the police, prosecutors, and corrections officials all signed off on the private center and did not pay significant attention as the two judges began filling them up with kids who otherwise would have gotten a couple of hours of after-school detention (Interbranch Commission on Juvenile Justice, 2010, p. 60). And, most egregiously, the judiciary, which should be the least political, best-trusted branch of government, generated the scandal through conflicting interests in the construction and operation of the private centers and by hiring relatives and friends in key positions in the court. The extortion and vacation rental payments are the first things that attract our attention, but staffing the court with uncritical supporters undermines professionalism and public confidence and virtually eliminates the possibility of whistleblowing.

The public was also uncritical. Even though Ciavarella was well known for giving juveniles harsh sentences, he was re-elected in 2004 with 59 per cent of the vote. In hindsight, the Interbranch Commission warned against using campaign slogans like zero tolerance as a substitute for thoughtful philosophy (Interbranch Commission on Juvenile Justice, 2010, pp. 60, 62).

Outcomes and Lessons Learned

After criminal charges were brought against the two judges, the State Supreme Court removed both judges from active judicial service in January 2009. Conahan pled guilty to conspiracy and was sentenced in September 2011 to 17-and-a-half years in prison and ordered to pay nearly USD900,000 in fines and restitution. Ciavarella opted to go to trial and was convicted in August 2011 on 12 of 39 counts, including racketeering[8] and conspiracy. He was sentenced to 28 years in prison and ordered to pay USD965,000 in restitution (Kalinowski, 2014; Sisak & Sweet, 2011a, 2011b; *The Citizens' Voice*, 2011).

The facilities' former co-owner Powell pled guilty to federal criminal charges and was sentenced in November 2011 to serve 18 months in prison and pay USD60,200 in fines (Sisak & Sweet, 2011a; *The Citizens' Voice*, 2011).[9] The developer Robert Mericle was sentenced to a one-year prison term and fined USD250,000 in April 2014.[10] He had in 2009 been charged with failing to tell federal investigators and a grand jury about the fraudulent scheme and later entered a plea agreement, which included his promise to contribute USD2.15 million to child welfare programs (Allabaugh & Kalinowski, 2014; U.S. Department of Justice, 2014).[11]

The companies of the two businessmen paid out millions in compensation to juvenile victims. In one of these law suits Powell agreed to pay USD4.75 million and Mericle agreed to pay USD17.75 million in a civil rights action (Halpin, 2016; Janoski, 2011b, 2012; LaFreniere, 2015; Schuppe, 2015; U.S. District Court for the Middle District of Pennsylvania, 2012).

In the Luzerne County court new policies were enacted after the scandal. The county negotiated its way out of its 20-year contract with PA Child Care. Detentions were significantly reduced, including those imposed pre-hearing, and home confinements replaced them (Janoski & Sisak, 2010).[12]

But could the scandal have been prevented or the harm limited? The first complaint about the behavior of the judges was made by the Juvenile Law Center but dismissed by the State Supreme Court after the District Attorney of Luzerne County argued that its facts were not established, and the Administrative Office of Pennsylvania Courts was satisfied that corrective measures had been taken, i.e. Ciavarella was not acting as a juvenile court judge after May 2008. It was when the Center filed a second complaint, in February 2009, that the State Supreme Court agreed to a review of the Luzerne juvenile court and the appointment of a special master (a remedial administrator assigned by a court) (Interbranch Commission on Juvenile Justice, 2010, pp. 8–9).

The State Supreme Court took full jurisdiction over Luzerne juvenile court proceedings and appointed as special master Arthur E. Grim, the former presiding judge of Berks County, who was also chair of the Pennsylvania Juvenile Court Judges Commission. Grim reviewed all cases in which Ciavarella had placed juveniles in the two private facilities and/or denied them the right to counsel (Interbranch Commission on Juvenile Justice, 2010, p. 10).

In October 2009, the State Supreme Court adopted Grim's recommendations. He had identified 1,866 cases where juveniles appeared without a lawyer before Ciavarella between 2003 and 2008 (54 per cent of juveniles were unrepresented) without having waived their right to counsel. All juvenile court decisions by Ciavarella were vacated and related records were deleted (Interbranch Commission on Juvenile Justice, 2010, pp. 10–12).

The Interbranch Commission (2010, pp. 60–61) report found no evidence of a similar breakdown of juvenile justice anywhere else in Pennsylvania and therefore did not recommend systemic reform. It did stress the role of the Supreme Court of Pennsylvania in ensuring the quality of the justice system, and being responsible for "adjudication, education, oversight and, where justified, sanction" of misconduct. Juvenile cases require special understanding from judges, prosecutors, and defense attorneys, based on education, experience, and professional commitment. Relatively few juvenile cases involve serious criminality. More often, children who are before juvenile judges have psychological problems caused by abuse or neglect. Finally, the Commission (p. 54) recommended discontinuing the use of leg shackles and handcuffs attached to leather belts for juveniles in court.

Case Two: The Swedish National Audit Office

In the summer of 2016, the Swedish National Audit Office (NAO), the highest-level (supreme) accounting and oversight agency in Sweden, was rocked by allegations that the Auditors General (AGs), the chief officials of the NAO, had favored former colleagues for certain jobs, used personal contacts in investigations, and had intervened in investigations, in violation of NAO standards (Delin, 2016). This was reported in several articles in one of Sweden's most important newspapers, *Dagens Nyheter*. These reports led in short order to the resignations of all three AGs (Riksdagen, 2016a).

This case differs from the juvenile court scandal in Pennsylvania in that neither criminal charges were laid nor allegations made of personal financial gain and bribery. In the NAO case formal rules were ignored and favoritism became acceptable, in part to reach performance goals. We will consider the relation to individual and organizational corruption in this case in a moment. What should be noted at the outset, though, is the systemic cost of an ethically compromised oversight agency as important as the NAO. It is the NAO that is supposed to keep the system honest. If it can't be trusted, where does that leave us?

Let us first look at the media revelations and the actions of the AGs in the institutional context. The NAO is an independent authority under the Swedish Riksdag (Parliament). The Riksdag's laws guide the extent and focus of auditing activities. The Riksdag also funds the NAO and assesses its performance. Thus, oversight of the NAO comes down to the Riksdag. Three AGs, appointed for non-renewable seven-year terms, head the NAO. Their independence has strong constitutional protection (Instrument of Government, Chapter 13, Article 8), without which a supreme audit agency is useless. The AGs decide how to divide work among themselves and each is responsible for how to conduct the audits he or she is responsible for and what conclusions to draw from the results. One of the three has responsibility for the administrative management of the organization (Riksrevisionen, 2017).[13]

When the three AGs that headed the NAO at the time of the scandal took office in 2014 and 2015 (Riksdagen, 2016b; Riksrevisionen, 2016c, 2016d) they considered it to be inefficient, characterized by low competence, low productivity, and high overhead costs (Ackum, 2016; Carlsson & Delin, 2016f). They initiated reforms to improve the conduct of performance audits of various government functions with an emphasis on efficiency and effectiveness. The strong emphasis on efficiency had consequences for organizational-level factors and how bureaucratic routines and formal rules were interpreted and implemented.

The Swedish rules on public access to official records in the Freedom of the Press Act[14] provide constitutional protection for public officers who give information— "whistleblow"—to the media. Whistleblowers played a critical role in how the scandal was revealed. *Dagens Nyheter* received tips from inside the NAO in the spring of 2016 about favoritism in hiring and later more specific information targeting the AGs. During the investigation the newspaper asked the NAO to turn over documents, audit reports, official notes (Delin, 2016), e-mails, and telephone and mail logs; material treated as official public records which agencies under the Freedom of the Press Act are obliged to provide on request.

What Happened and Why

In late June 2016 *Dagens Nyheter* published the first articles. These concerned how AG Ulf Bengtsson had allegedly interfered in an audit of the Skåne County Administrative Board despite it being the responsibility of his colleague, AG Margareta Åberg (Carlsson & Delin, 2016i; Delin, 2016). Bengtsson discovered that the audit report included criticism of a decision by an agency, the Swedish Agency for Government Employers, the consortium that bargains with public employee unions, which he led at the time of the decision.

To assess the seriousness of these actions the paper consulted the Swedish Inspectorate of Auditors.[15] The director of the Inspectorate found it inappropriate to comment on the case given his previous role as director at the NAO and instead referred to a colleague (Delin, 2016). Reporters later discovered that in an e-mail to the chief auditor at the NAO, the Inspectorate director commented on and complained about the investigation by the paper. Reporters interpreted this as a heads-up to the NAO about the upcoming investigation, while the Inspectorate director said it was not about warning the NAO but done out of concern for the effects of the pressure the investigation would put on affected persons (Carlsson & Delin, 2016g).

The criticism centered on an audit report that criticized the county governor/ Lord Lieutenant of Skåne (Scania) for overreaching her responsibilities when making a severance payment or golden handshake of more than SEK2 million (USD200,000) to a deputy county governor as settlement of a dispute. The county governor countered that she acted on the advice of the Swedish Agency for Government Employers, which Bengtsson then directed. Bengtsson read the report once he had become one of the AGs and disagreed with its conclusion that the severance payment was inappropriate. Seeking support for his position, he contacted a former co-worker, the chief legal officer at the Swedish Agency for Government Employers, who then discussed the matter with the NAO chief legal officer and the NAO chief auditor, the supervisor of the auditor who wrote the critical report. Bengtsson also contacted his colleague AG Åberg and argued that the auditor was wrong, but did not tell Åberg that the agency that provided advice in the decision had done so under his leadership (Carlsson & Delin, 2016i). Bengtsson had also been in contact with the county governor to give support to her decision.

According to the auditor responsible for the report, he and his colleagues were told by Åberg that they did not have adequate grounds for their conclusion about the severance payment. However, Åberg said she did not put any pressure on the auditors to change their conclusions (Carlsson & Delin, 2016i).

After AG Åberg's criticism and a review by the NAO Legal Department the chief auditor instructed the responsible auditor to formulate a new report and change the assessment, in line with a review made by the Legal Department. The Legal Department supported Åberg's position after consulting the chief legal officer at the Swedish Agency for Government Employers. This was the same officer that Bengtsson earlier had contacted for support and with whom he had continuous contact about the matter up to its completion in the spring of 2016, shortly before the whole affair became public (Carlsson & Delin, 2016i).

After being instructed by the chief auditor to change the report's conclusions, the responsible auditor found his independence threatened but decided not to resign. The critical audit report remained but the NAO issued an official note that the Legal Department had reviewed the matter and that criticism of the severance payment should not influence the annual assessment of the Skåne County Administrative Board.

Both Åberg and the chief auditor said that they had not known about the previous involvement of AG Bengtsson in the case. Bengtsson argued that there was nothing wrong with his looking into the case once he was an AG. He said that the advice in favor of the severance payment was issued by the chief legal officer at the Swedish Agency for Government Employers without his involvement. Further, he said that he had not contacted or tried to put pressure on the responsible auditor at the NAO (Carlsson & Delin, 2016i). But then another allegation of audit interference by Bengtsson was reported in the media, so he resigned at the end of August 2016 (Riksdagen, 2016b).[16]

The key issue in this case is AG Bengtsson's previous and undisclosed involvement in the case and the effects of his involvement on public confidence in the impartiality and independence of the NAO. This is a case of interest conflicts, mainly at an individual level. But the case also relates to conflicts of interest at the organizational and systemic levels. Further reports were to raise concern about consequences of favoritism and conflict of interest at these levels. It was later revealed that many of the recruits to high positions in the performance audit division at the NAO came directly from previous positions within the Government Offices. These reports centered on how AG Susanne Ackum recruited former colleagues from the Government Offices, where she had been undersecretary at the Ministry of Finance (Bringselius & Lemne, 2016), for these positions (Carlsson & Delin, 2016h, 2016k). Job descriptions were tailored to the resumes of her former colleagues who she had promised jobs. They received higher wages than other NAO employees at their rank and were asked to audit policies and decisions that they had themselves implemented in the Government Offices (Carlsson & Delin, 2016k).

This recruitment policy created a flow of placements based on informality and personal contacts. This caused NAO staff discontent, which led to resignations, criticism from union representatives, and claims by whistleblowers that the independence of the NAO was threatened.

Let us look at some examples of the impact of interest conflicts in the NAO. One instance concerned a recruit who had been assistant head of the Ministry of Enterprise and Innovation responsible for answering NAO questions when the Ministry was being audited. After joining the NAO the recruit became head of a new unit auditing the performance of the same operations that he had previously regulated. In a second instance, another NAO recruit, a former Ministry undersecretary, was simultaneously a board member of an agency that is audited by the NAO. In a third example, the recruit in question was a former colleague of AG Ackum from the Ministry of Finance and got a position at the NAO as head of performance audits and chief economist, receiving a salary higher than most state agency executives (Carlsson & Delin, 2016d, 2016k).

Further revelations detailed a breach of the NAO's standard of secrecy in the preparation and writing of reports. AG Ackum had consulted people external to the NAO to comment and give feedback on working drafts of audit reports to determine whether the reports should be terminated.[17] AG Ackum handed in her resignation in July 2016 (Riksdagen, 2016b), just as *Dagens Nyheter* was about to publish new information about the case.[18]

The Role of Bureaucratic Routines, Administrative Culture, and Inspection

As a consequence of these revelations, in July of 2016 a special group within the NAO was appointed to adopt a new policy for dealing with ethics violations and conflicts of interest (Carlsson & Delin, 2016e). Before resigning, AG Åberg commissioned Hans Gunnar Axberger, a former parliamentary ombudsman and professor of constitutional law to investigate various allegations (Riksrevisionen, 2016a). Axberger's (2016) report in October (Riksrevisionen, 2016b) concluded that Bengtsson should not have tried to intervene in the case concerning criticism of the large severance payment in Skåne County due to his previous involvement. The report also faulted the AGs for not performing risk assessment as required by law in relation to the efficiency reforms. The recruitment processes were criticized for reducing confidence due to the use of personal networks and some cases of remarkable pay rises. Axberger (2016) further criticized the AG that used external persons to review working drafts and the termination of reports in violation of the Act on Audit of State Activities. *Dagens Nyheter* had reported how justifications in termination decisions were meagerly expressed and how AGs, in less than a year, terminated nine investigations, which was considerably higher than in previous years and had cost the NAO USD1 million. One investigation was terminated two weeks after one of the AGs discussed it with an officer at the Government Offices who a couple of weeks later got a job at the NAO (Carlsson & Delin, 2016d) (see also Carlsson & Delin, 2016a, 2016l). Among the overarching findings, Axberger recommended that the NAO no longer recruit directly from government ministries, in order to uphold its audit objectivity. Axberger also recommended more external control of the NAO to check the informal management culture that encouraged formal rules to be sidestepped. He also pointed out that the rules regulating the NAO were deficient and that the Riksdag had not made clear just what performance audits should do.

Oversight

The Riksdag has the most important and most visible role in oversight of the NAO. But given the need to preserve NAO independence, Riksdag members walked a careful line in the immediate aftermath of the revelations. The Riksdag Committee on the Constitution, which nominates AGs, heard testimony from each of them. The Committee did not find adequate evidence for the removal of the AGs, but was concerned that trust in them had been damaged (Carlsson & Delin, 2016f). The Committee initiated an overview of the NAO where issues included the role of the AGs, relations between parliament and the NAO, and conflict of interest rules (Riksdagen, 2016a, 2016b, 2016c). The Committee's later report included several recommendations concerning the regulation and strengthening of the independence of the NAO, and more leverage for the Riksdag in reviewing the behavior of the three AGs (Riksdagen, 2016d).

Governance or Exchange Corruption?

At the organizational level of the NAO, lax recruitment processes and violation or neglect of formal employment rules were tolerated and, for a couple of years, normalized. It should be pointed out that there were no reports of financial gain at the individual level by the three AGs, but the use of personal networks, favoritism, and sidestepping of formal rules can still enhance their authority over the audit report process, which is an ill-gotten, personal benefit. Given the critical role of the NAO in the Swedish system of governance the distortion of the audit process was very serious. A former supreme audit head was among those who called for the AGs' resignations (as did Transparency International Sweden and the Swedish Institute of Authorized Public Accountants), stating that the reported behavior by management would have been "bad enough at any agency" but happening at the NAO it was truly "scandalous" (Carlsson & Delin, 2016b).

Case Three: Stop, Question, Frisk – The New York Police Department

The following case study explains that the aggressive street policing tactics used by the New York Police Department (NYPD) between 2002 and 2013 were the product of institutional bias and can be considered corrupt (Anechiarico, 2016, p. 81).

The NYPD underwent significant changes in the aftermath of 9/11 as it built up counter-terrorism operations. Ethnic and religious profiling became a professional area of expertise in the intelligence and demographics unit in the NYPD, and the Department adopted new performance measures driven by a new crime data system, Compstat. The Compstat management system was a very important factor in the way the organization operated and how it interacted with the public. This system was instrumental for deciding the priorities of the Department. It provided real-time updates of how police resources were used and of criminal activity on the ground. It produced a regular and detailed audit of productivity at street level in terms of how effective resources deployed were in bringing down crime (Anechiarico, 2016, pp. 93, 98). At its peak in 2011, the use of Stop, Question, Frisk tactics (SQF) by the NYPD led to about 600,000 stops. Crime went down during this period, but it is not clear what role SQF played in the reduction, since this trend began before the institution of Compstat and the use of aggressive, zero-tolerance policing tactics.

Eighty-seven per cent of those stopped were of men of color, out of a population that is 54 per cent African-American and Latino. This raised questions about whether racial profiling rather than reasonable suspicion, the constitutional standard for a street stop, caused the racial disproportion. Also, only about 10 per cent of the stops led to any further legal action, which is another indication of stops being made for reasons other than suspicion of crime (Anechiarico, 2016, p. 99).

A particular incident serves to describe, on the individual level, how SQF, driven by the performance pressure of Compstat, played out on the street:

> On April 13, 2011, around 11:00 p.m., [Nicholas] Peart was walking on 144th Street between Lenox and Seventh Avenue—the block on which he resides—on his way to the corner store. Peart was wearing sneakers, jeans and a red hooded sweatshirt. He was sending a text message while walking when two uniformed officers appeared directly in front of him. … One of the officers took Peart's cell phone and instructed Peart to put his hands up against the wall of a church. Officer A patted Peart down outside his clothing over his entire body and put his hands in his pockets. Officer B

also put his hands in Peart's pockets, removed Peart's keys and wallet, and searched the wallet for ID. Officer B did not ask permission to search the wallet and Peart did not consent. During the search Peart asked, 'Why is this happening?' In response to questions about what building he was coming from, he explained that he was coming from his apartment in the Frederick Samuel House, which is a NYCHA[19] [public housing] building. Officer A then grabbed Peart's sweatshirt with his fist near Peart's chest area and handcuffed him. Officer B, who had Peart's keys, asked which key opened Peart's door, and Peart identified the key in order to prove that he lived where he said he did. He did not give Officer B permission to enter the apartment, but Officer B entered the building and remained for about five minutes. While Officer B was in the building, Officer A, who was still holding Peart's sweatshirt, placed Peart, still handcuffed, in the back of an unmarked police vehicle parked in front of the church. Officer A removed Peart's sneakers, patted down his socks and asked Peart if he had weed on him. Peart said he did not. Eventually, Officer B came out of Peart's building. The officers opened the car, let Peart out, removed the handcuffs, and returned his keys, phone and wallet. The officers explained that Peart fit the description of someone who had been ringing a doorbell at the Frederick Samuel House. Peart was then free to go.

(Anechiarico, 2016, pp. 81–82)

Based on this incident together with many others, a federal judge found the use of SQF by the NYPD to be in violation of constitutional rights against unreasonable search and seizure and the guarantee of equal protection under laws (Anechiarico, 2016, p. 82). The long-term tolerance and encouragement of racialized policing by the NYPD is an indication of governance corruption.

What Contributed to These Violations of Rights?

Among the questions raised by this case is how large, public organizations like the NYPD end up promoting corrupt behavior. In line with our definition of governance corruption in Chapter 2, we should return at this point to Warren's discussion of deceitful exclusion and Johnston's emphasis on democratic participation (Anechiarico, 2016, p. 91). To do this we need to consider contextual and organization factors (see Vaughan, 1996, 1999) which show how aggressive street policing tactics resulted from and then reinforced institutionalized bias and corrupt policy. The role of bureaucratic routines, in this case, as they were structured by Compstat's performance standards and by an "us versus them" administrative culture, shaped how the constitutional SQF guideline of "reasonable suspicion" was interpreted and implemented at the organizational level, and then transmitted to patrol officers. This is directly connected to negative effects of SQF on certain groups of citizens, in this case men of color, who were "un-named", i.e.

by the NYPD's refusal to acknowledge the disproportionate impact of its policy. The SQF policy turned young men of color into a "surplus population", which happens when technical solutions—like assuming the criminality of a subgroup—lead to the omission of the human component of a societal problem.

The highest leadership in New York City, the mayor and the police commissioner, never acknowledged the racial implications of their street policing policy despite its disproportionate racial impact; Latinos' and African-Americans' share of stops was almost twice their proportion of the population. Instead city leaders used another indicator in terms of "suspect" population, pointing to statistics of reported suspect descriptions to conclude that Latinos and African-Americans were overrepresented among identified violent crime suspects. The police commissioner argued that since African-Americans constituted about 70–75 per cent of the people identified by victims and witnesses in the commission of violent crime, and, since they added up to 54 per cent of the stopped population, they were in fact being "under-stopped". (However, this benchmark neglects the fact that identification by race occurs in a much smaller percentage of cases.) This fits the surplus population definition: here, an entire racial group was labeled as suspect. Reasonable suspicion was redefined as suspicion of any young man of color encountered by the police. Thus, on the streets, young men of color were excluded from equal treatment and citizenship (Anechiarico, 2016, pp. 93–96).

The adoption of the "population of identified suspects" indicator at the highest leadership level meant reduced discretion for police officers through strict compliance rules, performance quotas, and acceptance of racial disproportion (Anechiarico, 2016, p. 96).

Compstat was driving the increase in stops. Precinct bosses in several recorded conversations with patrol officers told them to make stops based on race. Testimony by police officers in the federal SQF trial explained how performance targets were used for the number of stops and arrests in a given period and how this in practice replaced individual judgement by officers of what is suspicious behavior. Patrol officers' service ethics and discretionary judgement were replaced by centralized performance criteria. The expectations and goals of Compstat were over time replaced by a routine in which precinct commanders laid down quotas for stops, arrests, and summonses (Anechiarico, 2016, pp. 95–98).

Routines, together with the highest management's support of the effects of a racialized policy, served to normalize outcomes and effects that otherwise would seem deviant. Performance targets were put ahead of the public values, that is outcomes that would serve "the long-run survival and well-being" of the public (Bozeman, 2007, p. 12). This case is an example of how a warped definition of efficient performance can cause the failure of public values (cf. Bozeman, 2002, p. 150).

The long-term misuse of SQF in New York City shows how entrenched normalized deviance can be in an organization, how it leads to governance corruption, and how difficult it is to reform. The racialized nature of street patrols, as approved by the highest leadership of the NYPD and the city, was extensive and chronic. Further, it undermined the value of participation and inclusion in democratic decision making about public safety. In most of the cases reviewed in federal court, SQF did not seem to indicate individual corruption among patrol officers, most of whom were responding to performance standards set by the Compstat management system. However, the way that Mayor Bloomberg and Commissioner Kelly supported, justified, and defended racialized street patrols hardened the policy of racial exclusion.

Case Four: Child Sexual Abuse in the Irish Catholic Church

Ciarán O'Kelly (2016) explains the sexual abuse scandal in the Roman Catholic Church in Ireland as an example of corruption on the part of both the Church and the Irish government. The case included the heinous crime of sexual abuse of children by clergy and centers on a non-state organization, the Church, that exercised governmental authority, relatively free of inspection and oversight. The case explores how the Church dealt with knowledge of the abuse, possible intervention by the state, and, finally, public demand for accountability and punishment. It concerns governance corruption in how victims of abuse were denied voice and justice, and how injustice was covered up.[20]

The scandal dates from the mid-1990s, after a Catholic priest, Brendan Smyth, was imprisoned in 1994 in Northern Ireland (O'Kelly, 2016) for the serial abuse of children. Smyth confessed to sexually abusing 50–100 children but added that it could be "double or perhaps even more" (quoted in Collins, 2017) in spite of having received psychiatric treatment for his obsession. Smyth's crimes were known to the Norbertine Order, of which he was a member, and to the Church hierarchy, since he had been reported by a fellow priest. But instead of the Church and Order reporting him to the police he was moved from parish to parish across Ireland, which enabled him to find more victims (Collins, 2017).

In the aftermath of the Smyth scandal, many other reports of sexual abuse in parishes and Church-run institutions followed. The reports followed a pattern whereby the Church silenced victims and colluded with the government to hide the abuse from the public. Due to the need to prevent law enforcement from exposing the extent of the abuse, it is clear that the Irish government knew what was happening early on. Those who did complain to the police about sexual abuse by the clergy were referred back to the Church. The abuse took place in the context of the long history of deference to the Church by the Irish government (O'Kelly, 2016, p. 64).

Factors at the systemic level are important to understanding this case. The Irish Church has historically had a very important role in the social and political life of Ireland, where the overwhelming majority of the population is nominally Catholic. Given this history, the Church has, for generations, exercised autonomous authority over the Irish population. Further, the Church plays a key public role as provider of government-tax-supported education and health-care. It has also played an important role in government-funded, Church-operated carceral institutions, including children's homes, laundries employing unmarried mothers, and psychiatric hospitals. These activities provided the Church with revenue and strengthened its role as a regulator of public morals and conduct (O'Kelly, 2016, pp. 59–61).

What Was the Response of the Irish Catholic Church?

The Church saw abuse as an internal matter that should be handled by its leadership, with priority given to its own institutional interests rather than to justice for its victims. A 2011 report showed a lack of recognition on behalf of senior clergy of the scale of child sexual abuse, and a lack of interest in the matter. The Church had in 1996 adopted a framework document on how to handle clergy sexual abuse, but these procedures were not followed. Intervention by the Vatican, which at the time did not support involving local law enforcement, indirectly gave individual bishops freedom to ignore the 1996 procedures and lent support to those who opposed the 1996 rules (O'Kelly, 2016, pp. 65–66).

What Were the Causes of the Scandal?

O'Kelly's analysis tells us to look at the relationship between the organization, the Church, and the system, the Irish government, if we want to understand why sexual abuse of children continued for so long in Ireland. The case points to how government authority is shared and mediated by many actors, public and private, and that the boundaries of government authority are fluid. How the abuse within the Irish Catholic Church could evolve and why it was not stopped is directly related to how authority over criminal behavior in the Church was shared. Citizens, O'Kelly reminds us, are governed by rules set both by governmental and non-governmental actors.

The diffusion of governing authority in Ireland allowed the Church to exercise unchecked power in ways that would not be tolerated if public officials were engaging in the same behavior. The fluid nature of governing authority in Ireland limited the authority of the law to define what was right and wrong and restricted information that the public needed to decide whether the relationship between the Church and the government was corrupt. As important as autonomy is for religious and other institutions in a free society, it can collide with two important values in a democracy: transparency and accountability. The Irish Church, after the Vatican blunted its attempt at reform in 1997, regarded transparency and accountability as threats.

Because of the horrendous levels of individual corruption by abusive clergy it is vital that we focus on organizational and systemic factors that allowed internal "resolution" of abuse claims against the Church (O'Kelly, 2016, p. 65).

As O'Kelly argues, "Naming corruption is a matter of being authorized to do so", and in this case neither the government nor Church leaders had an interest in naming the abuse. The government deferred to the Church, and Church leaders, prompted by the Vatican, used their power to protect the criminals in their midst, thus becoming criminals themselves (p. 56). The abuse was named as corrupt only when standards for judging the Church's behavior changed and then only because the extent of abuse was widely publicized.

At the organizational level bureaucratic routines and the administrative culture of the Church allowed for a long-term cover-up. It is clear that routines in the Church when meeting internal reports of abuse were focused on protecting the reputation and institutional prestige of the Church by dealing with victims internally. Institutional preservation, loyalty, and discipline defeated the rule of law (O'Kelly, 2016, p. 68). But Church leaders did not see their actions as corrupt or harmful; they were following core institutional values and rules. This applied also to cases when they broke the internal 1996 rules on how to report and deal with abuse. Moving abusive priests to other parishes; not reporting abuse to law enforcement, and instead enforcing a code of silence and non-transparency; and having victims agree not to disclose abuse, sometimes for financial compensation, was regarded as necessary, not deviant. Church values of duty and obligation grew apart from public values of justice and integrity. As a private organization but with public authority the Church made it very difficult to access information for accountability and made dissent within the organization very risky. Simply put, important social values and also the law were either obstructed or ignored. Together these conditions meant that the cover-up, which was considered corrupt from the outside, was regarded as good institutional service, stability, and loyal behavior from the inside. Harm that had been known by the Church hierarchy, but viewed by it as "unfortunate and morally uninteresting" when uncovered, became corrupt (O'Kelly, 2016, pp. 68–73).

Conclusion

All of the cases took place in political systems marked by influence market corruption where we are able to observe both exchange corruption and governance corruption (Table 5.2). The NYPD and the Irish Church cases demonstrate governance corruption, principally, and the Pennsylvania juvenile court scandal demonstrates both exchange and governance corruption as well as normalized deviance at the organizational level. The NAO scandal in Sweden is not, like the three other cases, a clear-cut corruption case but it relates to aspects of both individual exchange corruption and a failure of ethical controls in the organization. Taken together, the cases illustrate that real damage to the public and to government legitimacy results less from outright bribery and more from failures of democratic governance. It is governance corruption that is associated with the unjust silencing and exclusion of vulnerable groups like the victims of sexual abuse, racialized policing, or unjust sentencing in juvenile court.

TABLE 5.2 Summary of Cases

	Governance Actors	Type of Corruption	Main Problem and Contributing Factors
Case 1: Juvenile Justice	State and local government and a private/for-profit company	Extortion, conflicts of interest, profit-seeking sentencing decisions *Indicating:* Exchange and governance corruption	Tone at the top: individual actors exploiting opportunities and weak countermeasures at the organizational level. Systemic-level degraded public values and promoted market values.
Case 2: The Swedish National Audit Office	Government organization	Favoritism and institutionalized conflicts of interest. *Indicating:* In the gray zone for and related to both exchange and governance corruption	Neglect of oversight, ethically permissive administrative culture. Over-emphasis by leadership of efficiency and an informal culture that downplayed formal rules and enabled sidestepping of recruitment rules.
Case 3: The NYPD – Stop, Question, Frisk	Government organization	Normalized racial bias in street patrols, un-naming, and creation of surplus population *Indicating:* Governance corruption	Compstat-driven routines and administrative cultures, goal displacement in performance measurement, aggressive defense of racialized policing from leaders, failure of ethical leadership.
Case 4: The Irish Catholic Church	National government and a powerful, non-governmental organization providing public services	Sexual and physical abuse of children and adults, creation of surplus populations *Indicating:* Governance corruption	Autonomous use of government power, official deference to criminal activity in the Church, administrative culture in Church tolerating criminal behavior, normalized deviance, lack of transparency.

Source: Table created by authors

The cases show that we cannot identify misconduct neatly with one type of corruption or another but that cases often straddle both types. In this respect conflicts of interest are critical to understanding the links between exchange and governance corruption. A hypothetical example serves to summarize the link between the two types of corruption we find in the cases in this chapter:

> Let's imagine that Cindy Jones is an official in charge of letting non-bid contracts for a town government. If she substitutes another interest for the public interest in doing her job, she can be called corrupt. If that other interest is confined to her own profit or benefit, most likely by way of kickbacks from companies to which she grants contracts, we will call it exchange corruption and leave it at that. However, a closer look at the organizational and systemic context of her actions might put Cindy's behavior in another light. Say that the personal benefit from her official duties is known and tolerated or perhaps even encouraged by others in her agency. We must then add to the individual perspective an understanding of contributing factors at the organizational level; the corrupt organization adds to our explanation of her behavior and makes it more likely. Further, if this exchange corruption in a corrupt agency continues unchecked by inspection and oversight, the exclusion of those not receiving contracts and the potential harm to the public from services rendered only by Cindy's "favorites" will add up to governance corruption.

When ethical awareness is low and organizational values do not support an emphasis on integrity, individual behavior will incline toward corruption. Similarly, organizational and individual behavior are influenced by factors at the systemic level. As we saw in the juvenile court case, systemic factors encouraging cooperative arrangements between the court and county officials and private companies seeking support to build detention facilities provided a setting that influenced opportunities and incentives at both the individual and organizational level, which resulted in governance corruption. In this case, powerful actors took advantage of their positions of discretion in light of weak ethics enforcement to thoroughly corrupt the juvenile justice system in a particular county. A web of unchecked conflicts of interest resulted in financial gain for the perpetrators and the systemic abuse of juveniles and their constitutional rights.

At the organizational level, all four cases illustrated how bureaucratic routine and administrative culture determine how corruption develops and persists. In each case, serious, consistent inspection and oversight might well have prevented the harm caused or at least brought it to public attention sooner. Here, again, balance is critical. If inspection regimes are too intrusive and aggressive, they may hamper flexibility and professional discretion to a degree that they displace the mission of an organization—not, in this case, with corrupt incentives, but with a dedication to rules that paralyze operations. On the other hand, if inspection is too lax, as it was in the cases in this chapter, we will allow corrupt officials to continue their misconduct unchecked and unaccountable. The Swedish NAO case illustrated how difficult it is to find the right balance. On the one hand the independence and protection of the agency from political interference is of paramount importance to uphold trust in its audit investigations. On the other hand, the Riksdag has an important role in ensuring that integrity standards are upheld and that the mission of the organization is followed.

These cases also show that non-governmental organizations like the non-profit Juvenile Law Center in Pennsylvania and the newspaper *Dagens Nyheter* in the Swedish NAO case had an important role in exposing misconduct and irregularities, rather than the formal instruments of government inspection and oversight. This is something important to keep in mind in attempting to reform systemic factors. The way that public–private sector relations are shaped can sharply raise corruption vulnerability. Transparency requirements in the public and private sector differ. When public services are operated by private organizations, freedom of information rules and transparency requirements may not apply at all or may be weaker than they are for government agencies.

Notes

1   "In the OECD countries today outsourcing makes up on average about half of government consumption and about 9 per cent of their GDP. The share of outsourcing has continuously increased over the past decades" (Dahlström, Nistotskaya, & Tyrberg, 2016, p. 22).

2   Our focus is to point to actors and circumstances that contributed to or were particularly favorable to the outcomes in the various cases (see Huberts & De Graaf, 2014, p. 161). In doing so, we should also keep in mind that contributing factors and circumstances and their effect may vary depending on what type of corruption we are dealing with, and the level of analysis may also have an impact. Also, this is not the same as establishing causality. Rothstein and Teorell (2015, pp. 81–84) have pointed out that establishing strict causality between a specific factor and corruption first requires establishing an effect from a factor on corruption and secondly that this effect would be absent if the factor were withdrawn.

3   A petition in cases of wrongful restrictions of freedoms or wrongful use of public, judicial, or corporate authority and failure to carry out that authority, in cases where individuals have no alternative ways of taking legal action.

4   Others were also found guilty in connection to the case or to other corruption cases in Luzerne County. The court administrator (below) was sentenced to 10 months' prison and to pay back in restitution the USD70,362 he had embezzled (Janoski, 2011c); a juvenile probation officer was sentenced to two years' probation (and a fine of USD3,100 and 100 hours of community service) for altering court records of a juvenile defendant to protect herself from liability in the civil rights and class action suits (Janoski, 2011a); county commissioner Skrepenak (below) was sentenced to 24 months in prison (and fined USD5,100) in 2010 for accepting a bribe from a developer whom he helped gain tax incentive financing for a project (Interbranch Commission on Juvenile Justice, 2010, p. 27; Sisak, 2010).

5   Its eleven members were appointed by the chief justice (four), the governor (three), and the leaders of the state legislature (four).

6 A finder's fee is a payment, by either the buyer or the seller, to the facilitator of a transaction for discovering the deal and bringing it to interested parties (Investopedia, 2017).

7 For example, in January 2003 Powell directed a transaction of USD610,000 to a company owned by Conahan, and in July 2005 another payment of about USD1 million was made to the judges, also arranged as a broker's fee, after a second center in Butler County, Western PA Childcare, of which Powell was owner, was built by Mericle and secured a county contract to house juveniles. After building an addition to the original center in Luzerne County Mericle paid the judges USD150,000 in February 2006 (Allabaugh & Kalinowski, 2014; Interbranch Commission on Juvenile Justice, 2010, p. 18; *The Citizens' Voice*, 2011).

8 An organized illegal activity, such as extorting money from business people by threat or violence; a dishonest scheme.

9 His sentence was reduced due to his role in helping to get Ciavarella and Conahan convicted; he secretly recorded them admitting to their involvement in the corruption (another judge was also convicted).

10 Sentencing was delayed as Mericle was supposed to give testimony in another corruption case against a former state senator (Allabaugh & Kalinowski, 2014).

11 His sentence was reduced due to the plea agreement and serving as a principal witness in the trial against Judge Ciavarella.

12 Butler County had likewise after its contract with Western PA Child Care ended in 2008 decided not to renew it, after which the facility changed to provide treatment beds instead of detention beds.

13 This concerns decisions about organizational structure and delegation, the proposed application for the yearly grant to the NAO, and the Annual Report of the Swedish NAO.

14 One of four fundamental laws, the others being the Instrument of Government, the Fundamental Law on Freedom of Expression, and the Act of Succession.

15 Before April 1, 2017, it was called the Supervisory Board of Public Accountants (Revisorsnämnden).

16 He referred to the questioning of his independence, and bad and deteriorating health (Riksrevisionen, 2016d).

17 One such example concerned the former colleague that became head of performance audit and chief economist of the NAO who previously had been head of the Socio political unit at the Swedish Confederation of Professional Associations (Saco). He had in that role been propagating for a new tax system with lower taxes for high-income earners. E-mail correspondence showed he had been consulted over coming audits of the tax system, and in his replies about priorities and dismissal of some of the ideas he also referred to reports he had conducted in his current Saco role and previously to work done at the Ministry of Finance, and weeks later he authored Saco's answer in the referral of consideration process of the analysis of the monetary policy of the central bank. Another instance concerned the cohabitant of AG Ackum and former head of the Socio political unit at Saco, who was consulted and provided feedback on the content and wordings of a report (Carlsson & Delin, 2016c, 2016j).

18 She referred to her actions making it impossible to carry on with confidence in her and the NAO (Riksrevisionen, 2016c).

19 The New York City Housing Authority provides housing for low- and moderate-income residents in the city.

20 For an example of how such cover-ups worked we can turn to the report by a grand jury in Pennsylvania concerning more than 1,000 victims of child sexual abuse by more than 300 priests over a period of 70 years. It concerned both governance and exchange corruption. Bishops and other leaders in the Roman Catholic Church in

Pennsylvania had persuaded victims not to report the abuse and law enforcement not to investigate. One example concerned how in 1964 the then district attorney Robert Masters had halted an investigation concerning a case where a priest had abused boys; he informed the diocese that he did so to protect the church from unfavorable publicity. In his testimony before the grand jury he said that he had done so because he wanted the church to support his political career (Goodstein & Otterman, 2018).

References

Ackum, S. (2016, August 5). "Riksrevisionens kompetens måste fortsätta att stärkas". *Dagens Nyheter*, p. 6.

Allabaugh, D., & Kalinowski, B. (2014, April 27). Attorney: Mericle's business will suffer. Mericle/kids-for-cash timeline. *Standard Speaker*. Retrieved from http://standardspeaker.com/news/attorney-mericle-s-business-will-suffer-mericle-kids-for-cash-timeline-1.1675898.

Anechiarico, F. (2016). Racialized policing in New York City: The NYPD and stop, question, frisk. In F. Anechiarico (Ed.), *Legal but corrupt* (pp. 81–104). Lanham, MD: Lexington Books.

Axberger, H.-G. (2016). 2015 års riksrevisorers utvecklingsarbete förändringsarbete m.m. Retrieved from www.riksrevisionen.se/PageFiles/25087/Axbergers%20rapport%20om%20Riksrevisionen_sammanfattning.pdf.

Bozeman, B. (2002). Public-value failure: When efficient markets may not do. *Public Administration Review, 62*(2), 145–161.

Bozeman, B. (2007). *Public values and public interest: Counterbalancing economic individualism.* Washington, D.C.: Georgetown University Press.

Bringselius, L., & Lemne, M. (2016, July 13). "Riksdagen måste axla sitt ansvar för Riksrevisionen". *Dagens Nyheter*, p. 6.

Buffer, M. P. (2011, February 1). Vonderheid to leave chamber by year's end. *The Citizens' Voice*. Retrieved from http://citizensvoice.com/news/vonderheid-to-leave-chamber-by-year-s-end-1.1098195.

Carlsson, M., & Delin, M. (2016a, July 25). Biståndspengar gick till pension åt riksrevisorer. *Dagens Nyheter*, pp. 8–9.

Carlsson, M., & Delin, M. (2016b, July 12). "De bör avgå frivilligt". *Dagens Nyheter*, p. 8.

Carlsson, M., & Delin, M. (2016c, July 11). Expert: "Det här låter som en lekstuga". *Dagens Nyheter*, pp. 8–9.

Carlsson, M., & Delin, M. (2016d, July 12). Granskningar för miljoner i papperskorgen. *Dagens Nyheter*, pp. 8–9.

Carlsson, M., & Delin, M. (2016e, July 7). Krisgrupp hanterar DN:s avslöjande om jäv. *Dagens Nyheter*, p. 17.

Carlsson, M., & Delin, M. (2016f, August 6). Mörk bild av myndigheten målades upp. *Dagens Nyheter*, pp. 8–9.

Carlsson, M., & Delin, M. (2016g, July 2). Riksrevisionen varnades: "DN har även jagat oss". *Dagens Nyheter*, p. 12.

Carlsson, M., & Delin, M. (2016h, July 9). Riksrevisor avgår efter DN:s granskning. *Dagens Nyheter*.

Carlsson, M., & Delin, M. (2016i, June 30). Riksrevisor på dubbla stolar avfärdade kritik. *Dagens Nyheter*, pp. 8–9.

Carlsson, M., & Delin, M. (2016j, July 11). Saco-anställd påverkade riksrevisorn. *Dagens Nyheter*, p. 9.

Carlsson, M., & Delin, M. (2016k, July 10). Så raserades förtroendet för riksrevisorn. *Dagens Nyheter*, pp. 8–9.

Carlsson, M., & Delin, M. (2016l, July 25). "Vi håller på att se över den här frågan". *Dagens Nyheter*, p. 9.

Collins, L. (2017, July 23). Brendan Smyth's evil deeds can never be forgotten. *Irish Independent*. Retrieved from www.independent.ie/irish-news/brendan-smyths-evil-deeds-can-never-be-forgotten-35958053.html.

Cooper, T. L. (2006). *The responsible administrator: An approach to ethics for the administrative role* (5th ed.). San Francisco, CA: Jossey-Bass.

Dahlström, C., Nistotskaya, M., & Tyrberg, M. (2016). Is the quality of the outsourced public services contingent on the quality of bureaucracy? (1653–8919). Retrieved from https://gupea.ub.gu.se/handle/2077/46050?locale=sv.

Dale, M. (2009, August 14). Luzerne builder latest to admit guilt in scandal. Associated Press/ *The Morning Call*. Retrieved from https://web.archive.org/web/20090903004413/http://www.mcall.com/news/nationworld/state/all-a16_kickbacks.6988485aug14%2C0%2C250767.story.

Delin, M. (2016, September 18). Tipset ledde till att Sveriges riksrevisorer tvingades gå. *Dagens Nyheter*, pp. 14–15.

Goodstein, L., & Otterman, S. (2018, August 14). Catholic priests abused 1,000 children in Pennsylvania, report says. *New York Times*. Retrieved from www.nytimes.com/2018/08/14/us/catholic-church-sex-abuse-pennsylvania.html.

Halpin, J. (2016, April 7). Lawsuit against ex-judges dropped in "kids for cash" case. Retrieved from www.mcall.com/news/nationworld/pennsylvania/mc-pa-wilkes-barre-kids-for-cash-lawsuit-dropped-20160407-story.html.

Huberts, L., & De Graaf, G. (2014). Why it goes wrong: Causes of corruption. In L. Huberts (Ed.), *The integrity of governance: What it is, what we know, what is done, and where to go* (pp. 144–166). Basingstoke, UK: Palgrave Macmillan.

Interbranch Commission on Juvenile Justice. (2010). Report. Retrieved from www.pacourts.us/assets/files/setting-2032/file-730.pdf?cb=4beb87.

Investopedia. (2017). Finder's fee. Retrieved from www.investopedia.com/terms/f/finders-fee.asp.

Janoski, D. (2009, July 2). Kulick testifies he met with Conahan, D'Elia. *The Tribune*. Retrieved from http://thetimes-tribune.com/news/kulick-testifies-he-met-with-conahan-d-elia-1.100703.

Janoski, D. (2011a, June 8). Brulo sentenced to two years probation for altering record. *The Citizens' Voice*. Retrieved from http://citizensvoice.com/brulo-sentenced-to-two-years-probation-for-altering-record-1.1159051#axzz1OhMSNqrK.

Janoski, D. (2011b, December 17). Mericle pays $17.75M to settle kids-for-cash claims. *Standard-Speaker*. Retrieved from http://standardspeaker.com/news/mericle-pays-17-75m-to-settle-kids-for-cash-claims-1.1246035.

Janoski, D. (2011c, June 9). Sharkey sentenced to 10 months in prison. *The Citizens' Voice*. Retrieved from http://citizensvoice.com/sharkey-sentenced-to-10-months-in-prison-1.1159533.

Janoski, D. (2012, December 15). Federal judge approves Mericle settlement for "kids for cash". *The Citizens' Voice*. Retrieved from http://citizensvoice.com/news/federal-judge-approves-mericle-settlement-for-kids-for-cash-1.1416602.

Janoski, D., & Sisak, M. R. (2010, July 1). Changes implemented at juvenile center. *The Citizens' Voice*. Retrieved from http://citizensvoice.com/news/changes-imple mented-at-juvenile-center-1.872550.

Johnston, M. (2005). *Syndromes of corruption: Wealth, power, and democracy*. Cambridge: Cambridge University Press.

Juvenile Law Center. (n.d.). Luzerne Kids-for-cash scandal. Retrieved from http://jlc. org/luzerne-county-kids-cash-scandal.

Kalinowski, B. (2014, November 6). Former judge in "Kids-for-Cash" scandal demands $130K from co-conspirator's in-laws. *The Morning Call*. Retrieved from www.mcall. com/news/nationworld/pennsylvania/mc-wire-pa-kids-for-cash-judge-wants-pay ment-from-coconspirators-inlaws-1106-20141106-story.html.

LaFreniere, M. (2015). $4.75M "Kids for cash" class action settlement preliminarily approved. Retrieved from https://topclassactions.com/lawsuit-settlements/lawsuit-news/97036-4-75m-kids-cash-class-action-settlement-preliminarily-reached/.

Learn-Andes, J. (2015, June 20, first published January 30, 2009). Powell may eat words about PA Child Care. *Times-Leader*. Retrieved from www.timesleader.com/ archive/262272/news-hottopics-judges-powell_may_eat_words_about_pa_child_ care_01-29-2009-html.

O'Kelly, C. (2016). Whose corruption? Which law? Law's authority and social power. In F. Anechiarico (Ed.), *Legal but corrupt* (pp. 55–80). Lanham, MD: Lexington Books.

Riksdagen. (2016a). Dnr 673-2016/17. Direktiv för en parlamentarisk utredning om översyn av Riksrevisionen. Retrieved from www.riksdagen.se/sv/SysSiteAssets/03.-pressmeddelanden/direktiv-parlamentarisk-utredning-oversyn-riksrevisionen/.

Riksdagen. (2016b). Konstitutionsutskottets betänkande 2016/17:KU14. Översyn av Riksrevisionen. Retrieved from www.riksdagen.se/sv/dokument-lagar/arende/betan kande/oversyn-av-riksrevisionen_H401KU14/html.

Riksdagen. (2016c). KU föreslår översyn av Riksrevisionen. Retrieved from www.riksda gen.se/sv/aktuellt/2016/nov/10/ku-foreslar-oversyn-av-riksrevisionen/.

Riksdagen. (2016d). Översyn av Riksrevisionen - grundlagsfrågor. Utredning från Riksdagsförvaltningen 2016/17:URF1. Retrieved from www.riksdagen.se/sv/doku ment-lagar/dokument/utredning-fran-riksdagsforvaltningen/oversyn-av-riksre visionen---grundlagsfragor_H4A5URF1.

Riksrevisionen. (2016a). Beslut om extern utredning. Retrieved from www.riksrevisionen. se/sv/OM-RIKSREVISIONEN/Pressrum1/Nyheter1/2016/Beslut-om-extern utredning/.

Riksrevisionen. (2016b). Hans-Gunnar Axberger överlämnar sin utredning till Riksrevisionen. Retrieved from www.riksrevisionen.se/sv/OM-RIKSREVISIONEN/Pressrum1/ Nyheter1/2016/Hans-Gunnar-Axberger-overlamnar-sin-utredning-till-Riksrevisionen/.

Riksrevisionen. (2016c). Riksrevisor Susanne Ackum lämnar sitt uppdrag. Retrieved from www.riksrevisionen.se/sv/OM-RIKSREVISIONEN/Pressrum1/Nyheter1/2016/ Riksrevisor-Susanne-Ackum-lamnar-sitt-upp-drag/.

Riksrevisionen. (2016d). Riksrevisor Ulf Bengtsson lämnar sitt uppdrag. Retrieved from www.riksrevisionen.se/sv/OM-RIKSREVISIONEN/Pressrum1/Nyheter1/2016/ Ulf-bengtsson-lamnar-sitt-uppdrag/.

Riksrevisionen. (2017). The Auditors General. Retrieved from www.riksrevisionen.se/ en/Start/About-us/The-Auditors-General/.

Rothstein, B., & Teorell, J. (2015). Causes of corruption. In P. M. Heywood (Ed.), *Routledge handbook of political corruption* (pp. 79–94). Abingdon, UK: Routledge.

Sandel, M. J. (1998). What money can't buy: The moral limits of markets. Lecture delivered at Brasenose College, Oxford, May 11 and 12, 1998. Retrieved from https://tanner lectures.utah.edu/_documents/a-to-z/s/sandel00.pdf.

Schuppe, J. (2015, August 12). Pennsylvania seeks to close books on "Kids for cash" scandal. NBC News. Retrieved from www.nbcnews.com/news/us-news/pennsylva nia-seeks-to-close-books-kids-cash-scandal-n408666.

Sisak, M. (2010, August 6). Skrepenak sentenced to 24 months in prison, fine. *Times Tribune*. Retrieved from http://thetimes-tribune.com/news/skrepenak-sentenced-to-24-months-in-prison-fine-1.927570.

Sisak, M., & Sweet, P. (2011a, November 4). 18-month sentence for Powell, kids-for-cash financier and star witness. *The Citizens' Voice*. Retrieved from http://citizensvoice.com/18-month-sentence-for-powell-kids-for-cash-financier-and-star-witness-1.1227829.

Sisak, M., & Sweet, P. (2011b, September 23). "Boss" Conahan sentenced to 17½ years. *The Citizens' Voice*. Retrieved from http://citizensvoice.com/boss-conahan-sentenced-to-17-years-1.1207996.

The Citizens' Voice. (2011, 4 November). Powell's kids-for-cash timeline. Retrieved from http://citizensvoice.com/news/powell-s-kids-for-cash-timeline-1.1227563.

U.S. Department of Justice. (2009a). Federal officials announce the filing of federal fraud and tax charges against two Luzerne county common pleas court judges in an on-going public corruption probe. Retrieved from https://web.archive.org/web/20090901151339/http://www.usdoj.gov/usao/pam/press_releases/Ciavarella_Conahan_01_26_09.htm.

U.S. Department of Justice. (2009b). News release: Two former Luzerne county court of common pleas judges indicted on racketeering, fraud, money laundering, tax and related charges. Retrieved from www.wbcitizensvoice.com/pdfs/racketeering_release.pdf.

U.S. Department of Justice. (2014). Robert Mericle sentenced to one year in prison. Retrieved from www.justice.gov/usao-mdpa/pr/robert-mericle-sentenced-one-year-prison.

U.S. District Court for the Middle District of Pennsylvania (2012). Case 3:09-cv-00286-ARC.

Underkuffler, L. (2005). Captured by evil: The idea of corruption in law. Duke Law School Legal Studies Paper No. 83: SSRN. Retrieved from http://ssrn.com/abstract=820249.

Warren, M. E. (2015). The meaning of corruption in democracies. In P. M. Heywood (Ed.), *Routledge handbook of political corruption* (pp. 42–55). Abingdon, UK: Routledge.

Vaughan, D. (1996). *The Challenger launch decision: Risky technology, culture, and deviance at NASA*. Chicago, IL: University of Chicago Press.

Vaughan, D. (1999). The dark side of organizations: Mistake, misconduct, and disaster. *Annual Review of Sociology, 25*, 271–305.

6

IS CORRUPTION INEVITABLE?
CAN IT BE CONTROLLED?

> We will never bring disgrace to this our city by any act of dishonesty or cowardice, nor ever desert our suffering comrades in the ranks. We will fight for our ideals, and sacred things of the city, both alone and with many.
>
> *The Athenian Ephebic Oath*

The first question in the title of this chapter is the more difficult, though there is nothing simple about controlling corruption either. To answer either question we need to be clear about what we mean by corruption. If we are asking a broad question about human nature and the inclination to cheat, steal, and harm the public, the first question becomes a lot easier, and the answer is plainly, yes, it is inevitable. But if we narrow the scope somewhat and refer to a particular agency or political jurisdiction, we might argue that, while we may never eradicate official misconduct, we can expect to reduce its frequency and severity. Coming down to the agency or city level makes sense of control as well. Control of corruption then becomes a matter of degree.

But should we settle for control and reduction? There have always been moral arguments that urge the total eradication of corruption. But zero tolerance is costly, over-inclusive, and largely ineffective, as we find in assessments of the Prohibition Era, the war against drugs, and sexual abstinence campaigns in the United States. Still, saying we will tolerate some or even a very low level of official corruption can be easily misinterpreted as being "soft on corruption", and can be used against us. As we note often in this book, the key is balance.

If the incidence and severity of corruption can be reduced or controlled in a given setting, what is the best, most efficient way to go about it? Since we have settled on a two-tier definition of corruption—the standard notion of private gain from public office, or what we call exchange corruption, and the conscious exclusion of those affected by policy from its formulation, or what we call governance corruption—the control of corruption needs to follow these two related but distinct tiers of the definition. Further, we need to find good examples of different approaches that are prominent enough to draw the attention not only of investigators and prosecutors, but also of journalists, scholars, and the public.

In this chapter we take the example of a single political jurisdiction to explain how corruption and control develop and change and how they are determined by cultural factors inside and outside of government organizations.

The Big Apple, Worms and All

New York City, in the space of a generation, went from a clear example of a kleptocracy to a model of honest, efficient government … and back again. Almost every modern technique of corruption control was either invented in New York City or tried out there, rigorously. Almost every type of corruption, including both tiers of our definition, has been apparent in one era or another of the city's history. And the strengths and weaknesses of each attempt to reduce or eliminate corruption have been well documented and analyzed. In short, the history of corruption and corruption control in New York City is as good an example as we are likely to find of the dynamics of corruption and corruption control.

Is It Something in the Water?

There are such stark, historical differences in the reputation of different nations for honest government that it is tempting to ascribe the level of corruption in any one place to embedded cultural factors, or what used to be called "national character": a mix of history, geography, and demography. Unfortunately, this approach is closely related to the ethnic, racial, and national stereotypes that damage the people tagged with them. But the idea persists that there is just something about the Finns that makes their country, by Transparency International's rankings, the most honest country in the world by reputation. Is it the cold weather, ethnic homogeneity, or perhaps religious traditions? It must be something, though it is probably not in the water. (One well-debunked explanation for the fall of the Roman Empire is that lead leached from pipes into the water supply). We argue that if we are interested in these matters, targeted case studies at the subnational level—New York City in this chapter—are more likely to reveal the effects of political culture over time than a focus on broad, national traits. The cultural and political DNA of government in New York City is worth exploring for clues to the intensity of both corruption and corruption control found there.

The DNA of New York City government goes back to the founding of a settlement in lower Manhattan by the Dutch in the early 17th century. As much as we might think that current problems of corruption can be solved by an understanding of current conditions, one of the key determinants in a study of public integrity in a particular place is how public values have evolved. The Dutch had a unique perspective on public life that shaped New York for better and worse. As the inventors of the international trading corporation—the United East India Company—the Dutch, in the 17th century, created a golden age of prosperity and artistic achievement through commerce and a strong belief that religious, ethnic, and racial tolerance were good for business. This openness and the remarkable deep-water harbor they found at the mouth of the North (Hudson) River created the most international and culturally diverse settlement in the Americas. Free traders, sailors, merchants, and farmers made their way to New Amsterdam from Europe, Africa, and the Middle East. While much of Europe was wracked by religious conflict and the Inquisition, the Dutch state, which had its origins in a war with Spain for political independence and religious freedom, legislated religious tolerance. One indicator of Dutch openness is that Jews from all over Europe emigrated to the Netherlands, where they were integrated into the life of the country to a greater extent than anywhere else in Europe.

The effect of this open, multi-cultural society on economic growth was positive and stamped New Amsterdam (which became New York City with the British takeover in 1664) as a place where tradition and inherited status would not repress entrepreneurship or stifle competition. However, there was a downside to the culture of openness and economic freedom in this bustling port. What we now call "corruption vulnerability" was everywhere. In the rush to make money, regulations and time constraints were the enemy, and many merchants and traders found ways around rules that got in their way. The result was poor building construction, bribery of customs officials, and illegal land deals with native tribes. As the last Governor General of the New Netherlands, Peter Stuyvesant cracked down on corruption but also became less tolerant of religious and cultural differences.

The trade-off between economic and cultural openness on one hand and public integrity on the other may seem obvious. If there are few cultural or legal barriers in a polity, there will be few restraints on bad behavior. On the other hand, if there are a great many restraints on bad behavior, there may not be much tolerance for minority religious or language groups or for the creative nonconformity that drives change. The values that are in competition are *tolerance and openness*, which facilitate entrepreneurship; *social order*, which restrains diverse behavior; and *public integrity*, which underlies democratic governance. Openness may come at the price of integrity and order. Order and integrity may come at the price of tolerance and openness. But if we are also interested in *democratic governance*, we should consider the possibility that an orderly, less open system is liable to *governance corruption*, even as it reduces *exchange corruption*.

Of course, it should be possible for a polity to be find the right balance among these values. This is the Holy Grail of democratic governance: an orderly, tolerant system that is open, honest, and democratically inclusive. But what we see over and over again is that one value comes to dominate and suppress the others. Cities and other political entities have never successfully legislated or planned just what the balance will be among these values—doing so is probably impossible. Nonetheless, if we are attentive, we can observe which value has outweighed the others and try to do something about it.

Openness, Integrity, Immigration, and Tammany Hall

On the centenary of American independence in 1876, the French presented to the United States a colossal and as yet unfinished statue. The Statue of Liberty was intended to celebrate the fruition of Enlightenment values in the creation of the American republic. But within a generation of the statue's dedication in 1886, it became a symbol of welcome for millions of immigrants entering New York harbor by ship. In a poem that recast its meaning, Emma Lazarus calls the statue the Mother of Exiles.

Between 1890 and 1920, the foreign-born population of New York City grew from 639,943 to 2,028,160, a number not exceeded until the year 2000 (Lobo & Salvo, 2004). The enormous influx of immigrants reshaped the city completely and challenged its political system in every way conceivable. In the late 19th century, as immigration was cresting, the power in New York City was still in the hands of the old Dutch/English elite, buttressed by German Jews who had arrived earlier in the century. A growing professional middle class led by this elite watched the influence of working-class immigrant voters threaten and then displace their control of municipal government. The political reform movement that began in the 1870s in New York City targeted the Democratic political organization or "machine" called Tammany Hall, which won the political loyalty of new citizens by connecting them with jobs created by public contracts let by Democrats in City Hall and with other support that we now expect from social service agencies.

To counteract the influence of the Tammany machine in immigrant neighborhoods, Republican elites organized charitable organizations "to morally manage the working classes and to mold the state's functions towards that end" (Johnson, 2006, p. 82). The most prominent of these, the Charity Organization Society (COS), was led and staffed by upper-class women who had two missions: first, to fight what they considered the corrupt alliance between Tammany and the Catholic Church by providing some limited material support to immigrant families, and second, to record and reform the moral behavior of these families. By 1895, COS agents had recorded 500,000 family histories, which were analyzed in terms of the Victorian moral standards of the Society in order to separate the deserving from the undeserving poor. The COS and other moral reformers were clearly more interested in *social order* and *integrity* than they were in *tolerance and openness*. If new citizens in New York City were to be accepted they would have to fit into the narrow mold of 19th century Protestant morality, socially and politically.

It was the Reverend Charles Parkhurst and his anti-Tammany City Vigilance League who gave voice to the anxiety of native New Yorkers about the growing influence of immigrants. Parkhurst made it clear that immigrants were not welcome in traditional governing circles and certainly not welcome in polite society. Parkhurst's famous denunciation of Mayor Hugh J. Grant, an Irish-Catholic Tammany operative, who was elected at age 31 and led the City from 1889–1892, made his animus very clear. Grant and his supporters, Parkhurst said, were "a lying, perjured, rum-soaked, and libidinous lot" of "polluted harpies" (Gunderman, 2016). The colorful rhetoric was in service to the goal of a new "civic manhood" (in an era when only men could vote) that Parkhurst pursued with energy and skill. This "exclusive and racialized construction of masculine citizenship" was widespread among the elite (Johnson, 2006, p. 82). Theodore Roosevelt, as a new member of the New York State Assembly, in 1882 bemoaned the lack of "respectable" young men in state politics (Johnson, 2006, p. 82).

An elite that is intolerant and closed—a change from the days of free-wheeling Dutch commercialism—exemplifies the corruption of democratic governance. Some citizens—native-born, economically privileged white men—were in a separate, hierarchically superior class to other citizens. But politics abhors a vacuum, and the collective influence of large numbers of new voters did not remain untapped.

Tammany Hall, demonized by Parkhurst, the women of the COS, and others in the city elite, was founded in 1789 as a fraternal society in tune with Jeffersonian principles of popular government and individual liberty. Early in the 19th century it was forced to open membership to Irish and German immigrants who used it as a base to oppose the hegemony of the social elite in city politics. Tammany's numbers increased, but the circle of elite power stayed closed. As a counter-weight to the elite's social power, Tammany politicians gained control of municipal government, which they used to enrich themselves and also to empower their immigrant supporters.

The epic corruption of the Tweed Ring at mid-century is a clear example of naked self-interest of office holders: the kind of self-dealing that we call exchange corruption. William M. Tweed, the Tammany Hall leader (Grand Sachem) was eventually convicted, with others in the Ring, of stealing somewhere between USD25 million and several hundred million dollars (in 2018, that would be somewhere between USD450 million and several billion dollars) through kickbacks, extortion, and padded contracts, one of which paid a plasterer USD2.9 million for a $20,000 job (Baker, 2002). Tweed died in Ludlow Street jail, but Tammany lived on and reemerged as the dominant political force in city politics until the 1950s, despite constant attacks and reforms aimed at its destruction. But, as Terry Golway (2012) and others argue, the self-dealing of the Tweed Ring was one side of the coin. The other side was a progressive interest in the welfare of the least-well-off New Yorkers. Golway argues further that it was Tammany Hall that led to many of the reforms of the New Deal.

But Tammany's good side could not save it. As Walter Hawley, reporter for the *New York Evening Sun*, put it in 1901, "Tammany is a fungus growth on imperfect social and political conditions that will decay and die in the light of universal intelligence" (Hawley, 1901). And Tammany did finally "decay and die". The Democratic Party reduced its influence from within, and it was gone by the mid-1960s. However, why it lasted for over 150 years and was so successful are important questions for this discussion.

The Roots and Legacy of Tammany Hall

If we return to the three factors that determine good governance (participation, duty, and inclusion; see Chapter 2) we can begin to see that corruption was inevitable in New York City in the 19th century and in the first half of the 20th. The rule-breaking and bribery that characterized colonial New York under the Dutch was initially an artifact of weak governance and a class of seafaring inhabitants unused to domestic order. But change came, as government became more powerful and particularly after the English took the city from the Dutch in 1664. British colonial authorities in the city and the Province of New York distributed land and shared political power with a small group of aristocratic families and other socially prominent Europeans including the old Dutch elite. Artisans, mechanics, sailors, and farmers were seldom included in decisions about criminal justice, sanitation, or taxation, among many policies affecting their daily lives and fortunes. We should also note the lack of basic education for anyone who could not afford tutors or school tuition, a condition closely related to relative degrees of corruption (see, for example, Asongu & Nwachukwu, 2015). Moreover, research also shows that levels of education at the end of the 19th century is an important predictor of corruption levels today as measured by the Corruption Perceptions Index (Rothstein & Uslaner, 2016).

By the mid-18th century, the governing elite opened up enough to admit successful merchants, but almost no one else. Colonialism, it has been observed, is a breeding ground for corrupt deals. By definition, the relationship between colonial governments and local populations is exploitative. But even more significant is the fact that, during the colonial period, both the Dutch and British engaged in the African slave trade. The first African slaves arrived in New Amsterdam in 1626. To this should be added the hostile relations and even war between the colonials and native peoples. Most residents of the colonial city, outside the tight circle of colonial administrators and large land-holders, lived in a political and social cage. To a large degree, realizing one's ambitions to move up socially and economically required breaking the rules or bribing your way around them.

Initially tolerant, open, disorderly, and corrupt, colonial New York City became less tolerant, closed, orderly, and … still corrupt. What changed was the type of corruption and its long-term effect. The earlier corruption was episodic and opportunistic: if I think I can persuade or pay off a colonial official to allow me to graze sheep on the common or keep an illegal number of pigs in my yard, I will. In this case, exchange corruption benefits both me and the official at the expense of the public good that the law seeks to protect by restricting grazing on the common and limiting the number of farm animals in populated areas. Very differently, corruption in the later colonial period was more deeply embedded in the economic and political class structure that developed under British rule. Solidifying class advantage by exploiting resources, both material and human, was the dynamic of governance for a century before the American Revolution.

Subjugation and Corruption

At this point, we need to understand a part of the story of corruption in the city that is too often left out of the discussion of public integrity in the United States and elsewhere: race. Shortly after the British took over what became New York City, it had an African slave population larger than any other city in North America. In fact, slavery was so popular with the ruling elite that there was little work to attract white laborers from Europe who might consider indentured work in the city. As Leslie Harris (2004, p. 340) puts it, "Racial slavery became the foundation of New Yorkers' definitions of race, class, and freedom far into the nineteenth century." But what does this sad state of affairs have to do with corruption? A great deal. The systemic corruption of democratic governance must be recast during this period of city history as the *prevention* of democratic governance. Both Dutch and British authorities surely used their positions to enrich themselves, but their gains depended not on episodic encounters with residents seeking some illegal benefit, but on a political system that subjugated classes of citizens identified by race and class. The exclusion we use to identify this kind of corruption cannot be seen more clearly than in New Amsterdam/New York, from its founding to the abolition of slavery.

Governance corruption was so thorough that slaves and whites working for suppressed wages joined together in 1741 to overturn the system by attempting to burn the city to the ground. They succeeded in setting a number of fires in the spring of that year. The revolt was suppressed and its leaders punished, but it caused many to question the role of slavery in the city. In the next generation, doubts about slavery in New York City were reinforced by religious objections that were part of the Christian fervor in the 1770 called the Great Awakening. The Revolution secularized these objections, and abolition became part of republican ideology in the Northern colonies. Still it was not until 1827, over 50 years after the Declaration of Independence proclaimed that "all men are created equal", that the New York State legislature abolished slavery. But the corrupt, political relationship between the ruling elite and the city's poor and working class did not disappear with the abolition of slavery. After 1827, many white New Yorkers feared the political influence of free African-Americans and joined the movement to "return" former slaves to Africa; even though the vast majority of them were born in the United States. And when the state government removed the property requirement for voting in 1826, it was kept in place for African-American citizens. The fear and hostility toward African-Americans are very similar in some ways to the reaction of the ruling elite to the waves of immigration beginning in 1880.

The roots of Tammany Hall are in the abortive attempt of poor whites and slaves to oppose governance corruption in the revolt of 1741. The total, political isolation of slaves and poor whites that was possible under autocratic colonial rule was more difficult in a regime of universal male suffrage at the end of the 19th century. Under these conditions, the elite could close its doors to the underclass, but it could not afford to ignore the economic resource of a large, cheap labor pool. So deals were struck between those financing the great infrastructure projects of the period like the Brooklyn Bridge, the subway system, aqueducts, and the electric grid, all of which were built largely by immigrant labor. The wealth of the Tammany bosses was the commission (*vigorish* or *vig* in local slang) for bringing labor and capital together. As middlemen in the economic development of the city, Tammany bosses were able to provide jobs and other benefits to their constituents, as well as feather their own nests. But their role as intermediaries also attached them to many of the interests of the elite. This attachment was most evident during the Civil War in the person of Mayor Fernando Wood, who also served in Congress during the debate over inclusion of abolition in the Constitution by way of the 13th Amendment, which he opposed.

During his second term as mayor from 1860 to 1862, Wood expressed his support for the Confederacy and for maintaining slavery. In doing so he was in line with the economic interest of New York's financial elite in cheap cotton produced with slave labor in the South. However, his inhumanity toward African-Americans contrasted with a remarkable act of compassion during his first term. In 1857, Wood persuaded the city council to allocate the large sum of USD50,000 (USD900,000 in 2018) for the purchase and distribution of flour, cornmeal, and potatoes to alleviate the effects of an economic downturn and mass unemployment (Golway, 2012, p. 114). The two sides of Fernando Wood remind us that whatever the Tammany machine did to counteract governance corruption in New York City, it was, with a few exceptions, part of the systemic exclusion of African-Americans from the political and economic life of the city. When white workers were as marginal as African-American slaves during the colonial period, they found common cause, as they did during the 1741 revolt. But once marginalized whites were organized by Tammany Hall and attained a degree of political power, their common cause with African-Americans disappeared. Worse, when the Civil War draft was enacted in 1863, Wood and the old elite whipped up white opposition that ignited days of rioting, leaving more than a hundred dead, including African-Americans, several of whom were lynched (see more about this below).

The tangle of political interests and the elements of democratic governance that leads to the anti-Tammany reform movement at the turn of the 20th century includes several components. Most obviously, the level of honesty in governance and in individual behavior in New York City had been low for generations. There are upticks when freedom, liberty, and equality are in the hearts and minds of New Yorkers, as they were during the Revolution. Otherwise we notice two factors that suppress honesty in the city's history. The first is the emphasis on order. The crackdown on the free-wheeling openness of Dutch colonial government began a period of diminished liberty and heightened class distinction. While free, propertied white men gained political power in the city, slaves, women, and men of little or no property did not.

Second, the property requirement for male suffrage came off in 1826, but it remained for free African-Americans. Women did not get the vote in New York State until 1917. Race and gender distinctions in voting are the clearest indication of governance corruption in New York City. Denying groups of people the vote based on birth characteristics violates both moral and democratic values. In addition, the way that those in power behave in a system based on mass subjugation is inevitably corrupt.

Connecting Governance Corruption to Individual Corruption

But how does race and gender subjugation relate to individual exchange corruption? If we try to put ourselves in the shoes of, let's say, the New York City police commissioner in the mid-19th century, we might be able to understand how city officials understood the values they were upholding. Let's think about three key parts of the job of police commissioner. The commissioner has to hire and train officers, enforce the law, and answer to the city council and mayor for his (all commissioners are men in this era) agency's performance.

Who Gets Hired?

Tammany Hall had a lot to do with how the police force worked and for whom. The New York Police Department (NYPD) dates from 1845 and it reflected the morals and politics of New York City very clearly. Recall that in the early 19th century, Irish and German immigrants *forced* their way into the Tammany organization and eventually took control of all its functions, including its role in the police department. We can assume, therefore, that our fictional police commissioner was selected by Tammany and would follow the standard procedure for hiring new officers: he would select recruits recommended by each neighborhood's alderman (city council member).

Who were the aldermen likely to nominate? To answer that question we should return to the word "forced" in the previous paragraph. There was remarkable opposition to inclusion of immigrants in the political structure of the city, not only from Rev. Parkhurst and the traditional elites, but from journalists, clergy, and even the young poet Walt Whitman, who wrote at the time:

> [S]hall these dregs of foreign filth—refuse of convents—scullions from Austrian monasteries—be permitted thus to dictate what Tammany *must* do?
> *(Whitman, 1842, p. 2)*

After facing down this kind of bigotry and worse, it is not surprising that once immigrants had a hold on Tammany they would use it to ensure and improve their economic and political status in the city. The new, immigrant Tammany did this by building a machine lubricated with payoffs and kickbacks. But the Irish and German politicians who replaced the old guard at Tammany shared several key attitudes with their predecessors. They agreed with and continued the political exclusion and subjugation of African-Americans and women. Whitman and the new, immigrant Tammany expressed fear of a "tide" of African-American labor (Hutchinson & Drews, 1998). In *How the Irish Became White*, Noel Ignatiev (2012, p. 2) shows "how the Catholic Irish, an oppressed race in Ireland, became part of an oppressing race in America". So, our police commissioner will fill the ranks of the NYPD with Irish and German recruits.

What Laws are Enforced?

There is a school of thought (Ehrenhalt, 1992; Golway, 2012) that praises Tammany and other political machines of the 19th and 20th centuries as exemplars of responsible, effective governance. Machine politicians must satisfy their constituents or they are out, this school argues, and that's good. Even better, they have the power to provide jobs and social services for their constituents, because of their control of public contracts.

This circle of benefits includes immigrants seeking work, public and private contractors seeking workers, and Tammany in the middle providing the jobs, letting the contracts, and diverting some of money into its own pockets. This is described by some as superior to the professionalized, bureaucratic governance that replaced it beginning with the New Deal in the 1930s. Our police commissioner would understand and agree that the law ought to be enforced according to what is good for Tammany voters. That view of law enforcement would be shared by rank and file officers who got their jobs through nominations from Tammany aldermen and by criminal and civil court judges who were so dependent on Tammany for nomination and election that they conventionally contributed large amounts to the Hall upon election. An 1899 article in the *Atlantic* summed up the effect this system had on the quality of justice in the city:

Being under obligation to his party for one of its most honored gifts, he [the judge] manifests his gratitude by becoming one of its most generous supporters. Even in office his zeal does not flag. He participates in party councils and takes the stump in political campaigns. The faithful servant and generous supporter of his party, he is rewarded with a re-nomination at the end of his term.

Meanwhile, in the community where he is prominent as a politician, he also sits as a judge. In the interpretation of the law and in the trial of causes he may have to decide between the very men, as litigants or attorneys, with whom he is associated or to whom he is opposed, in the arena of politics.

(Cook, 1899)

In addition to employment and help in time of need, Tammany constituents in the circle of benefits received favorable treatment by police and courts. However, if you were not in the circle of benefits, you were usually treated summarily and harshly. Of course, neither African-Americans nor women were part of the circle. The Tammany attitude toward African-Americans by the middle of the 19th century was painfully clear:

The stirrings of the Civil War were drawing near. In this crisis, Tammany, ever pro-slavery, dealt in no equivocal phrases. … Grand Sachem Nelson J. Waterbury, though expressing loyalty to the Union, averred that it was the President's duty 'to set his foot firmly upon abolitionism and crush it to pieces, and then the soldiers would fight unembarrassed.'

(Myers, 1917, pp. 195–196)

The low point for African-Americans in 19th century New York was the violent upheaval during the first days of the military draft in 1863. We mentioned this earlier in the chapter, but its lasting effect on the political culture of New York City warrants a more detailed description.

In the summer of 1863, the city was emptied of Union soldiers, who were in Gettysburg fighting the Confederate invasion of Pennsylvania. Two things sparked the violence. First, it was possible for anyone with USD300 (then a very large sum) to pay for a substitute and avoid conscription. Second, the recent emancipation proclamation shifted the focus of the war more directly on slavery. Recent immigrants were encouraged by Tammany, the Democratic Governor of New York State Horatio Seymour, and Tammany-connected Mayor Wood to see African-Americans as a threat to their economic position and social status. Further, African-American men, not yet considered citizens, were exempt from the draft.

Four days of rioting began on July 13. Groups of young men roamed the streets targeting the pro-war press and any African-American man they encountered. The overall death toll was between 100 and 200. There was also a great deal of destruction to property, including the Colored Orphans Asylum. The Draft

Riots, as they have become known, were the most obvious and brutal example of the corruption of social relations in New York City. Afterward, the African-American population of the city dropped by 25 per cent.

Is Reform Also Inevitable?

The Rev. Parkhurst and the other anti-Tammany crusaders had reason to object to the way the machine governed the city. But they did so in a way that replaced the racism in Tammany with ethnic bigotry. Tammany and its Irish and German constituents were slandered as thugs, drunks, and Papists. The last among these came from a deep-seated anti-Catholic prejudice that went back to 16th century Europe and survived into the 19th century intact. So, the "reform" of city politics by moral crusaders and Progressives, as reformers at the turn of the 20th century were known at the local and national level, was stained with ethnic and religious intolerance and exclusion.

It is tempting to look at the history of Tammany as a low point in the city's political history—especially in light of massive individual corruption that cost the city treasury millions and governance corruption that led to murderous violence. But what replaced it did not deal with the fundamental problem of race and gender exclusion. Instead, the reform movement added a new set of exclusions to those that Tammany established. These new exclusions were based on a new measure of social class: technocratic expertise. But, isn't that the kind of exclusion that we must tolerate or even hope for in a democratic society, meaning that those with superior training, education, and skill should be in positions of authority? At the turn of the 20th century, the answer was yes. Since that time, Americans largely have accepted and believed in "merit" as the way to select leaders and staff governments.

But when the Progressives spoke in moral terms about the need for reform, they generally did so by demeaning Tammany in the broadest terms. Nothing of Tammany should survive, they argued—"look how bad it was". Here's how one reformer, John DeWitt Warner, a scholar and later member of Congress, put it in 1902:

> [T]he Tammany methods of this [period] have been those of the garrotter, the sneak-thief and the pickpocket. The city was not only robbed; it was degraded. The police force, organized and maintained at a cost of millions to the taxpayers, to prevent crime, was made the instrument of crime, by an alliance between men high in police authority and those whose avowed business it is to break the law. The virtue of women, the vices of men paid blood money to the leeches, who now, shaken off from their prey, are investing their plunder in property at home and abroad, and resting until, as they hope, division in the forces of fusion, will give opportunity for another engorgement.
>
> (DeWitt Warner, 1902, p. 8)

What the reformers proposed to replace Tammany was a government devoid of party politics, or any other kind of politics for that matter. What has been called the "business affairs" of government—the production and delivery of public services—would be managed according to the then new sciences of administration and management. The elements of scientific management of a reformed city were tests of credentials, tests of knowledge, careful supervision of work, and most particularly zero tolerance of the corrupt bargains and self-dealing that Tammany used to govern. The downside of these innocuous elements was that they were based on a narrow notion of merit. The influential founder of the school of scientific management, Frederick Winslow Taylor, foresaw that "in the future the system will be first", not the people in it. The notion that any work, including governing, could be broken down into units and then structured for maximum efficiency did not only exclude those without entry-level credentials, it denied the reality of the whole person. People in scientifically managed organizations would become technical instruments.

Of course, it has not been possible to transform the work of government into a purely technical enterprise. However, specialization, hierarchy, impersonal rule-orientation, and the efficiency criteria of bureaucracy did come to dominate American governance, in place of the personalism and improvisation of political machines like Tammany. But is any of this corrupt? Life in the 21st century is shaped by bureaucracies from the Social Security Administration to the local department of motor vehicles to credit card and health insurance companies. It's hard for us to see such a pervasive system as corrupt.

One of the dangers of rule-oriented bureaucratic organization is goal displacement: over time the interpretation and application of rules become more important than serving the public fairly and effectively. In short, rule enforcement replaces public service. At this point we should return to the case of New York City, where we find an example of goal displacement in the operation of the Office of the Commissioner of Accounts (OCA). The OCA was an anti-corruption agency created in 1871 by reformers to prevent the kind of behavior for which they criticized Tammany. However, it was a generation later that the OCA began to make its mark on the city's political culture. Raymond B. Fosdick, a former social worker, was Commissioner of Accounts from 1910–1914 and brought with him to the job a belief in the role of government as the people's moral guide. While its formal role according to the City Charter was to discover and investigate corrupt activities, this goal was displaced in 1911 by a movement spearheaded by Fosdick to regulate what the city's 600 movie theaters were showing. Fosdick's "Report on Moving Picture Shows in the City of New York" recommended safety regulations for theaters and also that the Board of Education have the ability, without review or appeal, to prohibit public viewing of any film that the mayor found objectionable. The Folds Ordinance, which was based on Fosdick's report, failed, but Fosdick retained authority over so many other aspects of theater operations that his moral values had to be taken seriously by theater owners. While Fosdick's moral stance was not corrupt in itself, it redefined corruption to include behavior that was contrary to the values of a very few; in New York that meant Fosdick and the mayor.

Fosdick's moral stance as commissioner was typical of Progressive reformers, but it was something more than that. Fosdick's expansion of the definition of corruption and support of censorship was an early example of the kind of displacement that characterized New York City government as it grew in the 20th century. Some of this displacement, like film censorship, is moral arrogance, but, as the next section of this chapter explains, in many other cases goal displacement added up to so much exchange corruption that it had the systemic effect of governance corruption.

Individual Official Corruption in New York City, Then and Now

Boss Tweed may be gone, but greed lives on. The evidence since the bad old days of Tweed and his cronies is that corruption in New York City has been constant, though it varies in type and intensity. We will first look at what has happened since the end of Tammany in two key New York City municipal agencies: the Department of Buildings, which is responsible for the safety of the construction process and the habitability of new structures, and the NYPD, which is historically the most important local law enforcement agency in the United States.

NYC Department of Buildings

The Department of Buildings is the successor to the Tenement House Department, which was formed to regulate and eventually replace the inhuman housing conditions in the crowded, disease-ridden neighborhoods in lower Manhattan. The Progressive vision of housing policy was based on the scientific understanding of air circulation, fire prevention, and public hygiene. The crowning achievement of Progressive reformers was the Tenement House Act, passed by the State Legislature in 1901. The law gave the Tenement House Department significant authority to force renovations or condemn especially unhealthy and unsafe housing. But what actually happened did little to help the tens of thousands living in substandard housing. Those in the poorest neighborhood saw the least effect of the Act, while renewal and replacement was quite rapid in upper-class neighborhoods and in those where business was expanding (Page, 1999, p. 96). This is an unfortunate but clear example of the exclusionary effect of much anti-Tammany Progressive reform. While new laws at the turn of the 20th century look on their face to be humane, public-spirited reforms, whether we look at social services, recreation, education, or building regulation, the way the laws were implemented skewed to the interests of those much like the reformers themselves. Industrial and financial interests in the city, which had supported slavery 50 years earlier, had left behind their anti-abolitionism, but, once Tammany was side-lined, they reemerged as the governing elite. When we look at the Progressives' interest in integrity and good government, we see that Progressivism was not interested in rooting out exclusion and governance corruption, but in shifting power from Tammany and its constituents to themselves and their patrons; thus, we might consider the Progressives, as George Novack (1957, p. 84) calls them, "the left wing of the capitalist regime".

The Tenement House Department did not materially improve the lot of the worst off in the city, which was the Progressives' professed aim in lobbying for the 1901 Act. It might be said that the Progressives were complicit in the governance corruption surrounding the implementation of the Act. But we should remember that the main motive for the attack on Tammany was exchange corruption, and what the reformers considered Tammany's neglect of new efficient administrative methods in zoning and building regulation.

There has certainly been large-scale fraud and corruption in public contracting and building regulation since, but not on the scale of the Tweed Ring. What we do find more recently is chronic, almost continuous exchange corruption in contracting and building regulation. If we begin in the 1940s, after the first wave of Progressive reform had greatly weakened the old Tammany machine, we see a regular parade of Buildings Department employees arrested by the police and punished for accepting or extorting bribes to overlook building code violations, approve unsafe plans and site preparation, and issue final certificates of occupancy when violations remain. Table 6.1 lists the most prominent instances of individual corruption from 1940 to the present. If this long walk of shame is the product of new, more efficient administration, it is evidence that corruption in New York City is inevitable.

It's hard to read this list of bad behavior without thinking of its larger implications. Is it really a question of a few bad apples spoiling the barrel, or is it the barrel that spoils the apples? Each instance of self-dealing is shameful on its own, but collectively they point to a remarkable displacement of the goal of safe, durable building and construction in the city. What has replaced that goal is the economic elite's interest in the rapid physical development and redevelopment of the city and the political elite's interest in accommodating rapid development and redevelopment. It's logical and necessary for the two elites to cooperate: municipal law and public policy are the framework for economic growth, and the prosperity of the private sector stimulates employment and provides revenue for public services. But as this relationship grows—by way of large campaign contributions from developers to the state and local officials who regulate them—and becomes part of the structure of governance, other values and interests are left out.

More than 60 per cent of New York City residents rent their apartments and houses. They are not part of the structure of governance related to real estate development or building and construction regulation. Nonetheless, they live with the results of cut corners, overlooked violations, and unsafe conditions.

TABLE 6.1 Exchange Corruption in the New York City Department of Buildings, 1940–2018

November 1940: Mayor Fiorello LaGuardia suspended 26 elevator inspectors for extorting payoffs from contractors.

March 1942: Mayor LaGuardia suspended 32 plumbing inspectors for extorting payoffs in return for prompt inspection of newly constructed buildings.

June 1947: Department of Housing and Building clerks were indicted by the Brooklyn district attorney for destroying records and issuing certificates of occupancy for at least 12 buildings which had never been inspected.

October 1950 to January 1951: Several building inspectors were convicted of perjury after lying about the source of large amounts of money in their bank accounts. What turned out to be bribes amounted to several times an inspector's annual salary.

November 1957: Manhattan District Attorney Frank Hogan announced an investigation into the sale of condemnation permits by inspectors to realtors. After condemnation, realtors would buy the buildings for development at greatly reduced prices. The State Assembly's Committee on Government Operations also launched an investigation of the Department of Buildings.

March 1958: A Special Mayoral Commission on Inspectional Services reported allegations that realtors maintained special accounts for payoffs to Department of Buildings personnel. The Commission recommended daily, random assignment of inspectors in order to avoid the formation of corrupt relationships among the inspectors, contractors, and realtors.

January 1959: The chief inspector in the Manhattan Department of Buildings was arrested for taking bribes in exchange for ignoring building code violations.

February 1959: Kings County Judge Hyman Barshay ordered a grand jury investigation of the Brooklyn office of the Department of Buildings after the indictment of an inspector for "mutilating and destroying official records". A New York County grand jury was, at the same time, investigating the Department's Manhattan office, and the Department of Investigation (DOI) was conducting a city-wide investigation.

March 1959: A New York County grand jury criticized the Department of Buildings as being run so poorly that "essential services were administered in a completely disorganized, if not chaotic manner". The grand jury found that mismanagement resulted in "improper and corrupt practices".

January 1961: Buildings Commissioner Peter Reidy announced new anti-corruption efforts, including higher pay for inspectors, increased engineering staff, better liaison with the construction industry, and reduced time for application processing. Subsequently, the State Commission of Investigation, chaired by Jacob Grumet, released a report based on the anonymous testimony of architects, charging that corruption existed "at every stage of operations in the plan-examining division of the city buildings department".

February 1962: Mayor Robert Wagner suspended construction of residential developments in Canarsie and Mill Basin following revelations by a Brooklyn grand jury of fraudulent inspections and police shakedowns. A week later, the Board of Estimates created the position of special assistant to the buildings commissioner, responsible for "strengthen[ing] the control of the inspectional activities of the Buildings Department".

May 1966: Buildings Commissioner Charles Moerdler transferred 18 Staten Island construction inspectors suspected of "acts of impropriety and loose practices" as part of an effort to clean up the Department of Buildings' reputation. The city council rejected Moerdler's proposal that inspectors wear pocketless uniforms in order to deter them from accepting bribes.

June 1972: New York Times investigative reporter David Shipler described extensive corruption in the construction industry, including payoffs to organized crime and public officials. He found graft at every level, especially in the Department of Buildings' inspectional services. Builders, architects, and union officials interviewed during the *Times* investigation estimated that USD25 million per year was paid out in bribes, with an average of USD10,000 per year for each corrupt inspector.

1974: Following a two-year investigation, the DOI issued a highly critical report of the Department of Buildings. Using undercover techniques, DOI agents found the inspection system riddled with graft. Subsequently, 95 Department of Buildings employees were indicted, including nine managers, 15 supervisors, 43 inspectors, and 23 plan examiners and clerical employees.

February 1978 to December 1981: DOI Commissioner Stanley Lupkin reported that during this period, the DOI was responsible for 16 felony convictions of public officials and contractors for kickbacks given in exchange for awarding maintenance and repair contracts.

August 1986: Two building inspectors pleaded guilty to extorting more than USD40,000 in bribes and kickbacks from contractors engaged in a USD2 million masonry job at the Co-Op City housing project in the Bronx. One inspector was sentenced to five years in prison and a USD10,000 fine; the other received a three-year sentence and a USD10,000 fine. Eventually, 20 people were indicted, and 16 convicted for corruption, including bribery, kickbacks, and extortion.

June 1989: The Construction Industry Strike Force obtained an indictment charging a Department of Buildings supervising inspector with extortion and bribery arising out of a USD4,000 payoff from a Manhattan contractor to expedite two temporary and four final certificates of occupancy. In March 1990, the defendant pleaded guilty to bribe-receiving in the third degree and was sentenced to five years' probation, a USD3,000 fine, and 280 hours of community service.

1990: A joint investigation by the DOI and the FBI revealed that over a three-year period, 30 Department of Buildings Construction Unit inspectors and supervisors extorted over USD150,000 from building owners, contractors, and architects to expedite inspections.

March 1992: Twenty-three Department of Buildings inspectors were indicted on 124 counts of bribery and extortion for granting certificates of occupancy in exchange for cash.

September 1993: Twenty-five current and former Department of Buildings inspectors were arrested for extortion.

April 1996: New York Mayor Rudolph Giuliani suspended 42 of the Department of Buildings 58 elevator inspectors, citing evidence of a bribery and extortion conspiracy. According to one official, inspectors "extorted money from building contractors by citing buildings with minor infractions and offering to help cut through the city bureaucracy in exchange for cash payments" (Toy, 1996).

(continued)

TABLE 6.1 *(continued)*

June 2002: The U.S. Attorney in Brooklyn charged 15 current Buildings Department plumbing inspectors (out of a total of 24) with extortion of hundreds of thousands of dollars in small increments over a decade in exchange for approving work or overlooking violations. Those charged included the head inspector and supervisors in Manhattan, Brooklyn, Queens, and the Bronx (Rashbaum, 2002).

February 2015: Manhattan District Attorney Cyrus Vance, Jr., announced the arrest of 50 people, including 16 employees of the Department of Buildings involved in a scheme to bypass codes and safety regulations in exchange for vacations, sport utility vehicles, and, for the development director of the Brooklyn office of the Department, USD200,000 in mortgage payments (Mueller, 2015).

January 2018: Massimo Dabusco, a Buildings Department inspector, pleaded guilty to federal extortion charges. While serving as an inspector, Dabusco was secretly a partner in a construction company and used his authority to threaten developers to either hire the company or suffer the consequences of unfavorable inspections (U.S. Department of Justice, 2017).

Note: the incidents up to 1996 are drawn from Anechiarico and Jacobs (1996). Sources after 1996 are cited in the table.

Further, laws like Article 421-a of the property tax code, which relieves developers from paying property taxes on new residential buildings if they set aside 20 to 30 per cent of the units for moderate- to low-income tenants, mean that upward of 70 per cent of new housing in the city is not affordable for working-class families. After 45 years of high-end residential development—some of it the most expensive housing in the United States (for example, USD200 million for an apartment in a new building on 57th Street in Manhattan)—middle-class and poor New Yorkers are being excluded *physically* from the city. When a developer sees a chance to convert a moderately priced rental property into a haven for millionaires or billionaires (with a separate "poor door" for the 20 per cent that enable the tax break), it will be difficult for civil servants to hold back the tide of political influence, legal challenges, and bribery (Baker, 2018).

But it is the workers on the building sites in the city who have paid the highest price for the fast pace and corrupt regulation of the construction process: that is, the high number of serious injuries and deaths due to unsafe and illegal site conditions. A report by the New York City Committee for Occupational Safety and Heath was sharply critical of the way economic and political relationships leave out construction workers:

> When Carlos Moncayo, a 22-year-old Ecuadorian immigrant construction worker, had his life needlessly cut short in an unprotected excavation, the incident was not only foreseeable and preventable, but a criminal act on the part of his employer. Moncayo is one of nearly 500 workers in New York's

construction industry whose lives have been tragically cut short over the past decade. Many of these deaths were entirely preventable. The lives of construction workers who are building New York every day should never be sacrificed for the sake of higher profits.

(NYCOSH, 2017, p. 6)

The New York Police Department

The NYPD, as explained above, was an arm of the Tammany organization for more than a generation. The particular consideration given to Tammany constituents was, in some ways, a model of what we now call community policing. We must also remember, though, that not everyone in the city was treated with the solicitude shown by the police to residents of Tammany neighborhoods. African-Americans were generally excluded and, as in the rest of the country, women were kept to their role in the home.

After many years of control by a political party and involvement in its graft and extortion schemes, we would not expect the NYPD to become a paragon of virtue and neutrality overnight. In fact, the cycle of corruption scandals in the NYPD has been so regular that changes in ideology and party in the city's leadership seemed to make little difference. A good example of the imperviousness of the NYPD to reform is the frustration expressed by reformer Mayor Fiorello LaGuardia upon receiving a report on corruption in the Department from Police Commissioner Lewis Valentine. In his inimitable style, the mayor responded,

> Fortunately, the report is on the letterhead of the Police Department, written in great big black letters. Otherwise I would be at a loss to know whether such a report came from the boy scouts or from some student of a correspondence school on How To Be A Detective. It is the most idiotic, incomplete, stupid investigation that I have seen and I have seen a great many along the same line …
>
> It is this kind of conduct that brings scorn upon the whole department. A known crook is pointed out to the police and he is called in and says he is a good man and that is all there is to it.
>
> Hereafter you will be good enough to read the reports before submitting any such drivel and rot to the mayor. I am too busy to read such stupid writings, but I am not too busy to go over to headquarters and take hold of the department if that is necessary.
>
> *(quoted in Jeffers, 2002, p. 4)*

LaGuardia finally managed to persuade the NYPD to get tough with the mob and its connections inside the Department. Nonetheless, as the following list indicates, the corruption continued (Wikipedia, 2018).

Cases of Exchange and Governance Corruption in the New York Police Department

The following list, which we have supplemented with the indented text, is drawn from research by Ellen Belcher (2018) for the Lloyd Sealy Library of John Jay College of Criminal Justice at the City University of New York.

Lexow Committee 1895

The first body appointed to investigate New York City police corruption was created by the New York State Senate in response to a number of independent reformers' allegations of vice and corruption, headed by State Senator Clarence Lexow. The official name of the committee was the New York State Committee on Police Department of the City of New York.

> The Commission found that police engaged in a variety of corrupt practices, including intimidating and preventing individuals opposed to the Tammany machine from voting, taking monthly payoffs from gamblers and prostitutes, extorting money from legitimate businesses, and assaulting and harassing immigrants.
>
> *(Anechiarico & Jacobs, 1996, p. 157)*

The resulting report was titled *Report and proceedings of the Senate committee appointed to investigate the police department of the city of New York.*

Curran Committee 1914

> The Committee was formed after the murder of Herman Rosenthal, a professional gambler who was scheduled to testify for the prosecution in a case against police officers accused of conspiring with criminals and sharing the profits from their crimes. A police officer against whom Rosenthal would have testified was convicted of instigating the assassination and sentenced to death. The Committee reported that corruption and graft flourished in the Police Department and that an extensive system of extortion and blackmail thrived.
>
> *(Anechiarico & Jacobs, 1996, pp. 157–158)*

Headed by Henry Hastings Curran, this committee produced two reports:

- *A Report on the Police Pension Fund of the City of New York*, which is available in digital form from the Internet Archive (New York Board of Aldermen. Special Committee to Investigate the Police Dept, 1914b)
- *Report and minutes of investigation of clerical and administrative work performed by uniformed members of the Police Department* (New York Board of Aldermen. Special Committee to Investigate the Police Dept, 1914a)

Seabury Investigations [also known as the Hofstadter Committee] 1932

Chaired by State Senator Samuel H. Hofstadter, with an investigation conducted by former judge Samuel Seabury, this commission was formed in response to various reports of scandal and corruption. They exposed corruption in the New York City Magistrates' Court, including a conspiracy by judges, attorneys, police, and bail bondsmen to extort money from defendants facing trial. A report was issued: *The investigation of the Magistrates' courts in the First Judicial Department and the magistrates thereof, and of the attorneys-at-law practicing in said courts: final report of Samuel Seabury, referee* (New York (State). Supreme Court. Appellate Division, 1932/1974).

Helfand Investigation 1949

A response to newspaper reports about police bribery and gambling formed this commission, which was headed by Brooklyn Prosecutor Julius Helfand (New York (N.Y.), 1949).

Knapp Commission 1972–1973

The Knapp Commission (New York (N.Y.), 1972) was headed by federal Judge Whitman Knapp and formed by New York City Mayor John Lindsay.

> The Commission collected information from a variety of sources, including the testimony of two whistleblowers, Officers Frank Serpico and David Durk. According to the Commission, corruption in the narcotics bureau was one of 'the most serious problems facing the Department' (New York (N.Y.), 1972, p. 91). The investigations and hearings revealed rampant corruption, including police officers keeping money or narcotics taken during raids, obtaining drugs for informants, and using the fruits of illegal wiretaps for blackmail. The commission blasted the department for its hostile attitude toward any outside inquiry into its workings and for its refusal to acknowledge that a serious problem existed.
>
> *(Anechiarico & Jacobs, 1996, pp. 161–162)*

Mollen Commission 1994

The Mollen Commission's official name was The Commission to Investigate Allegations of Police Corruption and the Anti-Corruption Procedures of the Police Department. It was formed by New York City Mayor David Dinkins and headed by Deputy Mayor and former judge Milton Mollen.

The Mollen Commission hearings attracted a great deal of media attention as witnesses, some testifying from behind screens or wearing black
hoods, described police officers working in 'crews' who stormed drug locations and stole drugs and guns. One witness alleged that Officer Alfonso
Compres, known as the 'Abusador,' shot a drug courier in the stomach in
order to rob him of drugs.

(Anechiarico & Jacobs, 1996, p. 165)

The Commission presented its interim report in 1993 and final report in 1994
(New York (N.Y.), 1993, 1994).[1]

There have been numerous integrity violations in the NYPD since the Mollen
Commission issued its final report in 1994. Prominent among them is the case of
Detectives Louis Eppolito and Stephen Caracappa.

[W]hile they had been building their careers and passing themselves off
as gung-ho cops, they had been taking orders from the Mob. In dozens
of cases, they allegedly gave the Mafia the edge, allowing wiseguys to
get away with murder—literally. They revealed the names of individuals who were cooperating with the government, and as a result three
informants were killed and one was severely wounded. They shared
information about ongoing investigations and pending indictments
with the Lucchese crime family, one of New York's five major Mafia
clans. But most shocking of all, and unprecedented in the history of
the N.Y.P.D., they had acted as paid killers. The two detectives were
charged with taking part in at least eight Mob hits—including one where
they were the shooters.

(Connolly & Blum, 2005)

In March 2009, Eppolito and Caracappa were found guilty by a federal jury and
sentenced to life in prison.

The impact of police corruption is even more destructive to democracy than the frightful mess in construction and building regulation. Being
excluded from setting the priorities for law enforcement in a polity can have
dire consequences for the political and social stability of a community. The list
of police scandals includes a great deal of exchange corruption, but, as with
the cumulative effect of the Department of Buildings scandals, it adds up to
an organizational culture that is inattentive to corrupt behavior. Over time,
exchange corruption becomes exclusionary. If you don't have the money to
pay or if you find yourself on the wrong side of the law, your rights and very
life could be in jeopardy.

Chapter 5 explained the most recent policing scandal in the city, the racialized
use of relaxed stop-and-frisk standards.

More Effective Oversight

By the last decade of the 20th century, the city's DOI had moved away from the moralizing of "Fearless" Fosdick. By this time, the DOI had been insulated from arbitrary and biased political interference with a City Charter provision that requires the mayor to explain the reasons for the removal of the DOI Commissioner in writing to the city council. The DOI Commissioner is the only officer in the mayor's cabinet to which this unusual requirement applies. The result has been increasingly effective and efficient oversight of the city's administration of law and public policy.

As we see in the long, sad history of corruption in New York City, the way that organizations like the police and Buildings Department are administered and overseen has a great deal to do with the frequency of exchange corruption and with the extent of governance corruption. At critical points in the city's history, like the last quarter of the 19th century for policing and the decades straddling the turn of the 20th century for building, it benefitted elite political and economic interests to allow for lax administration, exchange corruption, and the avoidance of public values that were contrary to those interests. The administrative culture and accountability of organizations is both an indicator of relative corruption vulnerability and a cause of both exchange and governance corruption.

When the investigative function in New York City governance was invigorated and given significant independence, organizations were less likely to develop patterns of tolerance for exchange and governance corruption. This is not to say that corruption is gone, but it may be that it is harder than it used to be to get away with it in New York. But perhaps the most important innovation in how the power of oversight and investigation is used by the DOI in the city is the addition of policy and procedure recommendations (PPRs) to the public report on a scandal. These recommendations must be considered by the relevant agency's leadership and responded to in writing. The PPRs are tracked by a coordinator, who ensures the agency's response and transparency in implementing necessary changes. Since its inception in 2007, the PPR program has overseen more than 3,000 proposed changes.

A final New York City case study details not just the facts of recent corruption scandals, but also the PPRs associated with each.

CityTime Scandal

With around 300,000 employees (Goodman, 2017), New York City has one of the largest payrolls anywhere. In order to save administrative and processing costs, the Office of Payroll Administration (OPA) received authorization from the city council in 2002 to spend USD63 million on a web-enabled, automatic payroll system that would be known as CityTime. The contract was awarded to Scientific Applications International Corporation (SAIC). Ten years later, the system was not yet in place and the cost had exploded to over USD700 million, an overrun of over 1,000 per cent.

Since most corruption uncovered by the DOI in the past generation has been by way of favoritism or kickbacks of several thousand dollars, the CityTime scandal is remarkable for being closer to the rapacity of the Tweed Ring than to anything in recent memory. Unlike the inflated contractor bills in the Tweed era, the driver of the cost overrun in CityTime case was fraudulent billing and funds diversion by quality assurance and information technology contractors hired by the OPA, which, it is worth noting, is an agency operated jointly by the mayor and the comptroller. The chief consultant, Mark Mazer, had been hired by Spherion, the quality assurance subcontractor, for which the OPA Executive Director, Joel Bondy, also worked for a time. Bondy later said that he knew and trusted Mazer, and so gave him wide discretion. When the number of expensive consultants on the CityTime project reached 300, instead of re-examining the contract, Bondy allowed Mazer to spend USD15 million on new offices for the consultants, in which the two of them had adjoining offices (Gonzalez, 2013).

According to the DOI report on the scandal, the quality assurance and information technology consultants

> coopted and corrupted the project for their personal gain and used the project as a vehicle to steal hundreds of millions of dollars over the course of several years. The leader of the conspiracy was Mark Mazer, the senior quality assurance contractor on the project. As part of his duties, Mazer recommended multiple amendments to the contract with Science Applications International Corporation ('SAIC'), the lead software developer hired by the City to design and implement the CityTime system. As a result of the approval of these contract amendments, hundreds of new consultants were hired to perform work on the project which contributed to the dramatic increase in cost.
>
> Mazer used his authority and influence over the management of the project, including his personal and professional relationship with the Executive Director of the City's Office of Payroll Administration (OPA), the contracting agency, to cause many consultants to be hired by Technodyne, a 'single-source' subcontractor to SAIC that provided IT consultants for CityTime … In order to conceal the kickbacks, Mazer used a group of 'shell' companies controlled by his family and friends to engage in hundreds of financial transactions to distribute the proceeds of the fraud.
>
> *(New York City Department of Investigation, 2014)*

After trial on federal fraud and money laundering charges, Mazer and two associates were each sentenced to 20 years in prison. The City eventually recovered USD500 million from SAIC, the largest known state or municipal fraud restitution in U.S. history (Kovar, 2014). But how could the theft of such large amounts go on for a decade with none of the many law enforcement and oversight agencies in New York City stopping it—especially since it is oddly similar to a high-level corruption scandal in the New York City in the 1980s involving a company called CitySource (Newfield and Barrett, 1988)?

The DOI's report identifies six principal weaknesses in the way the CityTime project was administered (New York City Department of Investigation, 2014). Each of them raises important points about both the inevitability of corruption and the problem of controlling it.

Weakness#1: The City failed to properly supervise the CityTime project due to its inadequate executive oversight and lack of expertise in management of a large-scale technology project.

"Inadequate executive oversight" is so common that a researcher can be fairly certain of finding it in any organization of medium or large size in the public sector. The spread of large-scale bureaucracy in American government in the Progressive Era at the beginning of the 20th century successfully eliminated the personalism and pervasive exchange corruption associated with political machines like Tammany. In doing so, reformers created structures with built-in vulnerabilities. What organization theorists call span of control is perhaps the most obvious problem. With scores of employees to keep track of, agency administrators are generally unaware of a great deal that goes on—and that's just legal activity. Illegal self-dealing and interest peddling will be consciously hidden and very hard to detect. When the span of control is wide, supervision is done by written reports which flow upward. According to the McKinsey managerial consulting firm, in an administrative setting the "right" number of reports a supervisor should receive regularly is eight to 10 (Acharya, Lieber, Seem, & Welchman, 2017). However, the 300 consultants working on the CityTime project were supervised by other consultants and so largely beyond the control of not only their nominal bosses in the official hierarchy but also that of the chief consultants as well.

The problem with technical expertise noted by DOI is an odd one. While the OPA had around 150 employees at the time of the project and saw a need for several hundred IT consultants, another City agency, the Department of Information Technology and Telecommunications, at the time had over 1,000 employees. However, no one at the upper levels of government saw fit to include that department in the project.

Weakness #2: The City failed to assign an integrity monitor supervised by an independent agency such as DOI.

On big projects that the City finds are vulnerable to integrity violations or when dealing with contractors with either little or questionable experience, the DOI has the option of requiring that the contractor pay for a monitor that the DOI selects. These monitors or Independent Private Sector Inspectors General (IPSIGs) are often law, accounting, or investigative firms with knowledge of the procurement process. IPSIGs were used to good effect in monitoring the mammoth clean-up contracts let in the wake of the destruction of the World Trade Center on 9/11.

An IPSIG would have questioned the cozy relationship between Mazer and Bondy and would likely have deterred the theft of tens of millions of dollars, which the City later had to spend a great deal of time and money to recover. This is apparent from a basic explanation of the operational role of IPSIGs:

> Overall, Integrity Monitors work to create a culture of legal compliance and accountability, through training, adoption of practical integrity controls and compliance audits. Operationally, integrity monitors may provide risk assessments of existing operations to identify gaps; complete audits of internal processes and procedures; complete forensic accounting or engineering reviews; provide counsel and assessment of contracts and procurement; in an investigative capacity, complete employee and witness interviews and perform site visits to ensure compliance; and complete evaluations and audits of existing internal processes for susceptibility to fraud, corruption, and cost-abuse, among other areas of focus.
>
> *(New York City Department of Investigation, 2016)*

Weakness #3: The City did not properly evaluate the expanded scope of CityTime or contract amendments that increased the costs of the project.

As more consultants were hired and the project became more complex, Mazer took on a more official role, often representing the OPA at meetings with contractors and other government agencies. Of course, Mazer did not have an official position with the City. But his assumed authority allowed him to modify the contract, adding Amendment 6, which changed the terms of payment from a fixed rate to one that calculated time and effort. And as we noted in Chapter 5, there is a general tendency to put higher trust in information coming from people at the top of the hierarchy (Cooper, 2006). Amendment 6 was one of prime factors in the enormous increase in the cost of the project.

The CityTime project was not the first time that contractors were allowed to supervise themselves. The Government Accountability Office criticized very similar situations among American defense contractors who were tasked with awarding contracts during the Iraq War. These blatant conflicts of interest are normalized over the life of a project as the role of consultants like Mazer morphs into an administrative one that is regarded as legitimate by those responsible for overseeing it. As the DOI put it in reviewing Amendment 6, "No real oversight or analysis of this change occurred before approval" (New York City Department of Investigation, 2014, p. 20).

Once again, we should point out that the City has a large and well-resourced Department of Information Technology and Communications (DoITT), which in its own words was designed to do exactly what the OPA was so poorly positioned to do:

DoITT provides state-of-the-art IT practices to modernize and optimize the City's IT infrastructure by providing a unified set of shared services to a broad range of City entities, ultimately improving services for New Yorkers.

(New York City DoITT, 2018)

A nagging question is why the CityTime project was not given to DoITT in the first place. This translates into a more serious question: why did the two most powerful officials in the City government—the mayor and the comptroller, who are in charge of the OPA—fail to take an obvious step to reduce the corruption vulnerability of what was a large contract even at the start? There is no documentary evidence that will provide an answer, but we can put the pieces together to understand why the massive corruption on the CityTime contract was not inevitable, but predictable.

First, the City has a long history of undervaluing or ignoring the talent it has in its own agencies and departments. In this, it is not alone. Federal, state, and local agencies have similar attitudes about the superiority of private sector services. In our earlier description of New Public Management (NPM), you will recall the emphasis it places on the inefficiency and rule-bound stodginess of public service agencies. Much better, NPM advocates argue, to give service production and delivery over to the private sector, which is relatively unfettered by regulation and able to improvise and actually serve the public with elan and a consumer orientation. This leaves well-trained, ambitious professionals in public agencies out of the picture. As a public works agency engineer in the City government put it, "I've dedicated my life to public service and every time we have a new project in this office, it goes out to consulting engineers to design and we could have done it right here. It makes us feel useless" (New York City Department of Environmental Protection, 2006).

Second and more obviously, the place of the OPA in the City government guarantees confusion and makes effective oversight much less likely. As we have mentioned, the OPA is controlled by the mayor and comptroller … and that is the problem. Both the mayor and comptroller have large operations with high-visibility responsibilities. Worrying very much about a minor, administrative function like getting the paychecks out is unlikely. The OPA was largely ignored, so the evolution of the contract into a money-machine for Mazer and his fellow fraudsters was unseen by the high-level officials who were supposed to ensure that the OPA did its job efficiently and effectively. And, as it is put so clearly in the New Testament, "No man can serve two masters" (Matthew 6:24).

The remaining three weaknesses identified by the DOI are closely related, so we can consider them together.

Weakness #4: The City failed to *hold contractors accountable* for their inability to provide deliverables on schedule and within budget.

Weakness #5: The City failed to conduct *sufficient background investigations* on contractors and subcontractors that performed a significant portion of work on the project.

Weakness #6: The City failed to plan for *future City control* over management and maintenance of the completed project.

The emphasized words in each item point to the absence of even basic administrative control within the OPA. The executive director was neither an effective executive nor an evident director. In fact, he gave control of the contract to Mazer and the consultants. Disaster ensued.

Summary and Conclusion: What Can We Learn from the History of Corruption and Corruption Control in New York City?

1. History and political culture count and should be considered seriously when assessing corruption vulnerabilities in any jurisdiction.

The legacy and influence of racism and anti-immigrant bias had a strong influence on how government and public administration operated in New York City up to the New Deal. These attitudes were not universal, but were held by those in the old governing elite. Once immigrants took control of the City government, racism was reinforced and anti-immigrant attitudes were focused on groups that had arrived more recently, like Puerto Ricans. The ability to bend the system to help friends and exclude "others"—which we call governance corruption—can be traced to the culture of bias planted in the colonial period and coming to maturity in the late 19th century.

To test the validity of this thesis, we might compare New York City to other metropolitan areas in the United States and elsewhere that have very different political cultures. The history of race, ethnic, and gender relations in other places like Seattle or Amsterdam produced relatively more inclusive political systems, resulting in less exchange and governance corruption.

But political cultures change. New York's changed somewhat during the New Deal and in the wake of World War II. The end of Tammany Hall's influence and a focus by city politicians on fairness in the 1950s cut down on exchange corruption in particular. However, as the riots in the city's largest African-American neighborhood, Harlem, in 1964 and 1968—as well as the recent controversy over racialized policing—indicate, the old political culture is not gone.

The difficult and painful work of coming to terms with the past is how the political culture changes. This kind of change can be considered in an academic environment, where its dimensions can be better understood, but the most effective way of dealing with the consequences of exclusionary politics is by opening the electorate and policy-making process to as many people as possible. It is not for those currently in power to determine how to change the culture. Only with the participation of those who have been excluded from, for instance, setting rules for how the city is policed will the culture change to reduce both kinds of corruption. More simply, corruption will decline when we are unable to identify "us" and "others" in the population.

2. Reform movements aimed at reducing corruption should avoid moralizing and focus on the difficult problem of ensuring not only efficient but also democratic service provision.

The reform movements in the city's history are full of blistering attacks on the moral values and behavior of those presumed to be the cause of municipal corruption. The comments of Rev. Parkhurst and Walt Whitman are good indicators of the hostile motives behind the first wave of reform in the 1880s. By the turn of the century, the tone was more measured, but animosity toward the favoritism and ethnic networks that governed the city remained. What replaced them was technical expertise and bureaucratic structures. Academic credentials and relevant experience took the place of who you know and where you live.

But the effectiveness of public service production and delivery—from zoning to education to public safety—was measured without regard for how people used and were affected by these services. The important measures were outputs—how many students in how many schools, how many arrests, how much new development. Without measuring or considering public evaluation and experience, goals are easily displaced and deviance normalized: schools become unresponsive or even brutal to students, zoning creates racial and ethnic ghettoes, and the police become repressive. These were not the intended outcomes of the Progressive Era reforms, but each can be connected to the ethics of disinterested, apolitical administration that were the hallmarks of Progressive reform.

3. Oversight must be independent and cooperative.

The broad participation and open inclusion that are needed to prevent corruption will not arrive tomorrow. That being the case, it is best to be practical and plan to detect and control as much bad behavior as possible. This requires a serious investment in oversight. But too much oversight is also a problem and can lead to a stifling atmosphere of rules, reports, and surveillance that reduces efficiency and may eliminate certain services altogether.

A key and usually neglected part of oversight is participation by government employees in designing and enforcing integrity rules in their own agency. This requires a good deal of careful facilitation by agencies like the DOI, but where it has been tried it works remarkably well. What cities like Santa Rosa, California, have found is that the discussion around integrity enforcement leads to input from the rank and file in an agency on a variety of other, operational topics, which improves the work environment and the quality of service to the public.

Cooperative integrity enforcement and oversight requires a clear departure from the strict hierarchy and specialization characterizing most bureaucratic agencies. This will be no less difficult than developing a new perspective on political culture and the reform process. But there are models for it in government and in some corporate and not-for-profit organizations. Where it works, it invigorates public servants and makes it more likely that exchange and governance corruption will be taken seriously.

4. Corruption can be predicted and controlled, though not eliminated.

Political systems that are unconcerned with public participation and oversight or with accounting for the political culture in which they operate are more likely to spawn corruption of both types. The organizational level of administration, if left to drift toward bureaucratic pathologies, will provide perverse incentives—incentives to satisfy basic career and personal goals that are frustrated by a hierarchy and neglect by engaging in fraud.

If we remember that those who are the best public servants and those who are inclined toward corruption are not members of different species, we can understand that the way their work environment is structured and how they are treated will be more important in controlling corruption than another dozen investigators and more severe penalties. The broad inclusion we have been talking about must also include public employees themselves. This is what Denhardt and Denhardt (2015, p. 1) mean when they say, "Government shouldn't be run like a business, it should be run like a democracy."

Note

1 The Special Collections Room of the Lloyd Sealy Library of John Jay College of Criminal Justice (2013) holds records of the Mollen Commission, available for consultation by appointment.

References

Acharya, A., Lieber, R., Seem, L., & Welchman, T. (2017). How to identify the right "spans of control" for your organization. Retrieved from www.mckinsey.com/business-functions/organization/our-insights/how-to-identify-the-right-spans-of-control-for-your-organization.

Anechiarico, F., & Jacobs, J. B. (1996). *The pursuit of absolute integrity: How corruption control makes government ineffective.* Chicago, IL: University of Chicago Press.

Asongu, S., & Nwachukwu, J. (2015). The incremental effect of education on corruption: Evidence of synergy from lifelong learning. AGDI Working paper WP/15/036. African Governance and Development Institute. Retrieved from https://mpra.ub.uni-muenchen.de/69439/.

Baker, K. (2002, March 23). The courthouse that graft built. *New York Times.* Retrieved from www.nytimes.com/2002/03/23/opinion/the-courthouse-that-graft-built.html.

Baker, K. (2018, July). The death of a once great city: The fall of New York and the urban crisis of affluence. *Harper's Magazine*, pp. 24–49. Retrieved from https://harpers.org/archive/2018/07/the-death-of-new-york-city-gentrification/.

Belcher, E. (2018). NYPD – historical and current research: NYPD oversight – excessive force, corruption and other investigations. Retrieved from http://guides.lib.jjay.cuny.edu/nypd/oversight.

Connolly, J., & Blum, H. (2005, September). Hit men in blue? *Vanity Fair*. Retrieved from www.vanityfair.com/culture/2005/09/dirty-cops-murder.

Cook, F. G. (1899, June). Politics and the judiciary. *The Atlantic*.

Cooper, T. L. (2006). *The responsible administrator: An approach to ethics for the administrative role* (5th ed.). San Francisco, CA: Jossey-Bass.

Denhardt, J. V., & Denhardt, R. B. (2015). *The new public service: Serving, not steering* (4th ed.). Abingdon, UK: Routledge.

DeWitt Warner, J. (1902). Introduction. In M. T. Bogard (Ed.), *The redemption of New York*. New York: P.F. McBreen & Sons.

Ehrenhalt, A. (1992). *The United States of Ambition: Politics, power and the pursuit of office*. New York: Three Rivers Press.

Golway, T. (2012). *Machine made: Irish America, Tammany Hall and the creation of modern New York politics*. Doctoral dissertation. New Brunswick: Rutgers University.

Gonzalez, J. (2013, October 18). Witness testifies that top city official gave CityTime consultants free rein. *New York Daily News*.

Goodman, D. (2017, June 15). With largest staff ever, New York City reimagines how it works. *New York Times*. Retrieved from www.nytimes.com/2017/06/15/nyregion/high-number-city-employees-bill-deblasio.html.

Gunderman, D. (2016, November 20). A look at Rev. Charles Parkhurst, who exposed the "rum-soaked and libidinous" politicians at Tammany Hall. *New York Daily News*. Retrieved from www.nydailynews.com/news/national/charles-parkhurst-helped-tammany-hall-article-1.2879206&num=1&hl=sv&gl=se&strip=1&vwsrc=0.

Harris, L. M. (2004). Slavery, emancipation, and class formation in colonial and early national New York City. *Journal of Urban History*, *30*(3), 339–359.

Hawley, W. L. (1901). Strength and weakness of Tammany Hall. *North American Review*, *173*(539), 481–486.

Hutchinson, G., & Drews, D. (1998). Racial attitudes. In J. R. LeMaster & D. D. Kummings (Eds.), *Walt Whitman: An encyclopedia*. New York: Garland Publishing.

Ignatiev, N. (2012). *How the Irish became white*. New York: Routledge.

Jeffers, H. P. (2002). *The Napoleon of New York: Mayor Fiorello La Guardia*. New York: John Wiley & Sons.

John Jay College of Criminal Justice. (2013). Finding aid. Mollen Commission Proceedings Collection. Retrieved from www.lib.jjay.cuny.edu/info/speccoll/Mollen_Commission_Finding_Aid.pdf.

Johnson, V. (2006). "The moral aspects of complex problems": New York City electoral campaigns against vice and the incorporation of immigrants, 1890–1901. *Journal of American Ethnic History*, *25*(2/3), 74–106.

Kovar, J. F. (2014, February 3). SAIC to pay $500 million in New York CityTime Fraud Scandal. CRN. Retrieved from www.crn.com/news/channel-programs/232602640/saic-to-pay-500-million-in-new-york-citytime-fraud-scandal.htm.

Lobo, A. P., & Salvo, J. J. (2004). *The newest New Yorkers 2000: Immigrant New York in the new millennium*. New York: New York City Department of City Planning, Population Division.

Mueller, B. (2015, February 10). New York City buildings inspectors charged in bribe schemes. *New York Times.* Retrieved from www.nytimes.com/2015/02/11/nyregion/new-york-city-buildings-inspectors-charged-with-bribery.html.

Myers, G. (1917). *The history of Tammany Hall.* New York: Boni & Liveright.

Newfield, J., & Barrett, W. (1988). *City for sale: Ed Koch and the betrayal of New York.* New York: Harper Collins

New York (N.Y.). (1949). Helfand investigation. Retrieved from https://guides.lib.jjay.cuny.edu/nypd/oversight.

New York (N.Y.). (1972). The Knapp Commission report on police corruption. Commission report (with summary and principal recommendations, issued August 3, 1972). New York: G. Braziller. Retrieved from https://guides.lib.jjay.cuny.edu/nypd/oversight.

New York (N.Y.). (1993). Commission to Investigate Allegations of Police Corruption and the Anti-Corruption Procedures of the Police Department: Interim report and principal recommendations. Retrieved from www.lib.jjay.cuny.edu/info/speccoll/Mollen_Commission_Finding_Aid.pdf.

New York (N.Y.). (1994). Commission to Investigate Allegations of Police Corruption and the Anti-Corruption Procedures of the Police Department: Commission report. Retrieved from www.lib.jjay.cuny.edu/info/speccoll/Mollen_Commission_Finding_Aid.pdf.

New York (State). Supreme Court. Appellate Division. (1932/1974). The investigation of the magistrates' courts in the First Judicial Department and the magistrates thereof, and of the attorneys-at-law practicing in said courts: Final report of Samuel Seabury, referee. Supreme Court, Appellate Division – First Judicial Department. New York: Arno Press (John Jay College of Criminal Justice – Stacks – KFX2018.7 .S4 1974).

New York Board of Aldermen. Special Committee to Investigate the Police Dept. (1914a). Report and minutes of investigation of clerical and administrative work performed by uniformed members of the Police Department. Retrieved from City University of New York, Lloyd Sealy Library of John Jay College of Criminal Justice, Special Collections Room – HV 7597.E3.

New York Board of Aldermen. Special Committee to Investigate the Police Dept. (1914b). A report on the police pension fund of the city of New York, submitted to the Aldermanic Committee on Police Investigation by the Bureau of Municipal Research. New York: J. J. Little and Ives Co. Retrieved from https://archive.org/details/reportonpolicepe00burerich.

New York City Department of Environmental Protection. (2006, September). Interview by F. Anechiarico.

New York City Department of Investigation. (2014). CityTime Investigation: Lessons learned & recommendations to improve New York City's management of large information technology contracts. Retrieved from www1.nyc.gov/assets/doi/press-releases/2014/jul/pr13citytime_72514.pdf.

New York City Department of Investigation. (2016). The integrity monitor program: The role of the private sector in city contract oversight. Center for the Advancement of Public Integrity. Retrieved from www.law.columbia.edu/sites/default/files/microsites/public-integrity/images/the_integrity_monitor_program_-_capi_issue_brief_-_september_2016.pdf.

New York City DoITT. (2018). Services for agencies. Retrieved from www1.nyc.gov/site/doitt/agencies/for-agencies.page

Novack, G. (1957). The rise and fall of progressivism. *International Socialist Review, 18*(3), 83–88.

NYCOSH. (2017). Deadly skyline: An annual report on construction fatalities in New York State. New York City Committee for Occupational Safety and Health. Retrieved from http://nycosh.org/wp-content/uploads/2017/01/DeadlySkyline2017_NYS-ConstructionFatalitiesReport_final_NYCOSH_May.pdf.

Page, M. (1999). *The creative destruction of Manhattan, 1900–1940.* Chicago, IL: University of Chicago Press.

Rashbaum, W. K. (2002, June 26). Plumbing inspectors are latest charged in New York graft. *New York Times.* Retrieved from www.nytimes.com/2002/06/26/nyregion/plumbing-inspectors-are-latest-charged-in-new-york-graft.html.

Rothstein, B., & Uslaner, E. M. (2016). The historical roots of corruption: State building, economic inequality, and mass education. *Comparative Politics, 48*(2), 227–248.

Toy, V. S. (1996, April 19). In a corruption inquiry, Giuliani suspends 42 elevator inspectors. *New York Times.* Retrieved from www.nytimes.com/1996/04/19/nyregion/in-a-corruption-inquiry-giuliani-suspends-42-elevator-inspectors.html.

U.S. Department of Justice. (2017). Former New York City buildings inspector pleads guilty to extortion (U.S. Attorney's Office, Eastern District of New York, Docket No. 16-CR-559, DLI). Retrieved from www.justice.gov/usao-edny/pr/former-new-york-city-buildings-inspector-pleads-guilty-extortion.

Whitman, W. (1842, April 7). The mask thrown off. *New York Aurora.* Retrieved from https://whitmanarchive.org/published/periodical/journalism/tei/per.00398.html#n3.

Wikipedia. (2018). New York City Police Department corruption and misconduct. Retrieved from https://en.wikipedia.org/wiki/New_York_City_Police_Department_corruption_and_misconduct.

7
THE FUTURE OF PUBLIC INTEGRITY

Introduction

Like most discussions of complex issues, this book has relied upon ideas and concepts developed by scholars and practitioners, as well as several we have developed ourselves. This final chapter is an opportunity to revisit them in a way that identifies connections among them and their importance to our argument.

An overarching and important outcome of this work is that corruption, as we approach it, can serve as a point of entry for understanding the quality of democracy and challenges to good governance. The lack of inclusivity is a key factor in what we label governance corruption and for understanding dysfunctional politics in general. We have also argued that organizational pathologies explain the way that governance corruption develops and why it coincides with bribery and extortion. We have also demonstrated the connection between the definition and measurement of corruption and the way we fight it. Indeed, a narrow definition will make it hard or impossible for us to see the real enemies in our defense of public integrity.

In this final chapter, we start with our basic premises, followed by a review of key ideas and concepts we have used, and then a critical summary of the case studies in Chapters 5 and 6. In the final section we focus on inclusivity as the key part of ethics management strategies in preventing corruption.

Key Ideas and Concepts[1]

Definition of Corruption

The usual image of corruption we carry around is of a public official accepting or demanding a bribe or otherwise enriching him or herself. That image represents exchange corruption, the use of public office or position for private gain. Exchange corruption is a terrible problem wherever it is found. It is a political pathogen that turns trust into cynicism and legitimate power into oppression. If it spreads and takes root, exchange corruption can damage basic democratic values by limiting participation and obstructing access to benefits. But governance corruption is broader than chronic bribery; it also includes exclusion and obstruction due to bias, discrimination, and political repression.

The idea that democratic values ought to be included in the definition of corruption is inspired by the more comprehensive definition of corruption as decay and dissolution. Decay and dissolution are natural process that we do not seek to prevent unless they affect something of value to us. (We accept trees decaying in the forest, but not rot in the timbers supporting the roof.) But our values don't or at least shouldn't end with the honesty of public officials, as important as it is. We do or should also value the integrity of democratic decision making, broad participation, and inclusivity. Decay or dissolution of these democratic governance values is something we should seek to prevent.

A concept that we used in Chapter 6 to explain the way exchange and governance corruption were identified and either tolerated or controlled is political culture. This broad concept includes the historically embedded, transmissible understandings of power relations in a community and allows us to explain how and why some but not other behavior is considered corrupt and what the appropriate response, if any, might be. Political culture also includes the common social attitudes and biases that underlie power relationships.

Measuring Corruption

Corruption is hard to detect and investigate, so is also hard to measure. We argue that corruption measurement is not just a technical issue but should be seen in relation to what corruption is and how to prevent it. The most well-known measure of corruption in the early 21st century is the Transparency International Corruption Perception Index (TI's CPI), which includes a ranking of all the world's countries in terms of how they are viewed by others. The CPI has successfully raised the profile of corruption on the international scene; it was decisive in putting corruption on the international agenda. However, we should remember that information that is vital for reform is not included in the CPI. Its use of a single score for a whole country makes it impossible to account for differing forms of corruption and how they vary across countries and between levels of government within a country. And if we want to take action against corruption this information is important. A combination of measures is needed for this, and is particularly necessary for understanding governance corruption at the systemic level.

Overall, in this respect we are not convinced of the usefulness of these country-level quantitative measures. Much more useful for reform purposes would be tightly focused tools for evaluating and comparing subunits of government, and particular agencies and programs, over time and across locations. Surveys of citizen experience with public officials can reveal relative amounts of exchange corruption, but governance corruption is a different matter. We find Michael Johnston's syndromes of corruption to be a useful typology for deciding where to look for damage to democratic values, though it will not produce a numerical score. Each syndrome indicates a different political structure and a different distribution of political power.

An important indicator of change is the seriousness and intensity of governance corruption that can be abstracted from Johnston's typology. An influence market may decay or shift into a system of elite cartels, or from elite cartels to a system dominated by clans and oligarchs or official moguls. It is also possible for countries or sub-governments to shift from more governance corruption to less. Johnston's specific indicators are a guide to the status and vector of governance corruption. For example, the early 19th century in New York City, during which the old Dutch and English elite had control, can be considered an example of Johnston's elite cartels syndrome, characterized by "networks of elites engaged in collusion, sharing corrupt takings while staving off rising political and economic competition" (2014, p. 246). The old elites were fighting against rising competition from well-organized Irish and German immigrants, who by the middle of the 19th century had taken over control of municipal government. The history of Tammany Hall's dominance of the city is replete with corruption of both kinds. The way Tammany ruled New York City fits Johnston's oligarchs and clans syndrome—"In a setting of insecurity, unpredictability, and weak institutions, oligarchs and followers contend in disorderly ways within both public and private sectors, often using violence to enforce contracts, collect debts, and protect assets" (2014, p. 247). In the century following the rise of Tammany, the city shifted back to elite cartels at the end of the century and then to influence markets by the middle of the 20th century.

Each syndrome entails both exchange and governance corruption, but the causes of corruption and the relationship between the two types change, depending on the syndrome. When the oligarchic bosses of Tammany controlled the city treasury and the letting of government contracts, we are directed by Johnston's typology to look at kickbacks, cost overruns, and overt conflicts of interest. Oligarchs and their clan-like followers use bribes liberally and, as we explain, exclude those who are not attached to the organization as operatives or constituents. That exclusion is the root of government corruption in this syndrome.

When we get to bureaucratic government after World War II, we look for favoritism curried through campaign contributions and promises of private sector jobs, which are hallmarks of influence markets and are both forms of exchange corruption. Governance is corrupted in this period by excluding those not in the public–private sector coalition that sets municipal priorities and distributes benefits—new schools, hospitals, recreation facilities—and imposes costs: abusive treatment by the police, prosecutors, and judges.

Organizational Structures and Processes

Political culture and systemic factors, like the quality of social services and the relative protection of marginal populations and children, are put into operation when they take organizational form. The form that is still dominant, though challenged by recent reforms, is bureaucracy, the hierarchical structure governed by written rules and norms of efficiency, specialization, and impersonalism.

The predominance of bureaucratic structures in public administration is critical in explaining the way corruption develops, is tolerated, and persists. We referred to two pathologies of bureaucratic organization in explaining exchange and governance corruption. The first is goal displacement, the erosion of the formal mission and purpose of a bureaucratic organization in favor of compliance with rules as interpreted by organizational managers. Researchers have found this pathology to be unavoidable as bureaucracies mature. The only effective safeguard is intensive oversight and the kind of self-examination and criticism that Argyris and Schön (1978) call double-loop learning, the regular assessment of operational premises and goals.

The second bureaucratic pathology that helps explain the failure of public integrity is normalized deviance. If they are unaddressed by organizational leaders, small errors or abuses will become embedded in ordinary operations and will be accepted as part of organizational history. Once the deviant behavior is normalized it can lead to corrupt outcomes that are acceptable inside the organization. Because of the routine nature of their operations, bureaucracies are the type of organization most vulnerable to deviance normalization.

Both of these pathologies are reasons for keeping a close eye on bureaucratic operations. Doing so helps us see how exchange corruption takes root and flourishes and how governance corruption develops and becomes embedded in political and organizational culture. Like political culture, organizational culture is a composite of transmissible norms and values that provide a lens which organizational members use to interpret their mission, understand and react to challenges, and either recognize or ignore mistakes and misconduct.

Critique and Reform of Bureaucratic Administration

The pathologies of bureaucratic government have not gone unnoticed. A critique based on democratic theory in the 1960s called for non-hierarchical, participatory forms of government organization, which had a marginal effect on the dominance of the bureaucratic form. However, the anti-bureaucracy critique of the 1980s, which was based on neo-liberal economic principles of market competition and consumer choice, caught fire and led, in many places, to the diminishment or replacement of bureaucratic agencies through privatization and contracting. This New Public Management (NPM) coincided with a parallel criticism of the costs of corruption control, which, it was argued, reduced the flexibility and efficiency of public agencies by making them ever more fearful of violating ever more extensive ethics regulations. The result was an unfettering of public organizations, which involved the replacement of ethics regulations with the profit motive of contractors and reliance on oversight of those contractors by agencies with fewer resources due to preference for the market. NPM replaced output measures of service quality with quantitative outcome measures that are used in making administrative decisions about employee status and resource allocation. This is called performance management.

The attack on bureaucratic administration was intended to counteract the effect of bureaucratic pathologies. The danger is that NPM's focus on market competition and performance management will warp public service toward performance targets and away from humane, democratic service. Where this happens, we are likely to find exchange and/or governance corruption.

Ethics Management

Ethics management is how we deal with exchange and governance corruption. We identified two strategies of ethics management: law enforcement and values-based. Law enforcement strategies use controls external to employees of public agencies like investigation, sting operations, transparency rules, and financial disclosure requirements to deter, detect, and punish exchange corruption. However, the net effect of external controls in law enforcement strategies on the level of exchange corruption is difficult to see and there are cases where even stringent controls are followed by bribery and extortion scandals.

Values-based strategies rely on the internal controls of public employees that are developed though experience, training, and peer support. While this is likely the most effective way to ensure public integrity, it relies on mutual trust, which may not be in vogue after a corruption scandal, resulting in increased or exclusive reliance on law enforcement and external controls.

The way we define and identify corruption has a lot to do with the way we decide to control it. In fact, as we will argue in the last section of this chapter, there is a close connection between the definition of corruption, the structure of public organizations, and the strategy of ethics management. A variation in one of these factors is reflected in changes in the other two.

An alternative to the opposed ethics strategies is a mix and balance of both. In real life ethics strategies often include both external and internal controls. But, as we noted, sliding toward law enforcement is quite common. What we suggest is a cooperative model of ethics management which entails participation by agency employees in the development and implementation of ethics rules and guidelines. This model is based on several successful experiments with participatory administration in public agencies and not-for-profit organizations.

Critical Summary of Case Studies

Each summary will highlight the ideas and concepts that are illustrated by the behavior of the individuals, organizations, and political systems involved. First is the juvenile court scandal in Pennsylvania. It is a case where those in leadership positions—judges, but also powerful developers and contractors—willfully exploited their positions for personal and financial gain. This naturally turns us to individual-level factors and the importance of oversight. This case raises especially difficult issues of ethics management, since it is judges to whom victims of misconduct must appeal. If those judges are themselves corrupt, it will be especially difficult to uncover and punish their corrupt behavior, as it was in this case. This case is also about raising ethical awareness among politicians and rights-oriented not-for-profits so that investigators and prosecutors become involved. This was necessary because the administrative culture of the local government either tolerated or ignored the corrupt use of sentencing power by the judges in question. For example, others could have sounded the alarm when juveniles were in court without legal assistance but did not, and existing rules on financial disclosure by the judges and others were not enforced. But we should also notice values and routines at the systemic level. Transparency and freedom of information makes it more likely that civil society can serve as a watchdog regarding bad behavior. Here again the confidentiality that is part of juvenile court proceedings was an obstacle to ethics management. Neither law enforcement nor values-based strategies had a chance to work, because neither was in place.

In the case of the Swedish National Audit Office (NAO) the performance measures put in place by the leadership were important causes of ethical misconduct. The emphasis on efficiency allowed one Auditor General to import a number of trusted former colleagues in violation of formal rules on open access to government employment. This action, while a logical and even necessary one in the eyes of the Auditor General, would not pass Terry Cooper's test of asking how a given action would reflect on you if it appeared in the media the next day. Systemic factors are also important to consider in this case. Complying with the open access rules would slow down the process at some cost to efficiency, a value strongly emphasized by the administrative system. Ferreting out interest conflicts is time consuming, but it protects basic public values of fairness and administrative neutrality. The Auditors General in this case lost sight of this and in doing so attracted the attention of the Riksdag and created doubt about whether the NAO could be trusted with the high degree of independence necessary for the mission of a supreme audit institution. Here law enforcement ethics management was successfully bypassed due to the very independence that is supposed to protect the integrity of its operations.

The history of corruption and ethics management in New York City demonstrates the long-term effects of bias and corrupt values in the prevailing political culture of a polity. It is also an example of the way in which "reform" can result in the exclusion of marginal populations and governance corruption. The reform of the old English/Dutch hegemony in the city resulted in Irish/German control of municipal government and the violent exclusion of African-Americans before and after the Draft Riots of 1863. By the end of the 19th century the desire by reformers to install professional, apolitical administration in the city was grounded in exclusionary Victorian moralism. The rise of bureaucracy and its discontents is a central part of this story. What we find by the middle of the 20th century in the city is an administrative structure shot through with exchange corruption and, as the New York Police Department (NYPD) case shows, the pathologies that lead to governance corruption. For most of its history ethics management in the city used a law enforcement strategy—intensifying most recently to a level of Panoptic surveillance and control. However, during the Progressive reform era around the turn of the 20th century, recruitment, credentials, and professional values were relied upon as a values-based strategy. If there was a period when a mix of the two was evident, it was the New Deal mayoral administration of Fiorello LaGuardia, who recruited and supported administrators of demonstrated virtue, but did not hesitate to "throw the book" at any government employee who violated his trust.

The NYPD case is a combination of data-driven (Compstat) performance management, an administrative culture shot through with goal displacement, and the ethical failure of the agency's leadership in their aggressive defense of racialized policing. The end product was the normalization of racial bias in street patrols and ultimately the creation of what Adams and Balfour call a surplus population: young men of color. This is clearly governance corruption. The ethical failure of the NYPD leadership indicates the needs for an alternative model of executive behavior, known as servant leadership, which emphasizes the value leaders should place on the involvement in decision making of rank-and-file organizational members. According to Robert Greenleaf (2002, p. 27) the test of leadership is whether those served are growing as individuals, becoming freer, healthier, and more likely to become leaders themselves, and whether the less well-off in society are benefitting from the organization's operations. In the case of the stop, question, frisk (SQF) policy in the NYPD, it was precisely those less powerful or less well-off who were poorly served.

The ethics management strategy used in the NYPD is hard to discern. Like the NAO in Sweden, the police in the city were given what was considered to be a necessary and high degree of independence. Up until recently, there was no inspector general assigned to the police department and it is still the case that validated findings of officer misconduct are sent to the Commissioner as advice that the Commissioner can and often does dismiss. Like the NAO, therefore, in practice ethics management was, if anything, values-based. The problem was that bureaucratic pathologies together with a closed, unaccountable organizational culture undermined any possible values basis of ethics management. In the NAO, in the aftermath of the media revelation about irregularities, an internally appointed investigation recommended a ban on direct recruitment from the government ministries to shield the independence of the NAO, more external control to check the adherence to formal rules, and clearer rules concerning the aim of performance audits.

In the NYPD case, it took court intervention and a change of leadership to reform the SQF policy and curtail consequent governance corruption. The policy and practice of SQF on the street was declared by a federal district judge to be a violation both of the fourth ("against unreasonable search and seizure") and fourteenth amendments ("guaranteeing due process and equal protection") of the U.S. Constitution. Various measures were ordered by the judge to remedy the problem, including use of body cameras for a trial period, an appointed monitor to oversee reform, and a period, though short, of required consultation with residents of areas most affected by the corrupt policy (Anechiarico, 2016, pp. 125–126). This led to changed routines of supervision, training, and discipline, so as to prevent and sanction "instances of racial profiling in street level law enforcement". Resident consultation involved a six- to nine-month joint remedial process, led by a court-appointed facilitator who would organize meetings in all boroughs that included various stakeholders such as community groups, NYPD staff, the district attorneys' offices, and representatives of local institutions such as public schooling and housing. The facilitator was to report to the court and monitor, who would recommend further reforms. This remedial process may well begin to counteract the exclusion experienced because of the application of SQF but given the short time period (nine months) it is difficult for interested citizens to organize, come up with proposals, and take leadership. Also, the remedial order of the court did not address the structural problem of normalized deviance and the organizational culture that allowed the classification of an entire demographic category as criminal suspects.

The Irish Catholic Church case concerned an organization with autonomous political power, enabled by the national government, with an organizational culture that tolerated sexual and physical abuse of both children and adults. Those who were abused, and their families, were denied voice and whole groups in the care of the Church were treated as surplus populations. Deviant behavior was normalized within the organization and covered up by the Church and the Irish government. Secrecy and lack of transparency further reduced accountability and contributed to governance corruption. The position of the Catholic Church in the foundation of Irish culture made it politically unchallengeable for generations. There were a number of applicable criminal and civil statutes that applied to the horrific abuse perpetrated by Catholic clergy over the years. None of them were used and abuses were suppressed and ignored. The Church has its own canon law that proscribes sexual relations of any kind, much less rape and pedophilia. There is also a traditional reliance in the Church on values-based ethics management based on years of clerical training and constant reflection and prayer. It was apparent to both the Church hierarchy and Irish law enforcement officials for decades that ethics management of priestly behavior had failed utterly. However, Church leaders and the government decided that the "reputation" and political authority of the Church were more important than the lives of thousands of victims. The moral collapse, corruption, and hypocrisy in this case is monumental.

Conclusion: The "Answer" Is Inclusivity

The story of both exchange and governance corruption is a story of exclusion. In the case of bribery and extortion, those who cannot or morally will not pay are excluded from the goods and services that corrupt officials put up for sale. In the case of governance corruption, displaced goals and normalized deviance that become embedded in political and organizational culture and pathologies of bureaucratic organization harm the victims in the cases we have explored. The victims of exclusion in the cases of governance corruption we present are:

- The children and their families in the bribery and kickback scheme in the Pennsylvania juvenile court.
- The average taxpayer in Sweden, whose interests in the integrity of government operations were subverted by favoritism and negligent oversight.
- Immigrant groups episodically and African-Americans and women who were chronically excluded by the systemic bias in political culture found in the history of corruption and reform in New York City.
- Young men of color defined as targets of racialized patrol strategies that were deployed as part of performance management in the NYPD.
- The child victims and their families in the sex scandals in the Irish Catholic Church, who were ignored by both the Church and the Irish government.

Those with most to lose, those most vulnerable, and those least able to assert their interests in the policy-making process were made to bear the brunt of mistakes, neglect, and abuse by public officials. Each is a case of governance corruption, but it is not difficult to see the parallel benefits to particular public officials as well as the broader damage to democratic values. The judges and prison contractors in the Pennsylvania juvenile court scandal had clear financial motives. Bribes and kickbacks were exchanged for the decision to build a privately-run jail and then stock it with children. The Auditors General of the Swedish NAO were able to grant favors, drop investigations, and provide employment to former colleagues, all of which can enhance their status and allow them to cultivate client relations. New York City politicians and administrators in the second half of the 19th century cultivated nativism and racism to ensure their own power and position. In the 20th century, it was reformers who asserted moral superiority to do the same. The elaborate and highly touted performance management system in the NYPD gave agency leaders the benefit of national celebrity and was supported even when it normalized racialized street patrol.

As we have mentioned, there are some cases of governance corruption in which the separable, personal benefits of exchange corruption are not easily found. These are usually cases of deep systemic bias and embedded organizational pathology that become part of standard operating procedure. However, at this point, it becomes evident that in most cases the initiation and maintenance of exclusionary policies will be perpetrated by those who see an obvious upside for themselves: status, money, recognition, and the development of a client network.

In our cases, both external and internal controls have failed. Neither law enforcement nor values-based ethics management have been effective in preventing damage to democratic values or individuals in any of the four cases. What we would like to argue in this final section is that inclusion and more extensive participation can help prevent exchange and governance corruption in two ways: by bringing the eyes and voices of the public into each stage of the policy-making process and by including the experience and values of rank-and-file public employees into the ethics rule-making and enforcing process.

If ethics rules are made and enforced by public employees at all ranks, the notion that organizational values are developed collectively will become part of organizational culture. Formal hearing and rule-making procedures will have to change to accommodate this shift in organizational culture, but they will no longer be in stark contrast to the top-down, punitive ethics management strategies used in most jurisdictions. The reason many participatory policy-making experiments fail is that those agency employees responsible for interacting with the public to produce public services are not trusted to govern themselves in their own workplaces. It is difficult for a regime of intensive external control to produce public servants who are free to interact creatively with the public to solve important problems. Can they be sure they aren't contravening a rule that was made and is enforced by those with little or no concern for the discretion necessary to effective collaboration with citizens?

Such collaboration will take a different form in each agency, so that potential for interest conflicts and self-dealing will vary from one agency workplace to another. It makes practical sense, we argue, to entrust those with direct knowledge of street patrols; solid waste collection; recreation; and environmental, housing, or homelessness policy to propose the dimensions of ethical conduct for their own work. These workplace ethics strategies might be made subject to approval by an interagency board that would ideally be composed of rank-and-file public employees elected from each agency in a jurisdiction.

In the United States, federal law requires that public employees accused of wrongdoing be given a hearing at which they can examine and rebut the evidence against them. This is a technical process that can't be left to even enthusiastic amateurs. However, referral to internal tribunals—or, for that matter, to public prosecutors—can and should be part of the inclusive, bottom-up process we recommend here.

"Eyes on the Street"

In 1961, the journalist and social critic Jane Jacobs published *The Death and Life of Great American Cities*, in which she rejected top-down urban planning for being sterile and destructive of social order. Areas dominated by high-rise buildings or cookie-cutter residential developments (which she dismissed at "dormitories") lacked the unplanned, eccentric street activity that, she argued, keeps neighborhoods alive and safe.

As she explains it, the more people on the street at all hours of the day, the safer an area will be. The more "eyes on the street", from stoop sitters to deliveries to people walking to the store or café, the better it is for the social integrity of a community. People get to know what looks "right" on the street and get to know each other well enough to act when something looks "wrong". Jacobs emphasizes the important role of mutual trust in urban communities. Not trust in the government or the police, but in each other:

> The first thing to understand is that the public peace—the sidewalk and street peace—of cities is not kept primarily by the police, necessary as police are. It is kept by an intricate, almost unconscious, network of voluntary controls and standards among the people themselves, and enforced by the people themselves. In some city areas—older public housing projects and streets with very high population turnover are often conspicuous examples—the keeping of public sidewalk law and order is left almost entirely to the police and special guards. Such places are jungles. No amount of police can enforce civilization where the normal, casual enforcement of it has broken down.
>
> *(1961, p. 32)*

It is a short trip from Jacobs' observations about order and safety in the urban community to understanding order and integrity and the government workplace. The same mutual trust is necessary and it develops in much the same way; by multiple, unplanned interactions and ground-level surveillance of behavior, not on the street but in the organization. Getting to a point where this evolves in a given public agency means "re-populating" the political space at the operational level of the organization by giving rank-and-file workers a say in the way the agency is governed. As it is, most bureaucratic agencies are very much like the sterile high rises and cookie-cutter suburbs that Jacobs said would require extensive policing and still not be safe. In essence, she is criticizing the law enforcement strategy in urban design and administration.

Jacobs has been proven correct in unfortunate ways. The way that public housing was built in the 1950s and 1960s—towers separated by open space devoid of commercial or other civic activity—was a disaster. Building on Jacobs' work, Oscar Newman (1973) labeled this kind of urban development as "indefensible space". Built in the early 1950s, the Pruitt–Igoe public housing project in St. Louis, Missouri, had become a symbol of the way tower-block projects concentrate social ills and exacerbate them. Pruitt–Igoe became a dangerous place to live that only got worse over time. By 1972, conditions in the project had gotten so bad that federal authorities relocated its residents and had all 33 buildings in the complex razed to the ground (Marshall, 2015).

That is what the anti-bureaucracy reformers in the 1980s wanted to do—raze government agencies to the ground. But like Pruitt–Igoe, the issue really is what you will put in its place. In St. Louis, a couple of schools now occupy the site of the housing complex (Pruitt Igoe Now, n.d.). In the 1980s, NPM was built to replace bureaucratic government. In both cases, the underlying problems of order and integrity—of community social structure or of official behavior in public agencies—were unaddressed. But there are models for rebuilding with integrity and order in mind.

There are successful examples of mixed-use development, which combine residential, commercial, cultural/recreational, and educational functions, rising from the ashes of indefensible housing complexes (Brown, 2018). The City of Santa Rosa, California, was mentioned above as a place that rebuilt its administrative structure around civic engagement and rank-and-file governance in municipal agencies (City of Santa Rosa, 2012, section 11; n.d.).

Labor–Management Relations as a Path to Cooperative Ethics Management

Public employee unions are an important factor in the identification of official corruption and how it is dealt with. While it differs between countries, the adversarial relationship between public employee unions and agency managers is found in a number of countries, including the United Kingdom and France. In the United States, rules laid out by the federal Office of Personnel Management (OPM) make it clear that discipline for misconduct and the way it is determined is the job of agency managers and agency legal counsel (U.S. Office of Personnel Management, n.d.). On the other side of the fence, the largest public employee union in the United States, the American Federation of State, County and Municipal Employees (AFSCME), cautions members that they are responsible for asserting their rights in any meeting with a supervisor that may entail disciplinary action. Comparable to the famous Miranda warnings that police must give to suspects in custody in America, another decision of the U.S. Supreme Court, *NLRB v. Weingarten* (1975), requires agency managers to allow employees to be accompanied by a union representative in disciplinary meetings, but the employee must *assert* the right. AFSCME suggests that its members carry a card with them that includes the following text:

> If the discussion in this meeting could in any way lead to my being disciplined or terminated or impact on my personal working conditions, I request that my steward, local officer or union representative be present. Without union representation, I choose not to answer any further questions at this time. This is my right under a Supreme Court decision called Weingarten (or cite a state law).
>
> *(AFSCME, 2017, p. 43)*

If an employee is accused of corruption, it will be supervisors and agency managers who determine how to interpret the law and behavior and whether their intersection constitutes a workplace violation, a civil offense, or a crime. In such circumstances, the use of the "Weingarten Card" makes sense. But the cooperative ethics management model we recommend requires buy-in from both agency managers and supervisors and also public employee unions. Research has begun to demonstrate multiple benefits from a cooperative public agency workplace:

> The past decade has shown that reshaping the labor–management relationship, and structurally reforming bureaucratic procedure and organization, can unlock enormous value. Rather than being defined by its stereotypes, the public workplace can be a place of productivity, human capital formation, and job satisfaction.
>
> *(Goldsmith & Schneider, 2003, p. 416)*

Research by Stephen Goldsmith and Mark Schneider identifies several specific strategies that help unlock public value and create a workplace where the goals of public service are not displaced by the litigious wall-building indicated by the OPM rules and the Weingarten protections. Most prominently, Goldsmith and Schneider mention cooperative agency governance. Based on their assessment of what works, they recommend that public agencies "[o]rganize employees in teams responsible for solving discrete problems. Enabling horizontal cooperation complements the reduction in vertical hierarchy. Teams, whether physical or virtual, should be flexible and able to form and then to reform as issues change" (2003, p. 422).

But no model will work everywhere. Rebuilding public integrity through cooperative ethics management requires rebuilding trust in public agencies from the bottom up. Perhaps the place to start this process is the same place we started this book, with an explanation of the two-part definition of corruption. If government employees are given a critical role in governing behavior both within the agency and in their relations with the public, the way toward democratic governance and sustainable public integrity will become clear.

Note

1 Citations for each of the terms in this section are found in the chapters in which they are first mentioned.

References

AFSCME. (2017). *Steward handbook: How to build a strong union and power in the workplace.* American Federation of State, County and Municipal Employees, Washington, D.C. Retrieved from www.afscme.org/news/publications/afscme-governance/afscme-steward-handbook.

Anechiarico, F. (2016). Conclusion: Accountability and the reform of legal corruption. In F. Anechiarico (Ed.), *Legal but corrupt* (pp. 121–140). Lanham, MD: Lexington Books.

Argyris, C., & Schön, D. A. (1978). *Organizational learning: A theory of action perspective.* Reading, MA: Addison-Wesley.

Brown, K. (2018, March 26). 10 urban projects that nail mixed-use design: These projects overcame the obstacles of mixed-use development in urban areas, offering vibrant designs and unique amenities. *Multifamily Executive.* Retrieved from www.multifamilyexecutive.com/design-development/10-urban-projects-that-nail-mixed-use-design_o.

City of Santa Rosa. (2012). Charter of the City of Santa Rosa California. Retrieved from https://qcode.us/codes/santarosa/view.php?topic=charter_of_the_city_of_santa_rosa_califo&showAll=1&frames=on.

City of Santa Rosa. (n.d.). Office of Community Engagement. Retrieved from https://srcity.org/250/Community-Engagement.

Goldsmith, S., & Schneider, M. E. (2003). Partnering for public value: New approaches in public employee labor–management relations. *University of Pennsylvania Journal of Labor and Employment Law, 5*(3), 415–425.

Greenleaf, R. K. (2002). *Servant leadership: A journey into the nature of legitimate power and greatness.* New York: Paulist Press.

Jacobs, J. (1961). *The death and life of great American cities.* New York: Vintage Books.

Johnston, M. (2014). *Corruption, contention and reform: The power of deep democratization.* Cambridge: Cambridge University Press.

Marshall, C. (2015, April 22). Pruitt–Igoe: the troubled high-rise that came to define urban America – a history of cities in 50 buildings, day 21. *The Guardian.* Retrieved from www.theguardian.com/cities/2015/apr/22/pruitt-igoe-high-rise-urban-america-history-cities.

Newman, O. (1973). *Defensible space: Crime prevention through urban design.* New York: Macmillan.

NLRB v. Weingarten (420 U.S. 251 1975).

Pruitt Igoe Now. (n.d.). Retrieved from http://pruittigoenow.org/about/.

U.S. Office of Personnel Management. (n.d.). *Managing federal employees' performance issues or misconduct.* Retrieved from www.opm.gov/policy-data-oversight/employee-relations/reference-materials/managing-federal-employees%E2%80%99-performance-issues-or-misconduct.pdf.

INDEX

Page numbers in *italics* denote an illustration; **bold** a table or box; n an endnote

Taylor & Francis Group
an **informa** business

Taylor & Francis eBooks

www.taylorfrancis.com

A single destination for eBooks from Taylor & Francis
with increased functionality and an improved user
experience to meet the needs of our customers.

90,000+ eBooks of award-winning academic content in
Humanities, Social Science, Science, Technology, Engineering,
and Medical written by a global network of editors and authors.

TAYLOR & FRANCIS EBOOKS OFFERS:

A streamlined
experience for
our library
customers

A single point
of discovery
for all of our
eBook content

Improved
search and
discovery of
content at both
book and
chapter level

REQUEST A FREE TRIAL
support@taylorfrancis.com

Routledge
Taylor & Francis Group

CRC Press
Taylor & Francis Group